PRODUCTIVITY ENHANCEMENT
in
MANUFACTURING
OPERATIONS

PRODUCTIVITY ENHANCEMENT in MANUFACTURING OPERATIONS

K.C. Alexander and Dr. A.K. Raj, PhD

Notion Press

Old No. 38, New No. 6
McNichols Road, Chetpet
Chennai - 600 031

First Published by Notion Press 2017
Copyright © K.C. Alexander & Dr. A.K. Raj, PhD 2017
All Rights Reserved.

ISBN 978-1-947429-41-3

Contents

PART 1: Motivation and Avoiding Common Mistakes

PART 2 : A Few Techniques or Tools Used for Productivity Enhancement

Foreword by L Ramkumar

K.C. Alexander (Alex), the author of the book *'Productivity Enhancement at Manufacturing Operations'* is known to me for more than two decades. I have had the opportunity to work with him closely when I was in Tube Products of India and on a few assignments later. I have seen Alex as a very highly committed and passionate individual who goes all the way to achieve his objectives with single-minded devotion.

Alex is an ever learning industrial engineer and he is constantly looking for newer challenges by which productivity improvements can be brought about in various types of industries. He was a lifetime TI professional with his stints in various SBUs of Tube Investments of India Ltd. His second innings of being a Consultant to various types of industry has been very illustrious and impactful as well on the businesses he worked with. The fact that Alex could contribute significantly to the productivity improvements of all CUMI Units, Rane Group companies, Best & Crompton units, Elforge units, Areva, IFPL, Pricol etc. is testimony to his commitments and caliber. He became a much sought after consultant with difference for suggesting and implementing various changes, such as, Layout modifications, lean man power, higher machine rated norms, with total flexibility work culture at shop floor operations along with zero over time practices etc. His contributions in all TII units with WIN: WIN Long Term Settlements are being appreciated even after 23 years after his retirement from TII.

I would like to recall the assignment in which he helped us at Fenner (India) Ltd. (when I was the President of the Company), at the oldest plant of the Company, at Madurai. Alex was able to give us a plan for improving productivity of the plant by more than 33%, in some shops, it was in the range of 50 to 60% also. This changed the fortunes of the plant that was otherwise considered inefficient. I am sure there are many more such assignments that Alex could be proud of!

In this book, Alex has given a number of examples and anecdotes that are very helpful to any reader. These are backed up by solid experience and evidences and hence one gets a practical approach to achieving productivity improvements.

The key thing that needs to be noted is Alex believes in working very closely with the employees who are involved in Operations to collate the various ideas for improvement. He motivates and encourages people to always look at name plate capacity of equipments. This process not only enables to get a "buy in" from the employees but also makes the results sustainable.

I wish the ever energetic and zealous Alex many more years of service to the industry and continue his contribution to productivity enhancements in manufacturing industries.

– L Ramkumar

Managing Director, Tube Investments of India Ltd.,

Foreword by Hussain Sehal

Mr. K.C. Alexander is a well-known brand in TII and well known to many other companies in South India for more than 3 decades. With a great career in TII in Industrial engineering and heading Operations of the largest Units of TII in Chennai, he has been instrumental to the growth of the organization. His contributions are immeasurable and significant in helping them grow from strength to strength. As a strategist, he played a pivotal role in initiating never before changes enabling maximization of human capital such as total flexibility in times of restrictive practices among workmen, cross functional working, zero over-time work culture, lean manning, enlisting people to become partners of progress for highest productivity that became benchmark practices. Right sizing by reduction of nearly 30% at a time when it was considered almost impossible task was a creditable achievement. His humility and excellent inter-personal relations skills are his great strength. He was accessible to all people regardless of level in the hierarchy. He was a good negotiator and motivator for raising the efficiency bars whenever needed. A man of expansive knowledge and experience, he broke new ground in application of Incentive schemes innovatively for organizations and for its successful execution. His schemes have been an integral part of every wage settlement signed by companies across the Group. Above all Mr. Alexander is a man of high integrity, convictions and very fair in approach.

Retirement was a new beginning and as a much sought-after consultant he provides his expert solutions for as many as 25 Companies across sectors, for raising their productivity levels and his association extends to Manufacturing giants like Murugappa group, CUMI units, Rane Group of companies, Best & Crompton, Elforge, Fenner, Areva, IFPL, Pricol etc.

I must say that this book on Productivity enhancement in Manufacturing, is a great gesture and a legacy to the professionals and managers who are striving today to achieve exemplary productivity targets.

– Hussain Sehal

Executive Coach

Formerly Country HR Director at Areva and Schneider Electric India.

Foreword by Mrs. Vanitha Mohan

It is always interesting to come across people from whom one can learn something. When such people decide to write a book, the learning becomes even more intense. One such interesting person that I have come across is Mr. K.C. Alexander whose book **"Productivity Enhancement in Manufacturing Operations"** is all set to create benchmarks for productivity in the manufacturing space.

Mr. Alexander came into Pricol as a saviour at a time when productivity had nosedived to abysmal depths as an aftermath of a labour issue. His diligent and committed way of weaving his way around people and processes during his stint at Pricol between 2010–2014 brought about a big change in our shop floor slowly but surely. Simple lay out changes which were hitherto not visible to the common eye yielded dramatic results in productivity enhancement. It went up to as high as 100% in certain cases the lowest being 25% mainly through lay out changes, capacity augmentation, lean manufacturing, set-up time reduction, assembly line balancing, simplifications, methods improvements, process improvements, automation and so on. Our supervisors who worked under him often referred to him as a University from whom they learnt to enhance productivity through several time tested tools. He walked the extra mile to build a team which bought into his ideas and techniques mainly because of their simplicity and easy to implement strategy. Having set things in order in 3 of our plants, he also helped to improve productivity in our Indonesian plant where a sizeable population comprises of young Indonesian girls who adapted themselves to the new techniques largely due to the ease of understanding and implementation.

This book has been very thoughtfully divided into 2 parts, one of which contains powerful and inspirational stories that even leaves you speechless at times and the other on productivity enhancement techniques which is a unique collection of practical and systematic methods which will go a long way to help the readers understand the subject thoroughly. I am indeed glad that he has thought of putting it all meticulously into what I think will be a Bible for the manufacturing team as well as HR which has to constantly battle with productivity norms. A book that can become part of a University curriculum.

What touched me most was his sincere intent to give back to industry all that he took from it by way of sharing his learning with the younger generation. I am sure this book will be a treasure trove for those wanting to dip into techniques to improve productivity in their work place through inexpensive means which is a must for a manufacturing set up in order to survive in a highly competitive business landscape.

I congratulate Mr. Alexander for this fine contribution and recommend this book as a must read for all in the field.

– Mrs. Vanitha Mohan

– Vice Chairman – Pricol, Coimbatore.

Foreword by
Udayakumar Gopalakrishnan

Though a luxury in the busy times, I nourish going down the memory lane of life. Often times, I become invigorated by ruminating special nostalgic era of the early career stint in HR invested at TI Cycles, during early 80s, where I was baptized by fire and love! I tend to pleasantly recall many role models, who influenced me. Mr. K.C. Alexander stood tall then and will ever remain so, for having invaluably contributed to my growth. He undoubtedly touched my life, with loads of authenticity and simplicity that were akin to his siblings. There was also an interim period, when I reported to him. Later during the second stint at Murugappa Group in the early 90s, (when I headed plant HR, at Tube Products), he anchored manufacturing operations.

Around six months ago, when he sounded me about authoring a book, I was elated on two counts. One was in simultaneous wonder as to why he didn't script this dream earlier and therefore happy that it would do a world of good to him, for he loved all what he did and this momentous step would add more love to his life. Secondly, I'm delighted about this gesture of creating a legacy for potential seekers to stumble upon untapped knowledge and for all those out there in the manufacturing sector at large who will certainly be able to consume, live and pass on his dream to live in eternity, as otherwise the world would be left impoverished, a thought that I would lament, forever.

Alex as he is fondly called, is a par excellence architect and Zen master in the arenas of industrial engineering, shop floor productivity studies and pre-settlement conflict resolutions which prepared robust platforms for Long Term Settlements (LTS), enabling many leadership teams and trade unions, to nurture harmony and collective ownership, beyond the normal confines of collective bargaining. Isn't proof of the pudding, in eating it? The productivity studies that preceded myriad LTS of the longevity type, spearheaded by him across diverse organizations have withstood the best of core values, business acumen and time.

Over a period of time, the lay outs in all shops became hazardous with safety issues along with congestion, low productivity etc. Mr. Alexander took the initiative of extending the manufacturing bays with better material handling equipment and low cost automation to reduce fatigue of various operators along with far better lay out changes. This by itself added considerable happiness in the minds of work men and volume and productivity went up very high

To the best of my knowledge, even after he hung his boots after almost four decades of corporate life at Murugappa Group, Alex has been associated with many organizations in a Consultant's role. Rane, Pricol and several units of Murugappa group, just to mention a few. Many institutions continue to utilize his services reaping enormous benefits. The accomplishments that he co-created with pride alongside leadership teams and unions alike have unleashed envious and inimitable legacy practices and are admired folklore! Breakthroughs resting on the expertise of Alex were institutionalized, to the ultimate fulfillment of all stakeholders. Let me add on with fervor – Alex possesses and more importantly demonstrates core values like integrity, authenticity, humility and compassion. These core values and traits, in consonance with the highest degrees of professional focus that he ushers, is a rarity in the emerging corporate world and needs to be welcomed, assimilated and internalized, by professionals who constantly seek productivity enhancements and whose hunger cannot just be withered, but also sustained and home grown.

This book on: *"Productivity Enhancement in Manufacturing Operations,"* explores the connected themes way beyond the basics of input vs. output ratio and transforms the traditional P&L account, into People and Love account!

'You can take a horse to water, but cannot make it drink'— so goes the old adage! Alex has interestingly distilled a concoction in this book: 'you can enable the horse to drink', by unleashing a motivating ambience for this to happen, with pragmatic insights.

What I liked best about this offering to the business world is that he deliberately chose not to place the cart before the horse. This is evident in the way he sequenced and packed Part 1 of the book, with inspiring storylines – stories that have a fair complement of struggles, challenges and mighty accomplishments. He has weaved as if in musical notes, the soft skills and motivational strategies that ought to be prerequisites before presenting Part 2 with a repertoire of time proven success tools and productivity techniques, which paved way for quality results.

This book in your hands is *'one stop solutions manual'*— definitely not just a cliché expression! This rich offering is a compendium for captains, owners and leaders, who can connect the past expertise they possess apart from connecting the dots of what they have not hitherto fathomed, to multiply success in manufacturing domain, as productivity enhancement is the mother of all innovative and benchmarking practices.

Alex has beautifully carved the book apt enough for a wide range of readers that could encompass academicians and students in engineering colleges, greenhorns who step into industry and corporate professionals, who wishes to transform themselves and cultures.

I wish Alex and his long time mentee A.K. Raj (my ex-colleague at TPI and an ardent practitioner of Industrial Engineering), who has co-authored this gift, the best and more to be part of the annals of epoch making history, that would easily include renaissance, whole scale systems transformation, renovation and innovation, at its zenith.

Before signing off – Alex, I'm humbled by your gesture to request me for a Foreword, for the book. Let the passions that you are wired with contagiously spread to those in the quest and were ignorant of a monumental source like you. May God bless you and the readers, to change the destiny to make this planet a better place, for contemporaries and posterity to tread, navigate and succeed, in tough terrains and unchartered frontiers! You have pushed the envelope and boundaries, for multifarious opportunities and possibilities, to emerge on this landscape. Horizons are never far away or remain untouchable, with your mighty creation.

Dear Readers! Fasten or rather unfasten your seat belts, for co-creating a wonder world by joining Alex and Raj, to revolutionize the industrial environment, which is beckoning to your clarion call. Go ahead and totally rejoice! What are you waiting for? The long wait is now thankfully over...

– Udayakumar Gopalakrishnan, CEO, CORE MIND

Professional Certified Coach, ICF

Institute Member, NTL - USA

Author of Seminal Book: *'What it Takes to be a Leader with Passion'*

Blog: *https://udayunplugged.wordpress.com/* | *www.coremind.in*

Foreword by DK Jairath

 My tryst with Alex, as I fondly call my elderly friend and colleague Alexander began in 2012 during my visit to the legendary factory of Indian Furniture Products Limited near Chennai as part of my Director induction process with the KK Birla Adventz Group. Amidst the familiar and large buzzing factory environments I had been familiar with, I was intrigued by the distant presence of a tall and frail elderly gentleman in Factory dress code, interacting with the shop-floor workmen. Have we forgotten to retire employees well past their working years, I thought. Queries led me to his introduction as our Factory Consultant with core expertise in Manufacturing & Productivity. What followed later was a casual interaction with him in his typical accent and I was mesmerized to observe ageless passion and hard work combined with practical knowledge and superb command on his subjects. Destiny took over from there and I soon possessed the "best productivity guy around" and "my senior most friend forever."

The book which I wish to introduce here has been in the making for quite some time and the idea was conceived by family and friends with the objective that the legacy of Alex must live forever. To be honest about it, this is not really any typical "book" or a "textbook." It is in real sense a "treatise" for practitioners of manufacturing, industrial engineering and productivity. Whether engineering students or manufacturing professionals working in industry, this handbook illustrated with the actual manufacturing environment challenges, best practices and practical solutions means a goldmine to all. It is in essence the nectar of Alex's legacy and real life manufacturing experiences, learnings and decades of contributions to the industry encompassing TII, CUMI, Pricol, Areva and IFPL among others.

Some of us have been fortunate to witness, assess, co-work, learn and apply the manufacturing and productivity improvements with great end-results along with Alex. Be it layout optimization for better throughput, low cost automation, process standardization, wastage elimination & material conservation, cost optimization, best class HR-IR practices, motivation, productivity targets, team building and output enhancement, incentive schemes or wage settlements etc., we have all learnt our bit in this wonderful association and journey. For most who may have missed, this handbook is the perfect way to get closest and learn the techniques, tools, skills, metrics and knowledge to make your manufacturing work life super successful.

My personal tribute and gratitude will always remain with Alex for the wonderful effort to share such invaluable knowledge with all of us and keeping the legacy in motion. For us, Alex will always be the Alexander of Manufacturing Productivity and the perfect gentleman ever!

Best wishes,

– DK Jairath

Corporate Entrepreneur & CEO

Commendation Notes

❖ My association with Mr. K.C. Alexander (Popularly called Alex) goes back to 1979 when I joined TI Cycles, Chennai as a Graduate Trainee.

❖ Alex has a strong manufacturing experience in TI Cycles and Tube Products of India (TPI). Basically an Industrial Engineer by Qualification, his keen focus on Productivity, Production and Cost Control improved the fortunes of all the businesses he was involved in very well. His strong Leadership in Management-Union relationship stood the test of time and he is fondly remembered by all his Colleagues.

❖ As a Colleague in TPI as Finance Manager, I had very interesting times with him. I used to push him for strong numbers in Production/Product Mix/Costs/WIP etc. Alex always to excel in achievements and we used to be proud of his role in TPI.

❖ I am happy that Alex is publishing a book which emphasizes on Productivity in Manufacturing. His long and illustrious career insights can easily be found in his book.

❖ I wholeheartedly recommend this book of my Senior Colleague in TI to any Professional trying to learn from other's rich experience.

❖ Kudos to Alex for sharing his Insights!

❖ All the Best!!

– Gopalarathnam S S
Managing Director-Chola MS

❖❖❖

As an HR professional, I have been associated with Mr. K.C. Alexander for more than a decade and have worked with him on different Operations & Productivity Improvement projects at two different organizations.

Passion is the only word I can think of when I see or hear of Mr. K.C Alexander. How else can one describe a Septuagenarian/Octogenarian (?) with such high energy and enthusiasm taking great efforts to pen down his experiences and thoughts for the benefit of manufacturing teams as well as for the students/professionals pursuing their career in manufacturing?

With his background of Industrial Engineering combined with the knowledge of business processes & operations, strong analytical and problem solving ability has made immense contribution in bringing about major changes in the shop floor and contributing to substantial productivity improvements in different organizations. He has played a major role in improving the operational efficiencies at our manufacturing plants. He corroborates his recommendations through scientific means and provides all the armour for convincing the Unions/Workmen. He takes complete ownership of his work and goes the extra mile in implementing his recommendations by working closely with the operations team.

This book is being released at the right time when the entire country is talking about "Make in India" as the key to help India become a developed economy. For Indian manufacturing to be competitive, we must have strong focus on continuously improving the productivity of all resources viz men, machines, materials, methods, money etc.

Mr. Alexander in his unique style has come up with an easily comprehensible book titled "Productivity Enhancement in Manufacturing Operations" wherein he has captured his invaluable knowledge & experience and also shared interesting and live case studies on how organizations have gone about improving their productivity. This book provides lot of insights and solutions to the numerous problems being faced by the manufacturing teams. This is a very handy and must read book for all those who are looking to pursue a successful career in Manufacturing Operations.

I am very happy to have been associated with a highly knowledgeable, hardworking and passionate professional.

Mr. Alexander, Congratulations and well done on your maiden book!

– Prasad N

EVP-Human Resources-TICO-TII

❖❖❖

Alex (Mr. K.C. Alexander) was my classmate during 1956–1960. We were studying for an engineering degree in Bangalore. Since then, we were in touch with each other. I can still remember how Alex greeted me with a warm, broad and bright smile when I entered my first class in the college. I knew then and there, that we were **friends for life.** There were a few boys from Kerala for the engineering course and I can tell you without any hesitation that Alex was the smartest and brightest of all and he still is!!

Alex has a photographic memory and he made full use of it to pursue his engineering course. Alex has been able to amass incredibly vast knowledge during his professional career and fortunately for the engineering and management world, he had the good sense to jot down all details of his experience and publish them in the form of a book "Practical Enhancement in Management Operation" I consider this a noble act by Alex, as he is graciously contributing his hard earned knowledge for the benefit of practicing engineers, students, teachers and researchers. Even a layman can use this book for its contents to inspire through the numerous quotes from famous people,

When you talk about productivity, it is not something you can see immediately in form or shape of an object. Productivity can only be evaluated in terms of enhanced values, higher production units, improved finance, reduced labor, higher output for less input, faster turnover etc. In fact, productivity is important in all aspects and facets of life.

What this book has achieved is, to materialize productivity and provide enough competent tools to achieve that material called **"PRODUCTIVITY"** This is fabulous. Many suggestive cartoons, pictures, humorous sketches etc. are included in the book, to explain what productivity is and methods to visualize it and achieve it.

I can very well appreciate all what is written in this book on productivity, as I can vouch for them from my 52 years of experience in professional engineering and top management fields.

I was with AMUL India for 15 years and was Asst.General Manager(Production) when I left, had worked with Nabisco (USA) in China as VP(MFG) and VP(Logistics) and with Danone as General Manager (Prod). During all these assignments, I had used many of the procedures mentioned in "Practical Enhancement in Management Operation" successfully and how I wish I had this book with me then, so that, I could have used this book to be more successful in my quest for more productivity with less effort !!!

Anyway, nothing much is lost for me. I can still use it for my social work, social engineering and inventions. I can derive great inspiration for my future inventions that are in the ANVIL now from this informative book.

I wholeheartedly recommend this Great Book to anyone, professional or otherwise to enable them to pursue a Golden Future.

Well done Alex. Let us have more creations from you, like this one!!!

– T.C. Chandran

Former AGM (Amul), VP (Mfg) and VP (Logistics) - Nabisco (USA)

Some books are for weeks, some are for months and some are for years. Mr. Alexander's book entitled -Productivity Enhancement at Manufacturing Operations, falls in the last category. What was the necessity of this when there are Productivity Councils, so many publications on this subject? Simple, what differentiates this one from others is its language which is lucid, easily understandable by anyone. And the illustrations from his rich practical experiences bridge the gap between Theory and Practice.

I have known Mr. Alexander when he was my colleague at TI, if someone enters his room without knocking, you will find hind him immersed in deep thought. He was a thinking man and the result is this book. I am sure, one will benefit immensely after going through this publication.

After reading the book, "What you will discover will be yourself"

– A K Sehanobis

Former President, Tube Products of India, Chennai

Mr. Alexander has been my colleague and friend for three decades, during the first decade we worked together at TI Cycles. It was in 1975–76, the fair and firm management had to crush the violence and strike imposed by the militant union, which ultimately helped to achieve fantastic productivity at this unit. In the last two decades of my association, we had a great time working and contributing together at Tube Products of India. During my tenure as President of TPI, the organization had great and useful service by him after his retirement, mainly for productivity enhancement and head count reduction which became essential for survival and growth of the organization. A WIN: WIN Long Term Settlement was the need of the hour in those years for sustained cooperation by workmen for getting rid of various unhealthy and undesirable practices such as overtime work culture, lack of flexibility among men to move from existing job to elsewhere on need base, too many indirect man power, very low productivity more by bigger crew size as compared to optimum or lean manpower concept, all these were achieved year after year.

Optimum utilization of costly man power and equipment and various facilities are of utmost importance in present day manufacturing units as everyone agrees to it. But then, why is it not happening is a big question that has to be pondered of it. Clearly there is a big gap between management team and work men on implementing the proposals which in my experience is largely due to lack of well thought changes which are to be discussed across all team members in full details irrespective of level or position of people in organization and finally it has to be agreed up on by workmen by and large before taking up for implementation to reap the benefits of quantum jump in productivity. In the absence of such leadership and tactics, the workmen often resort to pressure tactics, the shop floor managers resist on impracticability without adequate facilities or automation which ultimately end up in disruption of manufacturing operations. It may not be out of context to mention that such was the general situation in the period of 1975 to 1990 in most of organizations of Chennai, especially with militant union teams in some units.

With good lay out changes of machines, better material handling facilities, low cost automation, simplification of job contents, reducing fatigue of operators, reduction of crew size with concurrence of work men, planned tool changes, innovative tools, far better flexibility zero over time work culture etc., it would never be exaggerating to say that productivity can be almost doubled, well this is what happened at TPI. The importance of sharing the fruits of productivity should be shared among the workmen through highly motivating productivity incentive scheme for sustenance and full cooperation from the workmen. From a single digit incentive amount a few decades ago, today few units are paying 5 digit incentive amount, only to see steady growth of productivity.

I am very delighted to come to know the work done by Alexander in few other units based at Chennai and few units in South India, in fact he is a much sought after consultant with difference. I had the pleasure of working with him at Fenner, Madurai, a few years back just to cite one such case. My contribution was for innovative technological changes, whereas he contributed for fantastic labour productivity through drastic layout changes and norms increase with lean manpower at this unit.

Indeed I am happy to see that he has captured all salient experiences of five decades in his book on productivity enhancement in most simple way with lots of practical case examples and for sure, the readers will be able to make a note of change possibilities in their manufacturing units. This book can be thought provoking for both for manufacturing team from top to bottom and as well for HR professionals and it will certainly help you to achieve your dream of much higher productivity with lean man power provided you take up challenging task of implementation with full success by doing your prior homework good enough.

HAPPY READING with few interesting cartoons in light vein!

– G. Shiva Prasad
Former President of Tube Products of India

❖❖❖

I'm extremely happy to note that Mr. K.C. Alexander, a mentor, boss and above all a great colleague for last 40 years has penned down a book on productivity. When I heard Mr. Alexander is on this work, the first feel gone through me was "who else" is a better person to write this.

Mr. Alexander, a gifted industrial Engineer, talented in operation excellence in manufacturing with a focus on productivity is known for his passion, commitment and human touch. His innovative ideas, approaches and above all the task master in him made him successful making him most sought after in businesses of Murugappa group particularly in TII and outside for productivity enhancement.

Most of our long term settlements with union were with a focus on productivity and they all bear the stamp of Mr. Alexander. The human side of him has translated into trust with unions. I still remember the way we engaged Mr. Alexander, though he was retired, in convincing the union for the productivity in the bonus scheme, first time in TII. The comment from the union was "If Mr. Alexander says, we believe it and is okay with us."

When I look at the great work of Mr. Alexander and long association, one another colleague coming to my mind is the late Mr. A. Hydari whom we are all proud of for his great qualities as an Engineer, Manager and above all a great humanist who has given all the support and ambience to excel. I'm sure Mr. Alexander's work will be having reference to this great colleague.

As head of TQM & Training, my search for a faculty on productivity or manufacturing excellence naturally use to end up with Mr. Alexander who was most sought after in the system.

Times have changed and also the way we do business. The jungle's law 'Survival of the fittest' continue to be the order. Competitiveness in cost and quality is the mantra. For this, businesses adopts different approaches which all finally narrows down in addressing productivity, cost.

In the current scenario, a person with so much understanding on the topic who has experimented all his innovative ideas successfully and translated them into finer details, writing this book will be of immense value for the industry and certainly act as a reference document for Engineers and Managers.

I wish Mr. Alexander and his great work all success. Also I pray to Almighty God to give good health, happiness and the spirit of writing to do similar value adds in the time to come.

– T.M. Gopala Pillai

Ex. VP (TQM &Training),

Tube Investments of India Ltd, Chennai.

❖ ❖ ❖

Mr. K.C. Alexander with whom I was associated and worked for about 35 years is one of my professional friends. I was reporting to him at Tube Products of India in one of the main Product line for some years. It is unimaginable now to think back on our combined work to set right the workmen culture with horrible over time work culture, restrictive work practices, very low norms or productivity, more man power, bad lay out, highly non cooperative work force and so on. In a time span of 3 years by 1990, we were able to turn around the unit with double volume and productivity with zero over time and total flexibility, lean manpower etc., all because of my friend's initiative, total support from management and by mind set changes of workmen. It became a model unit at this big company.

Later on, when I became VP- T of TPI, I was able to put in to practice of earlier experience and doubled volume and productivity with lay out changes, automation and better material handling facilities along with lean man power.

I had again the opportunity to work at IFPL, a part of Birla group, where he was full time consultant. Together and with management support we did play our role to raise productivity by implementing product line lay out, low cost automation by avoiding third shift operations without drop of volume.

One remarkable achievement in these units was signing of WIN: WIN Long term Settlement with CITU union, much to greater satisfaction of both stake holders of management and work force with higher quantum of amount by way of productivity incentive earnings. I was his right hand for this turn around changes in these units.

Man power reduction and increasing productivity is a very tough job to get it done, being highly emotional and sensitive issues to handle the same successfully. It was successful where we worked together, all because of using various techniques mentioned in the book very methodically and by taking the operators in to confidence and by making them responsible as partners of the company.

He has worked as a consultant in about 20 organizations where he was able to achieve high level of productivity with various changes, all because of his working style of taking the team members in to confidence, made them as partners of the project, worked as one among them and not as a consultant who generally give good suggestions and then blame others for not being able to implement the ideas, took the workmen in to confidence by implementing simple automation to reduce their fatigue while working on job and by much higher of take home incentive amount month after month along with higher volume achievement.

I am proud to record that I was one among his friends who went on asking him to write a book on productivity enhancement based on his 5 decades of practical experience with stopping working at age of 80 years and for sharing with others who are looking for productivity growth in their manufacturing units. He has narrated few blunders which often happen in units by some reasons or other like lose norms which ultimately will become a pain in the neck of all supervisors of shop floor in Part 1 and in Part 2 lots of case study examples, some of which are quoted from the units I worked and fully implemented for great success. These practical explanations should make the shop floor engineers comfortable to understand and then implement in their problem areas, it is made humorous with live enjoyable cartoons too. At the end of reading, I am sure that you will agree with me some of them saying, "Reading this book has made much more confident to apply the techniques on need base for enhancing productivity and for head count reduction, which are the only two things my bosses ask me daily and hopefully my family may see my smiling face by month end, rather than frown face earlier"

Wishing the readers all happiness and benefits along with wishing my good friend, Alex and family all out happiness and health

– K. Perumal

Former VP-T of Tube Products of India, Avadi, Chennai

❖❖❖

Mr. K.C. Alexander, one of the authors of this book, has got a great reputation in the area of productivity enhancement, in Manufacturing Industries.

He played a key role in leading manufacturing industries in South India, towards improving the productivity.

He focused towards cycle time reduction, lay out modifications, crew size reduction as resultant of cycle time reduction and lay out changes.

He motivated employees to improve the productivity through effective incentive schemes.

Apart from enhancing blue collar productivity, he also focused on white collar productivity by educating and motivating the people in supervisory and management cadre.

He used to involve the front line employees, front line staff, and right from idea generation, data collection and implementation of projects successfully.

His transparency and commitment to create lot of enthusiasm among the group of people, who were involved in the productivity improvement projects was highly appreciable.

He was practical in his approach. Because of this, all the labour unions had 100% faith on him and he had no difficulty in convincing the unions whenever required.

I had the opportunity to get associated with him in Murugappa group in my role as GM-Manufacturing of TIDC and as GM-Manufacturing in Tube products of India and also in Rane group as VP-Operations in one of the units, towards enhancing the productivity.

I am sure that this book, will be a guide for all the young engineers in the manufacturing and engineering function. Also this book can be a reference to all the senior people, for productivity enhancement in the manufacturing operations.

– A.A. Ramalingam

Former GM – TI Diamond Chains,

Tube Products of India and VP - Rane

❖❖❖

After a deep contemplation, I break the protocol and surrender to my spontaneity to write this commendation note. Here I am in my authentic self. Let me narrate my first encounter with Alex 32 years back (Alex-this is how we fondly address him and he likes it). It was Monday afternoon in 1985 October, few days of my joining Tube Products of India (TPI) as a Special Officer-Canteen after my Hotel Management & Catering Technology graduation, the office phone rang up after a big commotion in the canteen for a shortage of side-dish. The company was going through a sensitive IR situation. The anguished union members were visibly upset with me for my unperturbed manner of dealing with them. They left my office challenging my existence in the organization with a loud noise. (I was 23 years old and they were experienced more than my age) In next 5 minutes I got a call from Mr. Alex's office to come and meet him. I was short of carrying my resignation letter but mentally resigned when I knocked his door. Believe me, Alex got out of his seat and greeted me with cheerful smile in Malayalam accented expression *'Hello Sayi, I know you have joined us few days back, I am so sorry that I got a chance to meet you only now'.* He continued saying *'I am personally very happy to meet a young professional like you, we are proud to have you part of our team'.* Not a single word he uttered about the canteen complaint that he received from the Union. After listening my background with caring attention, he escorted me to the doors with a warm touch on my shoulder. Outside his office, his secretary Swaminathan whispered to me, *'GM was upset with the Union guys for complaining about a new member who just joined'.* This is my first Alex experience. I saw the leader in him and I have decided to work with him.

He is a thorough professional I have ever seen in my life and a Karma-yogi who derives strength from work, nothing but work. I have worked with Alex in close quarters for 10 years and I have several experiences to share. Among many qualities that he is known for- like perseverance, humility, passion for productivity, result-orientation, servant-leadership and so on, I want to talk about two distinct qualities that inspired me. The first is-**humanizing the concepts and ideas**. The second is **Winning the End Result**. Secret of his success according to me is only these two unique 'gifts' that he is born with.

In today's modern world of manufacturing there is no dearth of tools and techniques for productivity and manufacturing excellence. But all these works in shop floor only when people who practice them are convinced and willing to adopt. The most critical challenge we face from shop-floor to top-floor is how to convince people and get their buy-in. In other words how to make the concepts work for us however great they are. Alex has the magic to manage this humongous task to deliver results. I would say he is a Human Relations specialist first and an Engineer next.

I was deeply inspired by his Servant-Leadership style like the way Mahatma Gandhi has influenced his fellow nationals. Alex keeps a low profile and makes others feel important. Loves fellow humans and would extend his help whenever they are in need. I can recall countless occasion of him being human than an authority. I want to emphasize the point that this was his nature not a management style. With this quality he has stolen the hearts of Associates and Union leaders and sowed seed of 'Progressive Industrial Relations'. His negotiation skills are out of the world. He will get into the spirits of people on the negotiating table and help them think his way. He is one among the very few veterans left in this country in to deal with any type of Union leaders in any IR situations. With his extraordinary business acumen and deep insights of human needs, he can freeze the volcano to glaciers. He is a win-win negotiator, but a double-winner always – winning the hearts along with the outcomes.

Book from a person of this caliber, **'Productivity Enhancement in Manufacturing Operations'** is a treasure for not only the practicing professionals, but the budding Engineers as well. I wish Professionals and Companies avail his wisdom and services through this book and his engagements.

I wish Alex all the best in his future endeavours!

– M.M. Durai Sayi

Vice President – Human Resources, Ashok Leyland

❖❖❖

In competitive manufacturing industry, productivity is vital and men, machine, material and money need to be synchronized continuously to deliver the output. Excellence becomes the key word to deliver the goods, at right time and right price. We need to be constantly innovate new methods, improve our process. Along with a cross functional team, Alex worked to study and improve the productivity. The team came out with several suggestions for implementation, which will enhance the productivity with minimum or no investments. Alex is a seasoned professional in studying and improving manufacturing process with inclusivity of the cross functional members across the organization. The methods suggested by him are based on the facts, scientific, easy to adopt, understand and implement. Implementation was possible as the people were involved at each stage.

Alex is completely a different type of Consultant from the traditional one's, more he works closely with shop floor employees and the Supervisors. He goes to the work areas to understand fully so that improvements can be carried out. This bring inclusivity and involvement of people cutting across different functions, in order to bring holistic approach and improving the productivity by implementing simple solutions to complex issues. Alex was with full of passion, commitment and brought the people together, cutting across function(s), made them to understand and deliver. Most of the solutions offered by him didn't call for investments and they are often change in the layout, simplifying the process and easy to understand and he puts his rich experience behind it.

– G Sathyanarayana

Vice President - Human Resources at TVS Srichakra Limited

❖❖❖

Conventional but Contemporary .... That's how, I would paraphrase Alex, as we fondly call him. Trained in the old conventional school of Industrial Engineering, he has evolved his applications of enhancing Productivity to suit the emerging trends. With extremely innovative and transparent systems of studying and improving productivity, he has helped us in many of our projects and negotiations with fearfully militant Trade Unions.

Alex has also this innate ability to customize, evolve and combine strategically and operationally impactful productivity linked bonus and incentive schemes. Always thinks Win –Win thereby maintaining equity amongst all stake holders.

As a person, he is extremely warm, affable, patient and open to contradictory opinion which is why he converts very successfully an opportunity to win friends and also goals.

He has always been a pleasure to work with

I strongly recommend the manufacturing and HR teams to make use of this book for enhancing productivity with lean manpower.

– Sukumaran.P.P

President - Group HR GVK Power & Infrastructure Ltd

❖ ❖ ❖

I was introduced to Mr. Alexander by my friend and colleague in Murugappa Group, Mr. P P Sukumaran about 15 years ago. In a manufacturing unit that I was managing, we had a need to conduct manpower study and productivity improvement possibilities. We engaged Mr. Alexander to help us on this. From the Day-1, I was mesmerized by the sheer focus, energy and highly people -oriented approach of Mr. Alexander. While obviously he has the subject matter expertise of Industrial Engineering, what makes him exceptional in my opinion is his people orientation, his energy level and his innate capability to motivate anyone he comes across.

He completed the assignment with us in a record time and convinced everyone including frontline employee about the possibility of a whopping 65% improvement in productivity without adding any manpower.

I am glad that through his book, many more people will be able to benefit from this epitome of knowledge, experience and practical guidance. I wish Mr. Alexander the very best of success.

– KK Bakshi

Consultant-Organization Development, Lean and TOC

Concentrate all your thoughts upon the work in hand. The sun's rays do not burn until brought to a focus – Alexander Graham Bell.

It's my absolute pleasure to write a commendation note on Mr. K.C. Alexander' s book on *"Productivity Enhancement at Manufacturing Operations"*

❖ ❖ ❖

Mr. K.C. Alexander and I worked together at TI Cycles of India from 2000 to 2002 and at Best & Crompton from 2007 to 2008. We fondly call him as Mr. KCA, who is known for his exemplary knowledge on Productivity enhancement techniques, be it white collar or blue collar productivity.

I thoroughly enjoyed my time working with Mr.KCA. He is honest, dependable, and incredibly hard-working. Beyond that, he is an impressive problem solver who is always able to address complex issues with strategy and confidence. Mr.KCA is inspired by challenges, and never intimidated by them.

As people have personalities, organizations have cultures. Some people are open to change and some are not. Some organizations embrace change as a catalyst for future growth and profitability, while some do not. Make no mistake; enhancing your productivity requires change. If any organization views change as an important business attribute, then ongoing productivity improvement will be their status quo. If the company is set in its ways, refuses to streamline its processes and shuns innovation, then productivity improvement is not required. Given today's business environment, the company will soon stagger under its own weight and fade away.

Over the course of my professional life, I have seen many great companies, small and large, get too set in their ways because of their incredible success purely riding on their productivity enhancement capabilities.

Mr.KCA' s knowledge of productivity and manufacturing techniques was simply amazing. He put this skill set to work in order to increase our total overall factory productivity by over 28% in just one quarter. This capacity enhancement not only eliminated the overtime culture but also brought in process improvements by simple layout changes and low cost automations. His contributions in making our entire workforce to perform multi-skilling and multi-tasking paved way for right sizing the operations crew and eliminating the man-machine imbalances. Going through the case studies he has presented in the book will certainly enrich a true professional's knowledge on productivity techniques.

His techniques not only enhanced the productivity for the management but also that of the workmen by a well-balanced motivational productivity incentive schemes. He is known in the industries for his craftsmanship in creating Productivity linked Incentive and Bonus schemes. Probably that is the reason how he got recognized by the leading Trade Unions and their affiliated bodies. He has been a member of the negotiating team for signing the wage settlements both during his service at various capacities and even after retirement.

I honestly appreciate and acknowledge his intention to give back the industry the knowledge and skill what he has learned in the form of this book. I hope everyone who is reads this book will find it valuable and the concepts explained with live case studies guide the reader about the techniques available to enhance their organization's productivity towards money, time and resources. I am sure this book will become a handbook for every individual who wants to drive productivity.

– F L Suresh

Former HR Head – TI Cycles, GM – HR Best and Crompton,

VP – HR – CRI Pumps, Coimbatore

❖ ❖ ❖

During my tenure of 36 years in Tube Investments of India, mostly in TI Cycles of India and four years in Tube Products, I had the opportunity of working with Mr. K.C. Alexander, as his subordinate and as a colleague later for many years.

I have not come across anyone like Alex, as we call him affectionately, who had his own style of Management in getting things done

When he was the Works Manager, I was responsible for Tool Room, and many incidents of tooling problems affecting Production and how Alex approached the Supporting functions like Maintenance and Tool Room in a very soft manner without an aggressive approach and got things done, revealed a unique personality.

Later, I was holding different positions as GM-Operations in TI Cycles and GM-Technical in TPI and TI Cycles as a colleague of Alex

The support he gave for the Technical and other Functions and the freedom he gives to his Team Members and his humane approach in problem solving, particularly handling the Labour, cannot be forgotten

I am really glad he has decided to share his abundant knowledge, of HR and Industrial Engineering and practical shop floor experience, through his Book. I wish Alex, all the best for his new venture.

– P. Shanmugham

Former GM – TI Cycles, GM – Tube Products of India, Chennai

❖❖❖

I have Known Mr. KC Alexander for the last 10 years – "a die-hard Engineer with a human touch".I first came across Alexander when I was heading Best and Crompton Engg as vice President –operation and he was engaged as a consultant to affect productivity improvements in the company and to help us formulate a Long Term settlement with the workmen.

Alexander's knowledge of the latest tools in productivity management and his down to earth approach in applying these tools to practical problems on hand, led to tremendous improvement in shop floor productivity and the work culture. For the first time, in the history of the company an agreement with the workers union for Zero Overtime was implemented. A clear win-win for all stake-holders. He had a holistic approach to problem solving and believed in interacting with the person involved in the actual work to bring in productivity improvements. With his help and advice, we were able to drastically bring down the rejection rate in the foundry by focusing on the principle of "first time right"

A man of very high integrity and strong conviction, he believed in transparency and fair play. During his engagement with the company, he always managed to foster positive discussions and bring the best out of both the workmen and the management team. A good communicator, who often drew cartoons of everyday happenings to put across his point of view in a light hearted but effective way. I have worked with many professional and consultants over my thirty odd years of professional career and Mr. Alexander stands out among them.

Mr. Alexander has now, in his new book, **"Productivity Enhancement in Manufacturing Operations"** captured the essence of productivity improvements gathered and painstakingly collated over a span of over 5 decades of his professional career. I trust this book would provide insight to generations of practicing engineers and management professionals in facing everyday challenges.

– MK Muralidharan

Director Vaishnavi Pumps and Valves Private Limited

Formerly - Vice President, Best and Crompton Engg. Ltd

and Retired Engineer Officer, Indian Navy

❖❖❖

I am a passionate Furniture industry man, having over 30 years of experience, out of which 22 years in Furniture. I started my Furniture career in 1997 as General Manager at Indian Furniture Products Limited (IFPL) and left them in 2005 to be rehired again in 2007. I worked there till end 2014.

When I rejoined in 2007, I was facing a hostile worker's union always at loggerheads with supervisors and management. They wouldn't adhere to instructions, quality consciousness was at the lowest ebb and on top it all, most of them would not work well in regular hours, to claim double payment on unwanted "Overtime".

I was completely perplexed and was sure that I would not be able to deliver results and I even started looking out of Middle East opportunities that came my way.

An elderly unassuming man with a certain "strict and tough" worn on his face came to us through our Production Manager who seemed to have worked with him in the past.

K.C. Alexander came, saw and conquered everyone's minds alike from casual labour to Managing Director. Unparalleled energy levels, a stickler to time and discipline, all of us learned immensely from him. I use to tell my supervisory staff that, work with him for 6 months, learn and you will be as good as an Industrial Engineering graduate with a management diploma.

We worked together on productivity improvement, wastage reduction, quality level enhancement and above all most important workmen productivity with significant measured more that 30% increased achievement in all aspects. The best is Overtime culture got completely abolished and workmen started to work and earn in real time. Needless to mention, company's costs came down and IFPL registered its best years from 2008–12.

Alexander Sir, called it a day at IFPL in 2014 and I was one of his "students" always requesting him to pen down his methodology and strategy into a book that could be useful for hundreds of organizations and managements.

I wish Alexander Sir, all the best and pray to God for his good health and long life. At this point, I must mention the ever-smiling Mrs. Alexander serving us her favourite mouth-watering lime juice and nuts during our several meetings that took place in his house at Anna Nagar.

– Satheesh Kumar

Former VP – IFPL, a Birla Group Unit

❖❖❖

Alex........, when I think of him, I am recalling and thinking of "Productivity". He was known or nicknamed as "Productivity Guru" even by all workmen, who used to say, seeing him in shop floor, "here comes the old productivity guru, he may again ask for more productivity today also."

I had close working relationship with him, ever since 2005 and till 2015 by working in two organizations. In the first organization, Borg Warner Tec, Murugappa, we were able to learn a lot from him by way of man hours, effective machine utilization, lean man power, line balancing, lay out changes, simple low cost automation to reduce fatigue of operators and so on. At the end we were able to turn around the unit by way of 30% man power reduction, 75% increase in productivity sadly, the implementation was tough having faced the labour strike then.

At the other unit of IFPL, a Birla group unit, fantastic achievements were achieved such as one shift reduction and that too with higher volume with reduced work force all because the total team involvement and by changing the mind set of workmen to raise productivity, along with product line lay out changes, a remarkable reduction from about 10% rejection of final furniture to almost 1% which is the best international standard. When the workmen started tasting closer to 5 digit amount by way of productivity incentive amount, their mind set changed for better along with total flexibility and zero over time work culture. It was like a miracle that happened in this troublesome unit which never made any profit except the period of change management taking place. His thoughtful practical productivity changes were like fulcrum which can move any mountain of low productivity, I am saying from my personal experience and after witnessing the proactive changes in the shop floor. The workforce generally felt that his teachings were a pleasant force on them to carry on productivity drive, somehow or other he was able to win over any of the worst operators with so much negative mind set which made the life of supervisors easy to manage them.

Currently, I am the Plant Head of a chain manufacturing unit near Delhi, I am very happy to share my experience of achieving great end results with record and mile stone achievements in the first year of my tenure for which I am most indebted by using my past experience of diversified management practices, many thanks to my productivity guru whom I am remembering with profound gratitude.

His book on productivity enhancement can be a saviour for any of the engineers struggling for quantum jump in productivity, this comes to you from my own vast experience of working with Alex or rather, productivity guru. You will love most of case practical examples amplified with interesting cartoons, at the end of the day, if you are under pressure like me to go for sky level of productivity with lean mean power, I strongly urge you to peruse this book, then you will also may join me to express happiness of going through it and for implementation of same. Best Wishes to the readers for achieving quantum jump in productivity in your manufacturing units.

– KA Nambi

Plant Head, LGB unit at Delhi

❖ ❖ ❖

Mr. Alexander, affectionately known as Alex, came to our unit of IFPL, the biggest manufacturing furniture company of Asia, and a part of Birla Group Company in the year 2007 and remained with us till about 2014 for helping us for productivity improvements and for facilitating the Signing of Long Term Settlement with hostile union. Sadly the management vs union relationship was at rock bottom with rampant Over Time work culture and riddled with total inflexibility practices by refusing to work anywhere else from his own machine job even on need basis, the supervisors were having very little empowerment to run the shop with union interference every now and then. With his guidance we were able to do a wonderful management charter of Demands which was presented to the union on the first day of Talks with union on LTS matters. The union expressed most dis satisfaction when it was made clear to them that no progress can come through unless it is agreed up on Touch Time or Machine Rated Norms by which only the company could arrive at a fair LTS amount after satisfying all management demands. At the end of 9 months discussions with lots of arguments and fights the new breath taking settlement was signed with more money on productivity linked Incentive schemes than fixed part of total affordable amount to workmen along with zero overtime work culture and total flexibility among the work men.

Things went on fine and the unit started making profit abolishing third shift of operation and still got more production in two shifts. Somehow the control got lost and situation became worse which resulted in strike for about 3 months and ultimately the war was won and another fantastic LTS was signed in 2013 and the workmen became partners of the company since then.

Alex, patiently guided us, took us to see few other companies such as Tube Products of India, Rane, Velacherry etc. which opened up our eyes by seeing the changes and after long interaction with both shop floor managers as well as union team and workmen. The greatest tribute in him is his capability to make us change our own self-belief by sharing all his work in elsewhere companies and making us positive minded for insisting changes from work men which were achieved as seen above.

Alex is well known as an effective change agent, savior, and highly demanded professional consultant with a difference, by many organizations of South India to bring unbelievable end results of productivity enhancement through well-organized study by way of lay out changes, lean manufacturing, right sizing of man power, various methods improvement along with low cost automation etc. and insisting on machine rated norms rather than bargained norms. Such productivity enhancement has been made part of wage settlements which often hailed as WIN: WIN for all stake holders of management, work men and customers.

This book on "Productivity Enhancement in Manufacturing Operations" aptly captures mantras for effecting productivity improvements in organized way with team work and along with taking the work men on board without which it can only end in failures. The distilled wisdom of Alex based on his five decades of practical implemented experience in many units captured crisply in simple language with plenty of understandable case studies can help readers in the area of productivity improvements and related space. In my opinion this book on most difficult task of achieving quantum jump in productivity is God send, it is amazingly inspiring, simple, and yet powerful book for both manufacturing team in shop floor and HR professionals. This statement comes to you having tasted and reaped the benefits in our unit and in many other units also because the insights he provides with help of cartoons, diagrams, lay outs etc in this book are most practical and relevant for all dynamic professionals who are under pressure to reduce head count and see the productivity graph goes up in all coming months of their stay in the company

– S. Palani

Former General Manager, HR of IFPL Zuari Group
- Furniture Division until 2015.

❖❖❖

Mr. Alexander is a well-known man who laid the foundation of "maximum productivity" with the optimum man power in many organizations. Earlier, there was disparity in incentive earnings of employees. After the revised incentive schemes introduced in 1987, we could see the positive change, people started talking about productivity, machine capacity, ideal time, down time, all the things took place beautifully well. As a union leader, we have raised many doubts, Mr. Alexander never denied in clarifying our doubts. He usually takes the even minor details into consideration and prepared detailed report with fairness. Always, he put his effort to make the people to understand and agree. Initially we had a scheme up to 1987 and by which the operators earned around Rs: 30. Today, it has crossed Rs: 10,000 in many departments and the scheme is taking care to achieve higher production levels. Whatever change taking place in process will be addressed in due course without making any loss to employee. That is the kind part of his work. We learned lot from him. He believed in cordial relationship and healthy conversation between union and management.

Over a period of time the lay outs in all shops became hazardous with safety issues along with congestion, low productivity etc. Mr. Alexander took the initiative of extending the manufacturing bays with better material handling equipment and low cost automation to reduce fatigue of various operators along with far better lay out changes. This by itself added considerable happiness in the minds of work men and volume and productivity went up very high.

Mr. Alexander is the person who takes care of both sides the management and the workers. The book purely speaks about productivity. Now the word is commonly used in many organizations, but thirty years back, the word was unheard until it was introduced by the people like Mr. Alexander with the help of M/s A.K. Raj/ Jackson along with all production teams. Mr. Alexander at that time when he introduced the word "Productivity," he made sure the people to pronounce, understand, utilize it and made both sides to enjoy the taste of productivity. His hard working nature, passion and people relationship are incomparable. He utilized the right persons to follow his schemes for the continuous successful implementations in successive years. He always believes in GOD. He treats all the human beings with utmost respect and generally takes care of them.

He still is remembered as a man who introduced the concept of Productivity in our manufacturing units some 30 years ago

– G. Udayakumar

Ex- secretary, Tube Products Employees Union, Chennai

❖❖❖

"It was the year 2000.I was in charge of Manufacturing of Grinding wheels at TVT plant in Chennai. We were having a long term settlement discussion with the Labour Union at TVT, going on. We were poised for a big change in the work culture. There were lot of restrictive work practices at the shop floor, tremendous overtime work culture, frequent Go-slow making the life of the Supervisor and the Manager that much more difficult to plan and manage day to day production.

This was the time Mr. Alexander was introduced to the core manufacturing team at TVT. What a meeting it turned out to be, when I sit back and think about it!!

Personally, I went through a transformation, when I heard Mr. Alexander's views on productivity. It gave an altogether different perspective for the word "PRODUCTIVITY."

He was sharing his experience at the shop floors of Tube Products of India and TI Diamond Chain plant. He also ensured to make arrangements for the TVT production team to visit these plants. I along with my colleagues visited both the plants. It was an eye opener for us. What can be done through simple layout changes, automation, flexibility in work place, all we could visibly see happening.

Once the shop floor visit was over, the seeding of the thoughts gained strongly and I returned as a rejuvenated person to implement what I saw elsewhere in my work place.

Mr. Alexander with his experience, guided us well and with his perseverance pushed and nudged us so much to be data oriented, so that we do not make any mistakes in our assumptions. All the while, the negotiations with the Union were on, and when we started presenting our proposals to them, even though initially the Union resisted, the resistance was much less, since all the proposals were meant to be making the life of the workmen simple and easier. With reluctance Union agreed to our proposals of flexibility, group output, lowering of losses and group incentive from individual incentive scheme payment. What a transformational change it turned out to be!

The Long term settlement (LTS) signed with the Union in the year 2000 was a historic one, and it became the bench mark for other industries in the TVT belt.

The results achieved were quite impressive with productivity increases ranging from a minimum of 25% to 50% in some places. This was after reducing the permanent manpower strength form a total of 600 to 400.

What a journey it turned out to be, if I recollect my thoughts. It was most satisfying, and professionally gave me lot of confidence, to address Productivity improvements, in many places, I went in my career after successfully implementing at TVT, CUMI Hosur plant also was transformed in the similar style, when I was given the responsibility as a Plant Head.

At a much later stage when I took responsibility in one of the ITES (IT ENABLED SERVICES) Company in Pondicherry, a similar change was made and we could see the productivity improving by 30–40%.

The Book on "Productivity" by Mr. Alexander is a wonderful gift to any person who loves to be a Production guy in any of the industries. It gives lot of, real time shop floor examples in one part and gives lots of insight what can be done in the other part.

At the age of 80, IT IS REALLY WONDERFUL, that Mr. Alexander has chosen to share his experience and knowledge through his book. ANY PERSON ASPIRING TO BE A PRODUCTION GUY should have this book with him.

– Nattamai Samyien Balasubramaniam
(NASA) – Former VP Manufacturing of all CUMI Units

❖❖❖

Acknowledgement & Remembering you with Gratitude

It would be highly unprofessional if I take entire credit for productivity enhancement of various organizations wherein I also contributed my humble mite. At best I may deserve the credit ranging from 1 to 10%. All the rest of 90% belongs rightly to the right team members of manufacturing and other departments besides the total support of top management. Not the least is the contribution that of workmen of various units for successful implementation of higher productivity with right sized lean man power. Mr. Thirunavakkarasu, the union leader, is remembered for radical mind set changes in the minds of workmen for higher productivity with right sized man power and he was well supported by Mr. Udayakumar for long period for sustenance of higher productivity along with much higher Incentive amount for the workmen.

Specifically, I would have never contributed for higher productivity but for the total support of M/s M V Subbiah, M A Alagappan, A Vellayen, M M Murugappan of Murugappa Group Companies for many years and in many units. It is difficult to find words to express my gratitude to each one of them .Even after retirement, I had many years of useful assignments mainly in the area of productivity enhancement in many units under their control, what more should I comment?

Mrs. Vanitha Mohan, Vice Chairman of Pricol, Coimbatore is greatly thanked and acknowledged for contributing towards significant productivity growth in all 4 manufacturing units. The support and guidance rendered by her and team members sustained me going for about 4 years.

Two other great professionals who helped the Tube Investments units to scale up on productivity ladder are the late Mr. A Hydari and Mr. L Ramkumar, the present MD. Indeed I had great innings with each of them and not out on scoring on productivity runs, how much I should be grateful to them! Thank you, Sehal, my great HR Professional friend forever.

One of my best experience towards the tail end of my consultancy work was working at IFPL under Mr. D K Jairath for the turnaround challenge of the organization.

Mr. Gopalakrishnan Udaykumar, CEO of Core Mind is one person who encouraged me to revive the book writing when I almost gave it up due to some health reasons. Thank You, Uday

M/s Ramkumar, Hussain Sehal, Mrs. Vanitha Mohan, M/s G Udaykumar and D K Jairath are profoundly thanked for their nice and wonderful forward notes.

My colleagues, team members or bosses like M/S, G Shivaprasd, AK Sehanobis, P Shanmugam, A A Ramalingam, K Perumal, SS Gopalarathinam, TM Gopalapillai, Durai Sayi, N Prasad, K K Bakshi, PP Sukumaran, NASA, G Sathynarayana, Muraleeedharan, F L Suresh, C M Satheesh kumar, S Palani, K A Nambi, T C Chandran, G Udayakumar the list goes on to whom I say BIG THANKS to each one of unique personality with tons of Gratitude. Thank You all for your wonderful commendation letters.

It is impractical and rather impossible to list down the names of all those people dead or alive who helped for productivity growth in respective units and therefore each one of them is remembered with gratitude for their wonderful support rendered for most difficult task of productivity enhancement and as such they are the winners to be thanked not only by me but my colleagues and seniors as well. Trust this observation is well taken by all those my dear friends, some of them are in touch with each other also.

Let me be honest and frank to acknowledge the enormous work and contributions rendered by Dr. A.K. Raj, PhD for shaping this book in the present form and format. I had the opportunity to work with him for about 25 years while at TII Units. After retirement and in recent months both of us decided to scribble our productivity experiences for sharing with readers of the book for the goal of enhancing productivity in their units. Well, this book is the combined efforts of both the author and co-author.

I hasten to express our profound thanks to Ms. Charmine and her wonderful team members of Notion Press for working like partners of this complex book publishing.

Introduction

Some of my professional friends used to ask me the question, "How long are you going to work as Consultant even at this age of 80 years and what foot prints or professional benefits are you going to leave for the Manufacturing team of any company as a whole at the end of the day in life?" This question prompted me to categorize all that I have done or contributed in the last 53 years of working in as much as 25 manufacturing units of various organizations of repute from 1962 to 2015. The entire work experience can be summarized under {1}, Productivity Enhancement in manufacturing operations {2} Lean Manufacturing {3} Productivity Linked Wage Settlements. The specialized connecting interlinking word of all the three topics is that of Productivity Enhancement which is as important as Oxygen supply to our body as proof of living on this planet!

As years go on, the pressure on manufacturing team from supervisors to manager to GM{Manufacturing} to VP {0perations} are so enormous to enhance productivity and reduce head counts month by month in changing business environments. It is most sensitive issue to be handled by management and if not handled, it can lead to disasters. The manufacturing team is not able to smile and enjoy the work or job since they are always hammered between management and workmen/union leave alone the demanding customers. Unless they are guided properly and unless they are highly self-motivated and determined before taking up this challenge, they are unlikely to achieve the desired end results.

This book on "Productivity Enhancement in manufacturing operations" is aimed to help and train the manufacturing team to become highly motivated and to avoid pitfalls by quick or fast changes without adequate thinking and then to suggest various techniques or tools to raise the productivity.

Part 1 of this book contains a detailed write up of Motivational stories of great people of this world. No woman be mother, sister or wife has ever delivered a baby without undergoing labour pain. No gain will come through without getting highly motivated, determined, and committed with high degree of persistence and passion. A few of the pitfalls by going for quick and fast productivity which have become disastrous are also highlighted.

Part 2 deals with various techniques which are applied in many organizations with proven good end results. The best way to impart or instill confidence in to minds of supervisors is by narrating the real experience of few companies. It is my experience while working in many manufacturing units and invariably they will say that we can also do it better for raising the productivity under their control.

At the end of reading of this book, it is hoped that the manufacturing team would be highly motivated and enthused to undertake the project with self-confidence and of course with the support of top management team. Sooner than later the SMILING FACES can be seen month after month which means more Oxygen supplies to the organization.

All the stake holders of the company from top management to management team to workmen to customers should be the beneficiaries of this change.

And if that happens, the purpose of this book is achieved, no matter whether I am alive or not, I will have the satisfaction of leaving good and useful foot prints for the manufacturing team to walk and achieve the goals beyond the expectations of the bosses with every possibility of good recognition from top management to the manufacturing team which will be highly pleasing to the family members at home and further no need to think of change of job and company too!!

LET IT HAPPEN IN YOUR MANUFACTURING AREA!

PART 1

Motivation and Avoiding Common Mistakes

1. Basic Need for Productivity Enhancement Study

"Productivity and Profit are like oxygen, food, water and blood for the body, they are not the point of life, but without them, there is no life, you have to initiate and no one else can do your job. You create your opportunity by asking for them"

– Patty Hansen

Just as oxygen is most essential for life, so is the Profitability of any manufacturing company for its survival and growth. The most important key for the Profitability is through Productivity of labour, machines, material and all other resources.

The Ball of Productivity is in your court. It is for you to score goals. But, we may have to change our age old manufacturing style of management. Our Attitude, our Aim, Desire and Passion have to be significantly higher level than it was before as days and years go on.

Days have changed. Today is not like 20 or 10 years or ever 5 years ago. Today is the day of change or else we may perish. Execute or Be Executed. Change everything other than your wife, as jokingly said by someone. Each one of us is responsible for making significant changes as of now and past team cannot be blamed.

"My fellow citizens, Ask not the Government, what it can do for you, ask yourself what can you do for the country'

– John F Kennedy

In our kaleidoscopic environment, Managers have to reach change, initiate change, plan for change and cope with change. The Manager is the only individual whose specific assigned function is coping, but more than that whose function is helping others to cope. Success depends on the success of other people. This is the basic rule for success. The only hurdle between you and what you want to be is the support of others.

Substantial Productivity enhancement is going to be saviour for you, the company and workmen. Make no little plans, they have no magic to stir men's blood and probably in themselves will not be realized. Make big plans, aim high in hope and work, remembering that a noble logical diagram once recorded will never die. Do initiate, do look for Quantum jump in productivity. If you think you can, you can. Display enthusiasm for productivity. Nothing great is achieved without enthusiasm. The wind and waves are always on the side of ablest navigators. Do uncommon things. Do things differently. Do not be satisfied with unsatisfied satisfaction of low productivity. Go all out for productivity and manage higher Productivity of all resources. Are we to expect the workmen to work with hands to the tune of say 85% level and go home? Or, do we want them to work as Partners of Progress, Prosperity, Productivity and Profitability using their talents of Skill Flexibility Planning skill, Positive Attitude and so on?

Nothing in this world can take the place of persistence. Talent will not, nothing is more common than unsuccessful men with talent. Genius wills not, unrewarded genius is almost a proverb. Educations will not, the world is full of derelicts. Persistence and determination alone are omnipotent.

Remember, that the creator God has designed you to do much more greater things by you in the shop. Do not despair. Do not feel bitter about low productivity, but feel better that you can take to sky limit. No more frantic and frenetic days in career. We ordinary people can do extraordinary things if we are committed.

Do We Have to Confront the Brutal Facts on Low Productivity?

"Confrontation doesn't always bring a solution to the problem,
but, until you confront the problem, there will be no solution"

– James Baldwin

How long you can afford not take action on Productivity? Remember today is the tomorrow you put off yesterday – on taking action.

In short, we need to be highly motivated with the highest degree of persistence. Perhaps a few of the greatest motivational stories of few people could highly motivate us for our present task of productive environment with commitment, determination, persistence and diligence

2. Motivational Breakthroughs - The Power of Persistence

Author Michael on Biography of Abraham Lincoln Commented

"To come from such a background where he really suffered from emotional malnutrition (his baby brother dies, his mother dies when he is nine, his father is unsympathetic and beats him, his older sister dies, his sweetheart dies before marriage, he has a terrible marriage, two of his children die, he suffers career failures many times, and has a difficult midlife crisis for a long period), and yet he overcomes all that to become not only famous but profoundly psychologically whole and mature, balanced and a model of moral clarity with unimpeachable integrity"

"I think that there is hope for all of us"

– Abraham Lincoln

The man who became the 16th president of U.S.A was nothing if not resilient, as the record of setbacks he overcame on his path to the presidency shows:

1832	Lost job
1832	Defeated for state legislature
1833	Failed in business and lost all his little savings 1834 Elected to state legislature
1835	Death of sweetheart
1836	Nervous breakdowns, many times.
1838	Defeated for post of Speaker
1843	Defeated for nomination to congress
1846	Elected to congress
1848	Lost nomination
1849	Rejected for post of land officer
1854	Defeated for US Senate
1856	Defeated for nomination for Vice president
1858	Again defeated for US Senate
1860	Elected President of United States of America

And do remember what a most wonderful shortest speech he gave at Gettysburg, possibly this world has never such a great statesman so far on this earth. What qualification he had inherited?

Winston Churchill

The political leader who navigated the world war-2 had a very bad start right from the birth. He was born two months before the due date. His aristocrat parents never had any time to look after him from the birth. He was sent to boarding school as a child. He did not excel academically well except in English and History. He had speech impediment. At the age of 19 he nearly drowned in an accident in Lake Lausanne and at age 57 he was hit by a car in New York City

A graduate of the Royal Military Collage joined British Army and travelled in many places and wrote newspaper reports and books. He resigned to pursue journalism and politics. He sought a seat in Parliament, but lost election. He then travelled to South Africa as a journalist covering the Boer War, where he was captured and thrown in to prison. He managed to escape to England and won the parliament seat. In 1940 he became Prime Minister and in the position, exercised brilliant, courageous, strategic, leadership that rescued Great Britain From the edge of seemingly certain defeat to victory in World War-2.

In 1941while visiting the school where had studied as a youngster, the then Prime Minister Churchill delivered a short speech. "This is the lesson: never give in, never, never give in, never, never, never- in nothing, great or small, large or petty- never give in except to convictions of honour and good sense. Never yield to force; never yield to the apparently overwhelming might of the enemy." He then exhorted the school boys in 1941- "Whatever you do never give in – and never, never, never give up."

His speech of just 733 words took about 4 minutes whereas Abraham Lincoln's Gettysburg address of 272 words took less than 2 minutes. Even today these two speeches are the greatest best ever speeches addressed by any Politicians of this world!

The True Story of Wilma Rudolph, an Outstanding Female Athlete

'The block of granite which was an obstacle in the pathway of the weak becomes a stepping –stone in the pathway of the strong'.

– Thomas Carlyle

On June 23rd 1940, Wilma Rudolph was born prematurely as 20th of 22 children in a poor family reeling from the impact of the Great Depression. She had scarlet fever, pneumonia and she was affected with polio from birth and had to be driven 52 miles per week to a hospital for blacks where she received treatment. There the doctor said as Wilma recalled, "I would never walk again. My mother said i would. I believed my mother." She started to walk with a brace until she was nine years old and by 12, she was able to walk normally within 4 short years, at age sixteen, she won her first Olympic medal. 4 years later at 1960 Olympics in Rome, she earned gold medals in 3 events and became an international super star. How? She wanted to see her desires fulfilled and she did because she never gave up.

This achievement led her to become one of the most celebrated female athletes of all times and won several state awards.

A True Great Motivational Story

The young man was the son of a horse trainer who would go from stable to stable, race track to race track, farm to farm, ranch to ranch, in the course of his work.

As a result the boy's high school career was constantly interrupted. When he was at high school he was asked to write a paper about what he wanted to be and what he would do when he grew up. He wrote about his DREAM in great detail (and not like some of you!!). He drew a diagram of a 200 acre ranch, showing the location of all the buildings, the stables, the track. Then he produced a detailed plan for a 4000 square -foot house that would sit on the 200 acre DREAM RANCH!

Two days later he got his paper back. On the front page was a large "F" with a note that read, "SEE ME AFTER CLASS." The boy with his DREAM went to see the teacher and asked, "why did I get an F?" The teacher said, "This is completely unrealistic dream for a young boy like you. You have no money. You have no resources. You need a lot of money to own a horse ranch. You have to buy the land. You have to pay for the original breeding stock and later you will have to pay large stud fees. You must be crazy. This is not the way to have your "DREAM."

Then the teacher with a kind sympathetic heart added, "If you rewrite this paper on your stupid Dreams with a more realistic goal, I will reconsider your grade for a pass"

The boy went home and thought about it long and hard.

Finally after sitting with it for a week, he turned in the same paper making no changes at all. He wrote in the margin, "You can keep your "F" and I will keep my DREAM."

The boy was MONTY ROBERTS, creator of the "horse whispering" concept and the author of several books on the subject. He was telling the story in his 4000 square feet house in the middle of his 200 acre horse ranch."

"Don't let anyone steal your DREAMS, he is telling you and me, "Follow your heart, no matter what."

A few More Glimpses of Motivational Stories

1. Bestselling author John Grisham's first book was rejected by 12 publishing houses and sixteen agents.
2. Enrico Caruso was told that "he could not sing at all." And yet he became the world famous singer.
3. Walt Disney was fired from newspaper on the ground that he "lacked imagination and had no original ideas."
4. A movie producer told Marilyn Monroe that "she was unattractive and could not act."
5. Elvis Presley was fired in October 1954 for poor performance and was advised to become a truck driver and yet he became the greatest of all time in singing and acting.
6. J K Rowling was totally broken, and severely depressed few years back. All publishers refused to publish her books and eventually Nigel Newton published Harry Potter books to please his daughter. Today Harry Potter books are sold more than 260

million copies, possibly the highest record and she is now one of the wealthiest women in the world.

7. You already know the true stories of Henry Ford and Thomas Edison, who was deaf and who invented maximum patents in this world including electricity bulbs. Edison was sent out of the school at the age of about 8 years when he was a third standard student, being too deaf and dumb to study. But his mother never gave up hopes of her son and together they worked hard. And he became the world's number one inventor with zero qualification. You know the story of Beethoven the famous deaf music composer.

There are many more successful people in this world. And all of them had the unique quality of "Never give up" and they exhibited determination, commitment, passion, perseverance, willingness for change with diligence.

Who knows from 5 years now, may be so much will be written on Narendra Modi!!

If we have such attitude, there is no reason, why we cannot achieve tremendous productivity enhancement in manufacturing operations. If you do not have such persistent positive attitude for facing all hardship of change management of achieving quantum jump in productivity, the reading of this book can be a wasteful exercise for you and that is the only purpose of narrating the true stories of great men to inspire you and instill you. If you are in the same wave length, please be patient to peruse the rest of this book.

3. Concepts of Productivity and Productivity Management

General Objectives of Production Management

- ❖ To carryout manufacturing, Operation at low cost
- ❖ To manufacture products at a predetermined quality level
- ❖ To manage a production schedule that maximizes Customer Satisfaction, yet gives manageable flow of works.

What is Productivity Management?

Productivity + Management→Productivity Management.

Productivity: Productivity is the optimization of all available resources. It is always expressed as a ratio of output to input.

Productivity = Output/Input

Management: Management concerns itself with the following three types of activities. Resources Input > Management Processes > Performance Output

Input: Money, Men, Materials and Capital Equipment.

What is Management?

Management is the organisation, motivation and control of human activity directed to specific needs.

In a typical company, the various factors effecting productivity are the responsibility of many different functional Managers. They may manage their limited area of responsibility effectively, but few can be truly said to manage productivity. This is a top management responsibility.

Labour Productivity

In National economics, the term productivity is often used in the sense of Labour Productivity.

Labour Productivity = Output/Labour Input

Every organization has products, either goods or service. Cars, Tyres, Bicycles, Tubes, Chains etc. are few examples of goods. Transportation and retail distribution are example of services.

What are the Other few Important Productivity Measures?

Machine Productivity

It is the ratio of Actual output/Cycle Time Output or Standard Output for the hour or shift.

What is Material Productivity?

Ratio of Actual Material content in the product/the material used for the product. It is almost similar to the yield of the material for the product.

What is the Productivity of the Enterprise?

According to Dr. J.E. Faraday

Productivity of the Enterprise = Output/(Labour Input + Capital Equipment + Raw Material/Parts + Miscellaneous)

Since our concern is mainly on Productivity enhancement, let us move on to labour productivity which substantial head count reduction, with all possible avenues.

Productivity is defined as the ratio of total outputs to total inputs, or the ratio of results of achieved to resources consumed, or the ratio of effectiveness with which organizational goals are achieved to the efficiency with which resources are consumed in the course of achievement. A basic and commonly and productivity measure is "Output per Hour."

$$\text{Productivity} = \frac{\text{Output realized}}{\text{Hours used to obtain the outputs}} = \frac{\text{Output}}{\text{Hour}}$$

Using specific example, let's say 10 units of output were produced using 5 units of labour, then:

Productivity = 10/5 = 2.0

Let's also say that in a following period of time 12 units of output were produced in the same work situation, using 6 units of labour, then:

Productivity = 12/6 = 2.0

Though the output has increased the amount of resources consumed has also increased, in this case in exact proportion to the increase in output, thus productivity remain same. To improve productivity we must accomplish one or more of the following changes. Note: The base Period referenced in the examples provided is:

Output/Input = 10/5 = 2.0

1. Maintain the same level of output while at the same time reducing the input or consumptions of resources. ie:

   10/4 = 2.5

   Note: Referring to the definition that productivity = effectiveness/efficiency in this example we have improved the efficiency of labour inputs, we have achieved the same result using fewer labour hours, thus productivity has increased from an output of 2.0 to 2.5 units produced per labour hour.

2. Maintain the same level of input while at the same time increasing the output, i.e., 11/5 = 2.2

   Note: Again referring to the definition that productivity = effectiveness/efficiency, in this example we have increased the effectiveness, or the magnitude of the results achieved or output, without increasing the labour inputs, thus productivity has increased from an output of 2.0 to 2.2 units produced per labour hour.

3. Increasing the level of output while at the same time decreasing the input, i.e., 11/4 = 2.75

   Note: In this case we have increased the effectives, or magnitude, of results achieved while reducing the quantity of resources consumed. In so doing, we have significantly increased productivity from 2.o to 2.75 units produced labour hour.

   In your manufacturing operations and in reality the operations could be much more complex with crew size of 3 to 7 operators for few machines in a complex layout. The challenge is to maximize the output with lowest number of head counts by the productivity enhancement team with various options and avenues for achieving the same. Let us move on the practical side of the challenge before us.

   Above examples are given in tabular form as shown below:

Impact of Input and output on productivity

Example	Scenario	Output(units)	Labour Input (units)	Productivity= Output/Input	%productivyty improvement over base level
1	Base	10	5	2	
2	Output↑ Input↑	12	6	2	0
3	Output↔ Input↓	10	4	2.5	25
4	Output↑ Input↔	11	5	2.2	10
5	Output↑ Input↓	11	4	2.75	38

↑ Increase   ↓ Decrease   ↔ same base level

4. Avoid Quick Fixing of Norms or Work Standards

A Tyre manufacturing company in South India was hard pressed during the years of 1961 to 1962 to increase the productivity of Tyre making section within 2 years of installation of all plants. Such an idea was initiated by head of production. Based on his earlier experience and intuition he fixed Norms with-out in depth study for various Tyres produced in the shop and he immediately recommended a quick fixed like fast food incentive scheme just for this section alone. The results were highly appreciated for about 3 – 4 months until things started changing. The incentive amount was linked to the then prevailing D.A {Dearness Allowance} fixed as per certain government formula based on cost of living. When the DA went on increasing the incentive amount also got multiplied which was overlooked by the concerned manager. When the money got increased the operators started reducing the production numbers having been satisfied with that much money and further on the attitude of "let us keep some cushion for next negotiation on increased Norms" Soon, the operators of all other sections started demanding for incentive scheme in their sections also. Some adhoc schemes were given and soon arguments started by the union on the veracity of Norms. Very soon the era of strike started in this unit and in the next 3 years the number of working days was far less than the actual working days. It went on for next 10 years at least with heavy losses for the company and wage losses for the workmen.

There are a number of other companies also that got into quick norms and poorly thought incentive schemes which invariably resulted into serious IR issues and conflict between management and changing union teams of the company. Once some money is given to the workmen and when they taste it for some time, it is almost an impossible task to get rid of, at best the union may agree for some changes provided the men get more money just for agreeing too few changes. In fact, it is worse than undergoing the pain of divorce of the spouse. It may not be out of context to mention that one company at Hosur [the name is withheld] was permanently closed down because of severe dispute on a wrong incentive scheme. There were so many issues especially during the period of 1970 to 1980 with regard to implementation of ill-conceived incentive schemes. It may not be appropriate if the names of such companies are disclosed and blaming any company is not our objective either.

> **The moral of this incidence experience is to say, "Be careful and do not be in hurry to set Norms or standards without the process getting well attained. Wait for achievement of at least 85% of expected Norms before setting the standards. Do check on the similar Norms of few competitors. Never go for fast food like incentive schemes."**

5. Avoid too Loose Norms or Tight Norms Which Will Boomerang Shortly

A well-known mass production torch light battery manufacturing unit in South India had the rejection rate at final stage of testing to the tune of about 1% during the year 1962 Translated in to numbers it varied around 10000 numbers per day. The practice was to salvage as many good parts like bobbin tubes from the rejected lot. This multinational company had a norm fixed at about 300 numbers of salvaging of battery cells. But the Head of production thought of fixing tight Norms in order to apply pressure on the workmen and supervisors and he fixed it to 350 numbers per person per shift. But the production rate never went beyond 250 numbers per person and the head count in this section went up to 40 people instead of sanctioned strength of 30 people. This was not acceptable to head office. The operators of this section were mainly from Anglo Indian community girls considered to be very smart. Every second month the non-achievers were sacked and new girls were recruited only to repeat the story worse with due training period to do the job. The cycle went on with more shouting by the factory manager on poor productivity and more manpower deployment in every shift having salvaging work. When the girls came to join the company for a temporary period of say 9 months, they had a mind-set of not able to stay on for more than 3 months however they worked hard, from the feedback of earlier girls who worked here. The poor senior supervisor who earned a good name in the same company lost all his credibility and the HOD went on shouting on him.

At this point of time in 1964, when I was hired by this multinational company which was 4th in the whole world in those years, the first assignment was how to set right the productivity of this section which was doing hardly 250 numbers as against the Norm of 350 numbers per girl per shift. Without any previous experience in this company, the best option for me was to see with own eye the things going on in the shop floor and as well the mindset of the girls working there. The repair work or salvaging work differed battery to battery and to say that they should complete 350 numbers did not make any sense according to my preliminary judgement. When some girls got a good name for completing about 300 numbers, they got good appreciation from the bosses, but the girls who could do around 200 numbers got nothing but abuse in spite of their genuine efforts! The entire salvaging work were classified in to major, medium and minor depending on the work content and the numbers recommended for these categories were 200, 300 and 400 numbers per shift per girl which was understood and agreed to by the supervisor and most of the girls. In order to monitor the daily output the equivalent factor of 1.5, and 1.0 and 0.75 were explained to them based on the broad work content according to the degree of salvaging work. Thus the girl who could do only about 200 numbers of major classified category would have the satisfaction of achieving the equated output of 300 by multiplying 200 x 1.5 and the girl with minor rework content would be asked to complete 400 to achieve 300 equated numbers by multiplying 400 x 0.75. This way the fairness was established in about 3 months' time and the girls started pouring more enthusiasm and came out with plans of having suitable rework table and various other low cost facilities in their work area and they themselves divided the battery repair work among themselves based on guidelines. They started things with their own planning with least instructions from the supervisors. By the end of 3 months the average number of repaired batteries went up to 325 from the earlier average of about 225 numbers per girl per shift that is they were able to achieve more than 40% productivity. This achievement credit went to USA headquarters because it was still higher than 300 numbers considered to be a landmark achievement. The supervisor who was denied increment started getting more increments and got promoted. Some of the girls who were more studious for innovative mind set changes got permanent position and 2–3 girls became management staff in due course.

If the experiences of few well known big companies located at Chennai on the ongoing disputes on NORMS between union and management are to be captured we need one exclusive big book. Our purpose is to understand the seriousness and to avoid such cases based on the real experiences of other companies.

The moral of this real story is, "Never set standards without in depth study and start blaming the poor supervisors and the operators for non-achievement. In any case such things will end up in disastrous end results only."

---

6. Assess the Real Morale and Happiness of the Operators Before You Think of Fixing the Norms

In 1967, the GM was very furious on the low output of only one Slitter available in a Steel processing manufacturing unit of a big group company. The low output of about 3 coils or about 15 Tons per shift was the bottleneck operation of this unit at that point of time. He was getting fed up with all sorts of rea-sons and excuses for not getting higher production such as old machine, high breakdowns and operators were not willing to raise the output and so on. He thought it would be better if he could spend one shift to assess the real causes and possibly they might give extra output in that shift by not wasting time. The GM, known as tiger Ram {name changed} stood in the shop floor for the whole shift and reluctantly he sat on a stool provided by one operator. The workmen or crew of 5 people were very clever and acted working hard without wasting any time at all. At the end of shift he was most angry by the output of just 2.75 coils!

On being asked by GM, I had to report to him on steps needed to raise the output beyond 4 coils to start with. From my earlier experience I knew nothing big could be achieved unless I took them into confidence and started discussing with each one of them on their difficulties and grievances. This attitude made all the difference, they said, "No one else bothered to ask our difficulties or concerns; they come and go without even listening on our issues. You appear to be different and so we will certainly cooperate with you provided you address to our concerns. The leather gloves supplied recently are not helping us to prevent our frequent finger cuts. Our main operator is paid less than the second operator without any skill level for this job because of his transfer from somewhere to this Slitter. The scissor sup-plies are extremely poor for cutting the steel coils. There are frequent breakdowns and there is setting delay frequently."

When all the above ongoing scenarios were explained to the so called tiger GM, he was more reason-able than thought of. He readily understood the prejudging on supervisors and the operators were a mistake and asked for quick implementation of the low cost proposals. Surprisingly the production level went to above 4 coils per shift with about 33% increase in productivity which was the demand of GM for achieving higher throughput from the unit by way of end products.

The moral of the story is to highlight the need of understanding the root and real causes of low productivity in any section before jumping in to conclusions. Let us remember that we need workmen cooperation for achieving much higher productivity in this era. Unless the workmen understand the actions taken by management including the genuine grievance addressing, they are unlikely to co-operate for higher volume and productivity anywhere and everywhere of the manufacturing operations.

7. Think Twice Before Introducing Rejection Control Scheme

In few Forging companies during the period of 1970 to 1980, the tendency to recommend incentive schemes to reduce rejection rates or speed up the repair or salvaging work was there, because the cost of material salvaged would be much more than the incentive amount paid to the operators. The scheme for example could be to reduce the rejection rates from say 5% level to about 1% level with attractive amount. In the initial months the operators could be happy with more money in hand and with lots of rejected forgings to salvage. But when the rejection rates started coming down with fewer actions initiated by management on furnace, dies and electrical maintenance, the operators did not have enough numbers to earn more money and in turn, the other operators started doing things favourable for having more rejection rates. Thus, the very purpose of having the usefulness of incentive schemes were defeated in such companies. The material wastage was much more than the incentive amount paid to the men.

In few grain manufacturing units for grinding wheels, the incentive schemes met partial success to bring down the costly rejection rates especially at furnaces. In one Steel processing unit, the need for having suitable incentive scheme was thought of many times. Finally suitable Yield incentive schemes were recommended in the year 2000 along with negotiation under wage agreement for about 4 years. The end result was good in few sections in few months, but the grievances and disparity in earnings became unbearable for union and even the management teams. Finally such schemes were scrapped in later agreements with the union

In one of the big furniture manufacturing unit in South India, they had the problem of high rejection rates detected at the final packing section resulting in to high level of rejection rates of about 7 to 8% or to the tune of about 800 to 1000 furniture products per month. Non completion of rejected WIP furniture meant very high loss to the company and severe customer dissatisfaction. The operators came out with reasons and excuses for not completing the WIP furniture processing in the month. A well thought incentive scheme was recommended and with difficulty in the initial months it got implemented by way of attitude change for timely processing of such WIP furniture instead of accumulating the same. At a later period, a few innovative steps were initiated to control the rejection rates to about 2.5 to 3.0% level from the earlier level of 7 to 8% levels. At the end of the day of the month, both management and workmen were most happy on the outcome and still they enjoy it with equal partnership.

The moral of the above real experiences of few companies is to highlight the need for thinking twice before coming out with incentive schemes to control rejection rates for the mutual benefits of both management and the workmen. If not done properly, it can end up in poor productivity after introduction of such schemes.

8. Always Rethink of Having the 3rd and 2nd Shift Operations

A well-known Bicycle Dynamo manufacturing unit in South India had 3 shift operations up to the year 1987 until the new Works manager was deputed to trim the organization for significant productivity improvements for the survival of the unit. By 1988, he came out with well thought plans of eliminating the 3rd shift operations except at heat treatment and furnaces where he recommended for reduced number of days to work to reduce the total cost of manufacturing. He demanded more output from all operators by eliminating the overtime work culture along with productivity linked wage settlement with the union and by trimming the strength of indirect man power and asking them to be part of productivity growth to earn more money. The reduction of 3rd shift got implemented with the involvement of union and workmen for the same volume achieved by having 3 shift operations. By 1990, by going for considerable bought out parts from Ludhiana, the need for having 2nd shift was questioned and all in all, the reduction of manpower and productivity were simply superb just because of rethinking by force or need of the hour!!

A well-known Pump manufacturing unit at South India had to go for 3rd shift operation in 2–3 critical ma-chines which appeared to be bottleneck areas by the year 2005. The shortage hours were hardly about 3 to 4 hours per day in these critical machines. In no time the union started pressure on management to go for complete 3 shift operations instead of partial 3rd shift operation at Boring and Drilling machines. In the subsequent years the productivity came down and the manpower went up, the electricity units went up and including the canteen expenses. The absenteeism rates also went up. A RETHINKING was initiated by management because everyone disliked coming in 3rd shift.

A series of steps were initiated such as lunch and dinner time working at those critical machines in the first two shifts by which nearly 3 hours of increased time was created with available machines. The unnecessary additional setting operations were reduced by better planning with more batch numbers each time since the wasteful setting time was huge in this shop. With all these simple agreeable solutions, the union and management agreed for cancellation of 3rd shift once and for all to the delight of workmen and supervisors!

The furniture company cited earlier was having 3 shift operations for about 11000 furniture per month with unimaginable overtime payment month after month up to the year 2007 right from 2000. Along with a highly productivity linked wage settlement, it was agreed to cancel 3rd shift operations by the year 2008 along with total banishing of overtime work culture. And these steps enabled to save about 85 men by abolishing the 3rd shift operations. The productivity went up by more than 50% for the same 11000 units and subsequently to a high as 13000 units per month by addition of few balancing equipment. When the demand has come down to about 8000 to 10000 units per month, the management has almost succeeded to cancel the 2nd shift operations also by the year 2014–15 by which huge fixed cost reduction is expected.

A well-known electronic assembly making unit in South India was having mostly single shift operations in many assembly lines. But with late arrival of material almost all days, a few assembly lines started working partial 2nd shift operations. With seasonal demand the need for 2nd shift came up although it was only for few months. Then there was the case of bottleneck operations here and there. All these meant huge man power additions with not much good end results on real productivity. Faced with severe competition, A RETHINKING WAS INITIATED BY TOP MANAGEMENT. Solutions started pouring including Line balancing for higher output at assembly lines with reduction of manpower and for better on time material supplies.

In about one year time things started changing with practically no more skeleton 2nd shift or 3rd shift operations. When the order load was very high justifying the need for additional shift operations, it would be considered on merit by the President. By these steps the avoidable additional shifts were avoided resulting in substantial increase in productivity.

The moral of all these case examples is to high light that we need to continuously think of the necessity of having additional shifts and in any case it should not affect the productivity already attained.

---

9. Need for Having Good Machine Utilization

The furnace capacity of 1 ton and 3 ton furnaces of a well-known foundry unit used to be hardly 80 boxes as against the possible output of 160 boxes per shift. On management suggestion, a study was undertaken in 2007. It was observed that the effective machine utilization was hardly at about 50% of the rated capacity utilization and in comparison to similar foundry units operating elsewhere. The following are the improvement scope of these furnaces.

Activities in Furnace Section

1. Loading the furnace with material.
2. Charging the material.
3. Heating the metal.
4. Tapping the liquid metal.
5. Ladle making
6. Ladle Pre heating.
7. Pouring.
8. To make lining in the furnace and sintering.

Present durations at which the furnace is idle due to the shift timing

1st shift – 120 minutes – 3rd shift crew stop production by 5 am & 1st shift crew start production by 7 am

2nd shift – 15 minutes from 2.00 to 2.15 pm

3rd shift – 45 minutes 2nd shift crew stop production by 9.30 pm & 3rd shift crew start production by 10.15 pm

Total idle time/Day 180minutes = 3 hrs/day

Observation and Comments

1. 1 Ton Furnace is by and large used as a mini heater for 3 ton furnace and no of boxes that are poured is hardly 50% of capacity output.
2. By the present method furnace operations, we can get around 110 boxes poured/shift, if various delays are minimized.
3. Due to various delays, breakdowns, shift timing, etc., the furnace output is about 80 boxes/shift on an average.
4. Thus the present furnace output/shift although is between 80–110 boxes (poured) it is largely limited by the present method of operations.

Improvement Scope – Furnace

Shift Timings to be re looked

1. Furnace should run continuously. It should not be in OFF between the shifts also.
2. Clear SOP to be made for Furnace operations.
3. Metal Composition to be established correctly.
4. Required lining thickness of the furnace can be re looked
5. Metal charging method to be changed. (Material to be crushed before placing in the furnace.)
6. The various Materials for Furnace charge such as pig iron, scrap, Fe-Si etc., can be made ready in the previous shift itself for next furnace charging.
7. Ladle pre heating can be done separately to avoid heat loss.
8. Furnace should always run with the lid close to avoid the heat loss.
9. Commitment of the furnace Operator is crucial since he is the HERO of the Furnace
10. Crane facility to be improved or reconditioned in the furnaces area.
11. The present Average heating time of furnace (1 & 3 ton) may be reduced by various improvements.

Further Improvement Scope – General

1. Shift timings to be re looked.
2. Sodium silicate tank to be fixed at top near the Muller Mixer.
3. Trolley can be made to carry CO^2 cylinders.
4. Sand obtained after opening the hand moulding boxes should be cleared regularly so that the available space can be used effectively.
5. Reduce the Break down%.
6. Few times hand moulded boxes are beaten with another hand moulded box using crane. Here we can have a shakeout machine to avoid damage of box & crane and to reduce power consumption. It also reduces the fatigue of the Operator.
7. Overall safety precautions to be taken.
8. House Keeping should be improved.
9. Unwanted things can be disposed and the generated Revenue may be used for improvements.
10. Gang ways to be marked.
11. Sand transfer (Manual) to be Muller point to be avoided. Sand can be brought regularly in a planned manner.
12. Gang ways to be marked.
13. Sand transfer (Manual) to be the muller point to be avoided. Sand can be brought regularly in a planned manner.
14. At the time of break down & Power failure Operators & casual labour are idle. They can be used for other activities.

15. Near the pattern storage area, few times, gas cutting work is done which is to be avoided.

16. From the safety angle, no. of fire extinguishers can be increased in the factory.

17. All the employees to wear safety shoe & helmets.

Scope of Productivity

Present Average furnace production per shift – 80 boxes.

Furnace capacity available for maximum boxes per shift with various improvements mentioned above — 187 boxes, say 180 boxes.

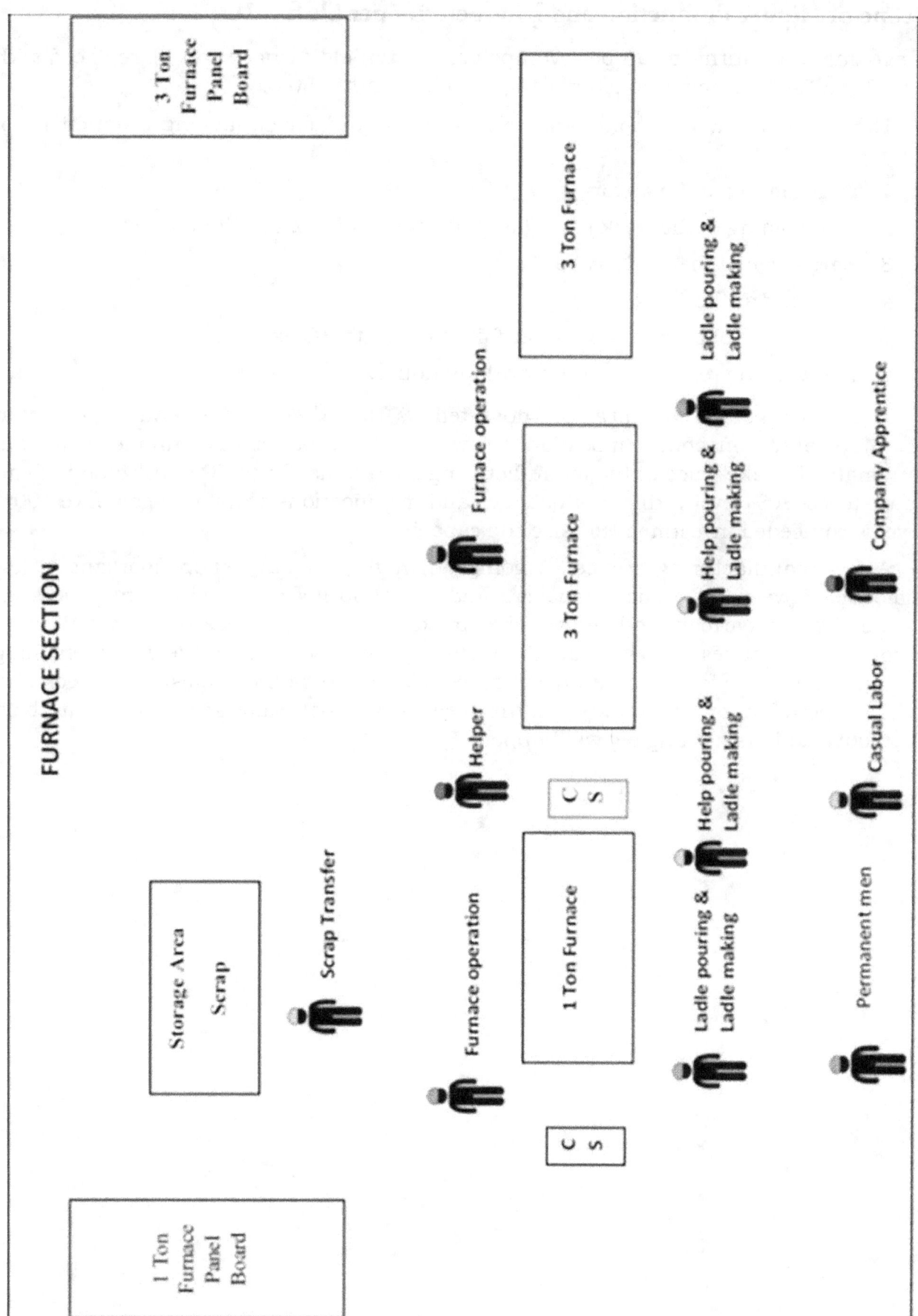

Scope of Higher Production and Productivity per Shift – 100%

If existing 3 ton furnace can be revamped and 1 ton old furnace can be replaced with new 3 ton furnace, the production can go up by another 50%.

The following unfair labour practices to be stopped for enhancing productivity of forge unit

1. Late coming to the factory.
2. Late coming to the work place (at start after lunch, after dinner etc.)
3. Early leaving the work place.
4. Smoking at the work place.
5. At the time of breakdown/power failure-operator/CL are idle
6. Being at the rest room during working hours.

The above actual case example does tell us that there is tremendous potential to improve the machine utilization by which the productivity enhancement will automatically take place in the manufacturing operations. From 50% utilization, if can go up to 75–80% level with minor changes and modifications and it can go above 100% level with needed investment to raise the capacity.

A few manufacturing scenes as going on in the Foundry shop floor and a few dialogue between the senior managers and the shop floor supervisors may be seen in the next few cartoons to highlight the constant pressure tactics used by seniors to resolve all the issues on low productivity and rigid work culture of the workmen along with most horrible low furnace utilization considered to be the biggest bottleneck and critical operation for this unit. But in the absence of a root cause study along with bold corrective actions nothing big will happen.

I am not happy at the House keeping, nor the Production levels. Why can't we get the 'Norm' level of production on daily basis? Why our Sales Value is going down, instead of going up? Look at OTD failures. Better not to talk on WIP bulging. What are you going to do? When? When can we see the Automation / Modernization / Material Handling system changes?

Look at the Trend of Production of Peak & Valley. I want steady and upward daily production. What the hell is going on in the shop floor? Tell me, can you do or not? Is Export happy with OTD? Are the Sales Value going up or down?

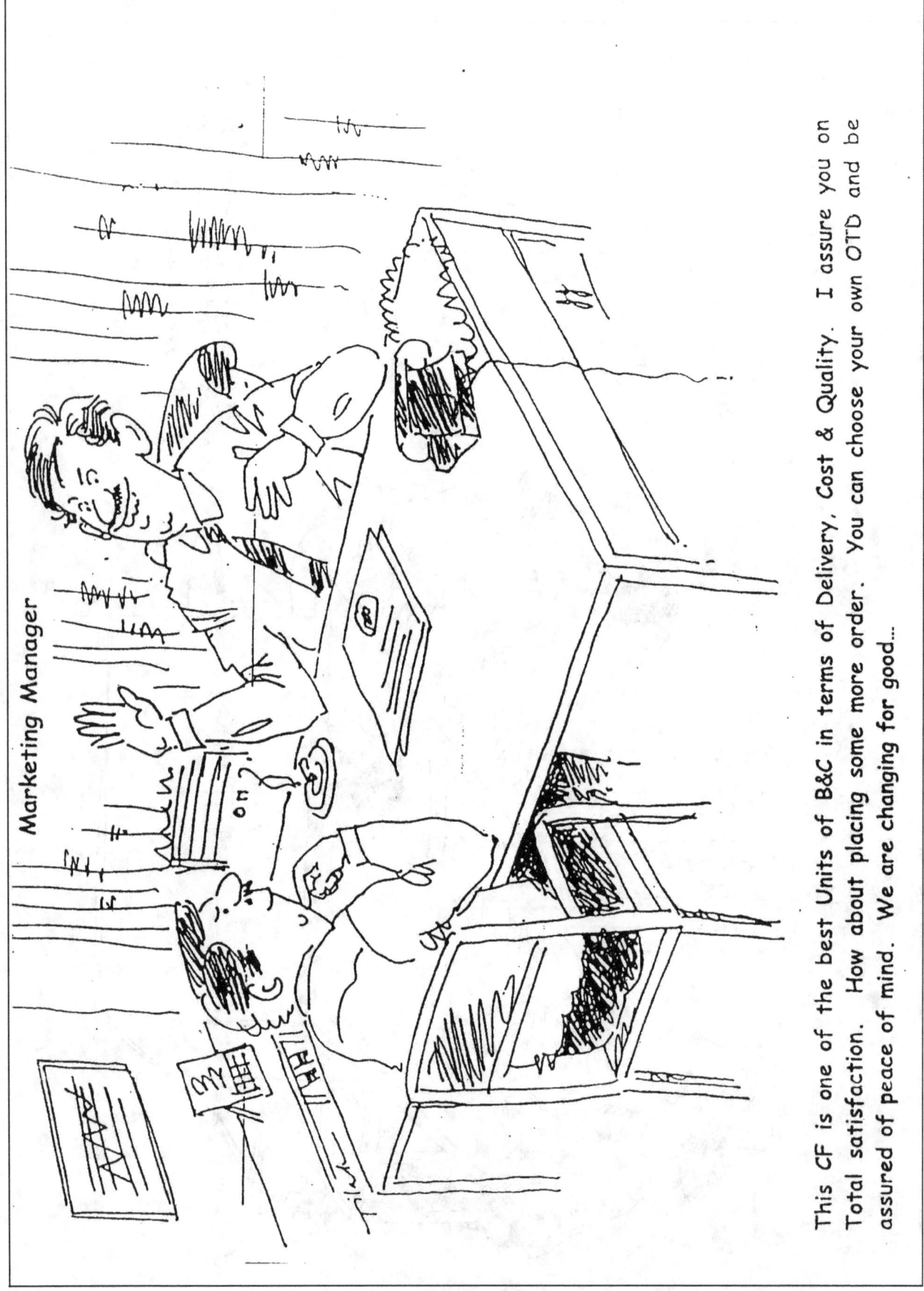

Please tell us what you want. We will then tell you why and how we cannot do it.

Be careful! He may be slow to understand; but he is quick to misunderstand.

See, He is Planning and in deep study to minimize the failures of OTD and for better Customer Satisfaction.

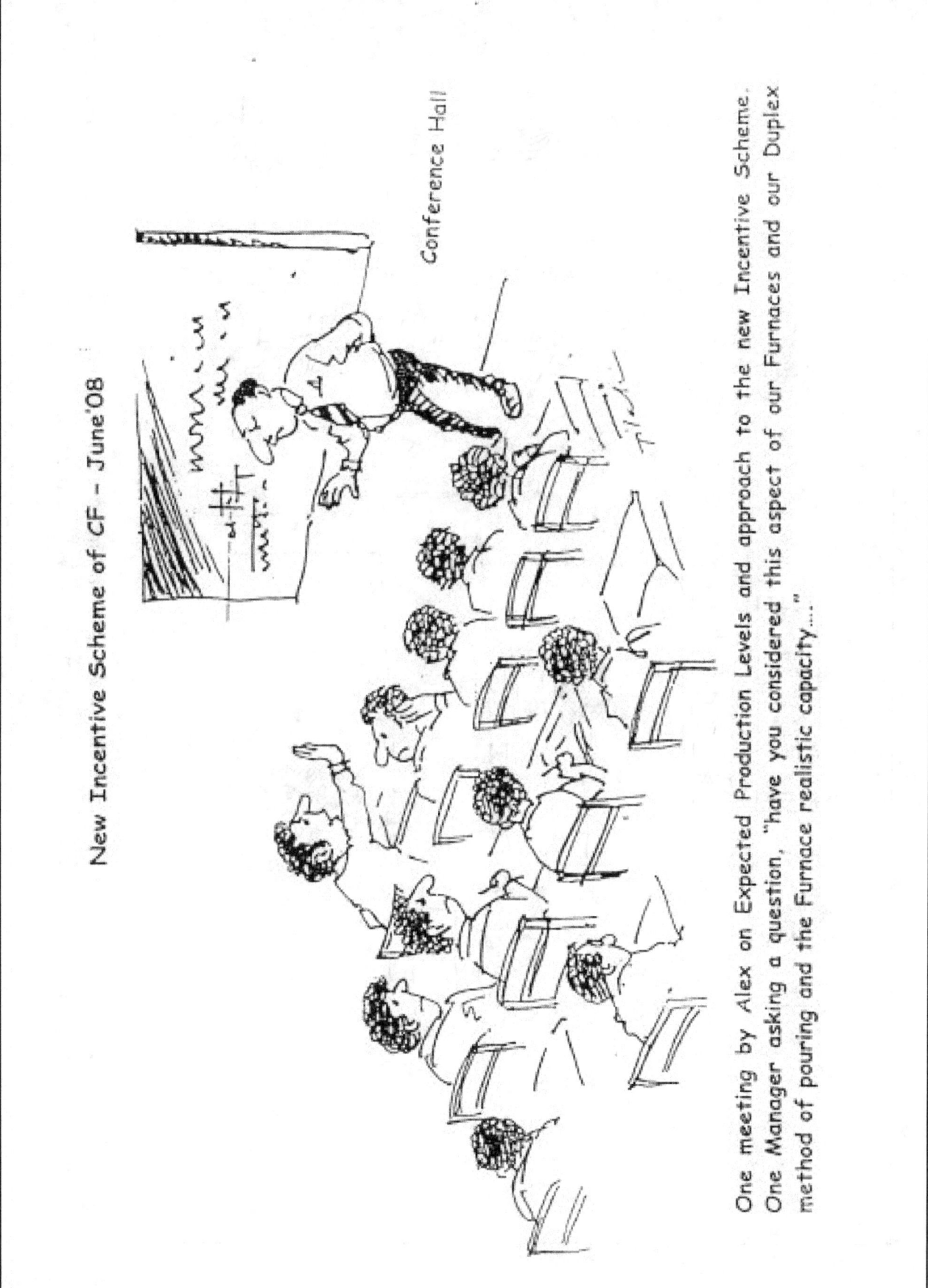

Before, I see, tell me, is it of good news on Volume and more so on Value? How about OTD? Have we increased or decreased the WIP? How many months the WIP is pregnant?

I cannot accept this sort of Low Production of 12B Models. I want you to meet the OTD of each order without any excuses. No reasons please. Can you or not? This month is very critical. How are you going to face the ORM & MD?

Take the case of low machine utilization of one of the major costly equipment of a large steel tube making company located at Jamshedpur

There was a case of low utilization of Tube Mill to be increased from 50% to 60% and possibly to 70% later on. This study was undertaken by Industrial Engineers of TATA Companies located at Jamshedpur in the year 1964 of which I was one member.

A few suggestions of minimum most Roll Changeovers, low cost automations to reduce operator fatigue, improved material handling system, preventive maintenance steps etc. were initiated which enabled Tube Mill utilization to go up to about 65%.

Like these cases, there could be hundreds of examples in any manufacturing unit.

Moral of the story is to try for much more machine utilization by which automatically the productivity will get enhanced.

10. At Times, Confrontation with the Union May Be Necessary

"Confrontation doesn't always bring a solution to the problem, but,
until you confront the problem, there will be no solution"

- James Baldwin

Three real incidences of enforced strike by the union are captured in brief to emphasize the need and guts to face it in the interest of sustained and improved productivity are narrated below:

In the year 1966, one of the biggest manufacturing company located at Jamshedpur faced a hostile union over the dispute of on the revised incentive scheme based on new NORMS in their Forge division. I happened to be the person responsible for changing the norm by about 75% more with the revised method of working which was practiced in 3rd shift, but not in the other shifts because the operators were scared to accept it in front of the shop floor management. Along with some other grievances, one fine morning in 1966, a few masked men came and beat very seriously, all supervisors including the seniors like GM who were not wearing the uniforms of workmen. Thanks to the then Resident Director, the strike was handled exemplary well giving safety to all staff,. After a few days of violence here and there, the strike fizzled out. The new NORMS got implemented and the productivity jumped by more than 60% in the most critical machine of this unit.

Exactly after 10 years in 1976, a famous Cycle plant located at South India, faced serious road blocks to raise the productivity by 5 to 10% more with staggered working days and with few flexibility changes. One fine morning a group of men assaulted a few management staff after seeing low payment of incentive amount for few workmen. Any amount of words and space will not be sufficient to explain the way the then CEO handled the famous strike which prolonged for about 11.5 months. At the end when the union and workmen came up with due apologies, he insisted for a flat 25% increase in norms and productivity which was reluctantly agreed to by them. It may look unbelievable, this unit registered about 66% more productivity in about one year time after the strike and by 1978. Just imagine, whether it could have happened without that strike!

A well-known small Chain making unit near Chennai had a very bad experience with the union on increased norms and other cultural changes by the year 2003. By 2005, suddenly the union went on strike which was handled by the then MD most meticulously along with HR manager. At the end the entire permanent work men whose head count was about75 went on VRS (Voluntary Retirement Scheme) and from the next month itself the trainee operators started working more and the company registered profit for the first time in last few years. Handling of strike was the saviour of this unit by enhancing the productivity.

It was in March 2013, the militant Union team went for a total strike of a big furniture manufacturing unit located near to the above company on the issue of not accepting additional productivity linked incentive scheme and the Union was adamant for not enhancing the wages through the productivity route. At the end of the violent strike for a period of 4 months, the top management team made the Union to accept the new productivity scheme for enhancing productivity. But unlike the above nearby company, this unit could not come out of the financial sickness, possibly by not taking adequate remedial steps for turning around the company during the strikes period.

With all humility, it is recorded that I was one of the contributors for creating unhappiness in the minds of the few Union team members of the above mentioned companies by demanding much more productivity and flexibility from the work force. And I was present in all these companies during the strike period.

Like these incidences many units of well-known companies like, Amalgamation group companies, MRF units, Ashok Leyland etc. faced strikes during the period of 1975 to about 1985 very frequently with strong arm twisting union of these companies. Thankfully, in all cases the management had the last laugh.

> **The moral of these incidences is to highlight the need for facing strike if it is imposed by union. It is good if it can be avoided but not on compromising on norms and productivity. Otherwise facing the strike very boldly is the right answer for achieving higher productivity.**

11. Does Your Incentive Scheme Payment Consider the Idle Time Hours While Computing the Efficiency of Production?

In many companies while computing the efficiency level of the shop, the IDLE TIME captured during the month is knocked off, on the thinking that it is not due to the fault of operators.

Say the expected level of production is 400 pieces for 8 hours with no idle time considered. If the actual production is 400 pieces, then the efficiency is 100%.

What happens when the level is 350 pieces with a booked idle time of 7 hours for waiting for material and breakdowns? Most probably it will be 350/7 = 50 pieces per hour which is the expected norm/hour and the efficiency will be declared will be 100%.

If the idle time booked is 2 hours, then also they will get 100% payment if the per hour production is not less than the norm.

Over a period of time the workmen will be able to record the needed idle time hours and supervisors will work will be silent because it got already established and change will create issues for him.

Even the indirect men will be declared as 100% efficiency achievers!

Such schemes will only promote the culture of booking more idle time hours and the company will never get full production expected of the shift. In 1966 one of the biggest companies at Jamshedpur was having such a scheme and the average efficiency level of the 6000 Ton Maxi press engaged for crank shaft forging never went beyond 40% level by these manipulations of idle time hours. When it was proposed to change the scheme without any concession for idle time working a strike was called by the then union with expected level of efficiency at about 70% level.

One big manufacturing at South India too has this culture of giving concessions to idle time hours with no increased productivity coming up in any month. The consultant employed gave some 10 headings by which various idle time causes could be written in printed sheet. Later another guy increased it to about 50 causes. With all these idle time cause bookings, no improvement in productivity happened.

Perhaps next to inflexibility and overtime culture, the passport and belief that it will help to reduce the idle time is the biggest culprit for standing in the way of productivity enhancement in any company.

The moral of all these incidences and experiences of few other companies is to highlight that no more concession to be given for idle time hours to promote cooking up by both workmen and supervisors in the interest of higher productivity.

PART 2

A Few Techniques or Tools Used for Productivity Enhancement

A few techniques or tools used for Productivity enhancement in manufacturing operations of few companies along with successful implementation.

1. Crew size reduction.
2. Automation/Autonomation.
3. Fundamentals of a Layout change study in a company from start to end.
4. Brief abstract summary of major Layout changes of a big company.
5. Brief summary of layout changes in a module of Bicycle manufacturing company.
6. Man power reduction methodology as done and implemented in a progressive unit of upper India.
7. Simple Productivity studies of few operations of a Manufacturing unit.
8. Productivity enhancement through yield improvement of a Manufacturing unit.
9. Process improvement studies of few assembly operations of a Manufacturing unit.
10. A brief summary of Productivity enhancement study of a Manufacturing unit through the route of automation, Simplification, elimination of co-workers, lay out and material Handling changes etc.
11. Productivity enhancement through Setup time reduction and the methodology.
12. Line balancing concepts applied in few assembly lines of auto component manufacturing unit.

1. Crew Size Reduction

Crew size reduction through the route of killing the terrorists of inflexibility & overtime work culture.

"It is high time for many individuals and companies to make a quantum leap in performance, a major shift in pattern, a healthy change of habits, otherwise, it is business as usual and that is simply not cutting it anymore"

- Thomas Peters – "In Search of Excellence"

Please note the key words, "Quantum Leap performance or Productivity and healthy change of habits. This is well explained in the following real experienced case study by killing the terrorist of inflexibility and over time work culture along with automation and taking the workmen on the board for change management

Many of old companies started by UK collaboration before 1970 had the culture of production by operators, setting by setters, quality by Quality inspectors, maintenance by fitters leading to compartment work culture. Over a period of time this culture led to established practice of do your job and not anyone else's job. There were days when the machine is stopped by the absence of any one or two operators, likewise the machine used to be stopped whenever absenteeism happens in other supporting functions. Even a little flexibility to help other operation was resisted more by union team than concerned operators.

Say the huge costly machine is manned as follows,

O-1 - Main operator with main panel control operation

O-2 - Second operator with entry or other panel control operation

O-3 - Loading assistant

O-4 - Unloading assistant

S-1 - Set up operator - 1

S-2 - Set up operator - 2

M-1 - Maintenance fitter - 1

M-2 - Maintenance fitter - 2

Q-1 - Quality check operator - 1

Q-2 - Quality check operator - 2

The crew size for this costly machine is 10, however, the setup, Maintenance and Quality operators have to cater to a similar machine located little away in the shop.

Apart from machine stoppage due to absenteeism in the absence of trained men for each of the job, there used to be waiting time when the supporting team operators are working in the other machine. When the production is going on invariably the supporting men would be idling and when the support job is going on, all others including production team would be idling. This was the real scenarios in those years under this traditional work pattern or culture.

Through the inflexibility and ongoing over time work culture, no one would do other man's job in any shift or day. If the Main operator is absent his job could be done by the Main operator of other shift, like wise for all production crew. If fitter is absent in one shift, his job could do only by the other fitter of any shift. And all these were done on over time payment. No day would go with someone absent and no day would go without over time payment. The work men had a plan to be absent and to get over time payment which used to be more or less same for all of them. The minimum over time hours were 8 hours, non-negotiable for them.

Under the above scenario, what else can we expect other than poorest productivity from the operators? The life of supervisors became miserable with union interruptions.

Once top management decided to break this work culture of total inflexibility and abolish or ban over time work culture in one manufacturing unit of a well-known company and was prepared for a show down if it was inevitable, but, wanted to do a good home work and by understanding the concerns of operators first, failing which, it was ready for show down.

The over time was totally banned. The flexibility was mandatory to do other man's job if necessary after due training period. Any supporting operators to do production job or vice versa on need base. Minimum absenteeism coverage was provided with trainee operators with more wage than ordinary temporary men.

It would be surprising to note the END RESULTS.

The crew size got reduced to just 4 men who had to do production job, do quality checkup when machine was stopped, they were told to do setting when the machine needed the change. In turn the operators got quantum jump in wages through productivity linked incentive scheme which was well prepared and tested to succeed for years to come.

Man power got reduced by 60% and productivity went up about 100% more. Several low cost automation steps were taken to avoid avoidable wasteful time, loading and unloading facilities were improved the manual fatigue considerably which were highly appreciated by the work men. Union interfering in day to day running by the supervisors vanished, they were respected and empowered.

The operators were designated as production cum setting cum quality cum maintenance operators at a much higher Basic wage considering the multi skill being taken with full responsibility and accountability. Indeed the resistance was much less than expected or anticipated and got it implemented most successfully, all because of the problem solving attitude and taking the work men on board for various changes.

The moral of this real incidence experience of a large company is that, there is abundant scope to go to much higher productivity provided we go in to root causes and willing to seek solutions and then get it implemented by taking the workmen in to confidence.

Few Byproducts of Inflexibility & Restrictive Practices in the Shop Floor

1. The permanent men are most reluctant to move from their traditional job to any other area even when there is considerable need. Some of them won't move to similar machine operation despite the request by the supervisors.

2. Indirect workmen belonging to Engineering, Stores, Inspection, Maintenance and Tool room etc. are not willing to take up the production pressure and not responding to production urgency and customer satisfaction. It looks they are from Venus and production men belong to earth!

3. Practically there is no urge from the workmen as a whole to achieve the monthly stipulated volume. They are more bothered about their free time, comforts and overtime working for the day. The workmen seem to think that the end product volume achievement is that of supervisors and they are paid for it.

4. The breakdown repair work, too many settings etc. seem to be the responsibility of supervisors and they do not wish to be questioned on it without any accountability.

5. No lunch and dinner time operation even on most critical machines in many places. Invariably 2 hours of machine time is lost in every shift due to late start, tea time, early lunch time, early stop etc.

6. Highly restrictive of norm and no one will go beyond norm even when they can do it. Some may do it provided it is not recorded in log book.

7. On the whole the operators are highly individualistic rather than believing in total team work culture.

8. In flexibility is the passport and visa for enabling them to get daily overtime on account of absenteeism of someone else!

9. When HR Managers go on advocate empowering of supervisors, in reality, they are more like slaves of workmen and taking instruction from the union team under this terrorist working atmosphere of inflexibility.

10. The motivation, spirits and enthusiasm of shop floor management from top to bottom are extremely low on account of inflexibility work culture created for a long period and now it has become the law for the workmen!

Desirable Flexibility and Cultural Changes Needed

1. Production workmen will have to work anywhere in the shop for any duration of time depending on the need.

2. There will be no overtime for anyone under any circumstances. The direct and indirect work men will be responsible for the gap of volume and it is their responsibility for making up the lost volume by cultural changes in the shop floor. Workmen to work in lunch/dinner breaks to avoid 30 minutes or more down time of the critical machines with staggered lunch arrangement along with total participation of indirect men

3. The Product line or module group men including direct and indirect should be totally accountable to give Production, Productivity and Customer satisfaction, as they may get same incentive amount linked to production and productivity.

4. Workmen will have to undergo multi skilling training meticulously and be willing to work anywhere in the product line or module or anywhere in shop floor without an iota of compulsion from the supervisors. It is nonnegotiable any more as the old days have become history.

Overtime Work Cuture Evils

1. In a shop that frequently gives OT, practically a few workmen do get bulk of OT Wages, making almost every one unhappy.

2. The root cause for supervisors conceding OT is because of less production in his shift or previous shift by which we are encouraging the OT work culture without solving the issue and the easiest way is to give OT and make up the lost production.

3. OT culture promotes absenteeism of almost all work men because any way management would be giving OT wages to make up his salary every month.

4. OT is the biggest culprit that stands in the way of true productivity. It is worse than cancer and it will spread faster and kill the organization in due course.

5. One of the causality of high OT is the lack of flexibility culture. With OT culture there will not be tendency for the workmen not to train others on their job, nor were they willing to give higher output.

6. It is an open secret that the output achieved in 8 + 8 {OT} hours can be easily achieved in 8 hours itself. They may effectively work for 4–5 hours in shift and will work for 3.3 to 4 hours output in OT work of 8 hours totaling 8 hours output!

In short the two biggest productivity inhibitor's hiding in the shop floor are INFLEXIBLITY & OT WORK CULTURE. On asking how to stop chronic drinking and smoking habits, some one answered, "Do not start in this adventure, once you get into this habit, it will be herculean task to come out even partially."

If your organization is addicted to these two evils, it is time for you to put a wakeup call and eradicate by any means. Otherwise for sure you will not achieve even an iota of true productivity.

It may not be out of context to mention that the writer has been able to kill these two evils in more than 20 companies where he worked as regular employee in senior position for 33 years and about 21 years as consultant responsible for implementation in a few companies. The biggest smiles came from shop floor management team from top to bottom in winning over the terrorists and at the end even more than 95% workmen also expressed total happiness in banishing these two evils from the shop floor and 100% of their families are happy on the implementation of these changes without diminished income. In fact the earnings of the workmen went up high with productivity rise!

2. Automation/Autonomation

A few automation cartoons of the then scenario of a well-known manufacturing unit may be seen in the next few pages along with proposed working scenario with little automation. This was done in the year 1990 and since then, hundreds of automations ideas were implemented in this unit along with full cooperation of the workmen, because it really reduced their fatigue of the manual work.

WCP > White Collar Productivity - Ideas from Management staff

Introduction and Methodology

Automation with a human approach to reduce the fatigue of operators is probably a very neglected area in most of the manufacturing operations.. We seem to forget how much today's youngsters have come this far on simple automation changes done in shaving the face on daily basis as compared to great grandfathers, say about 100 years ago. Our great grandfathers were using the knife like razors to shave their face with the usage of ordinary soap as lather, at least once a week with the help of known and good barbers. Our fathers or you when you were young started using the razor with single edge and double edge blades like seven o clock brand with better shaving cream to avoid the brushes. Today the youngsters may be using disposable razors with great gel or shaving cream and the whole process may be over in less than 5 minutes as compared to 30 minutes dangerous ordeal by great grandfathers to see blood coming out from faces with those knife razors. It is a necessity for today's smart youngsters to shave their face on daily basis. What a productivity improvement with innovations!!

Take the case of a continuous furnace with loading and unloading by 2 operators each, thus making the crew size to 6 men along with 2 needed main operators of the furnace including gas plant managing. Two operators are essential to lift the heavy tube or strips or materials. Their work load may be for a maximum of 3 hours per shift and the rest of the time they will be loitering around by being paid for it by the company and they may indulge in criticizing management on the apathy of not making any automation to reduce the fatigue. In the night, their wives may be applying oil for massaging the painful shoulders. When loading and unloading operations are automated which is not a big deal nowadays, there is no need for those 4 operators per shift and they can be engaged elsewhere. At the end both workmen and management would be happy by this automation implementation successfully. What do you think on the prospects of such automation process in your area of operations and it would surprise and so please avoid the delay any more!!

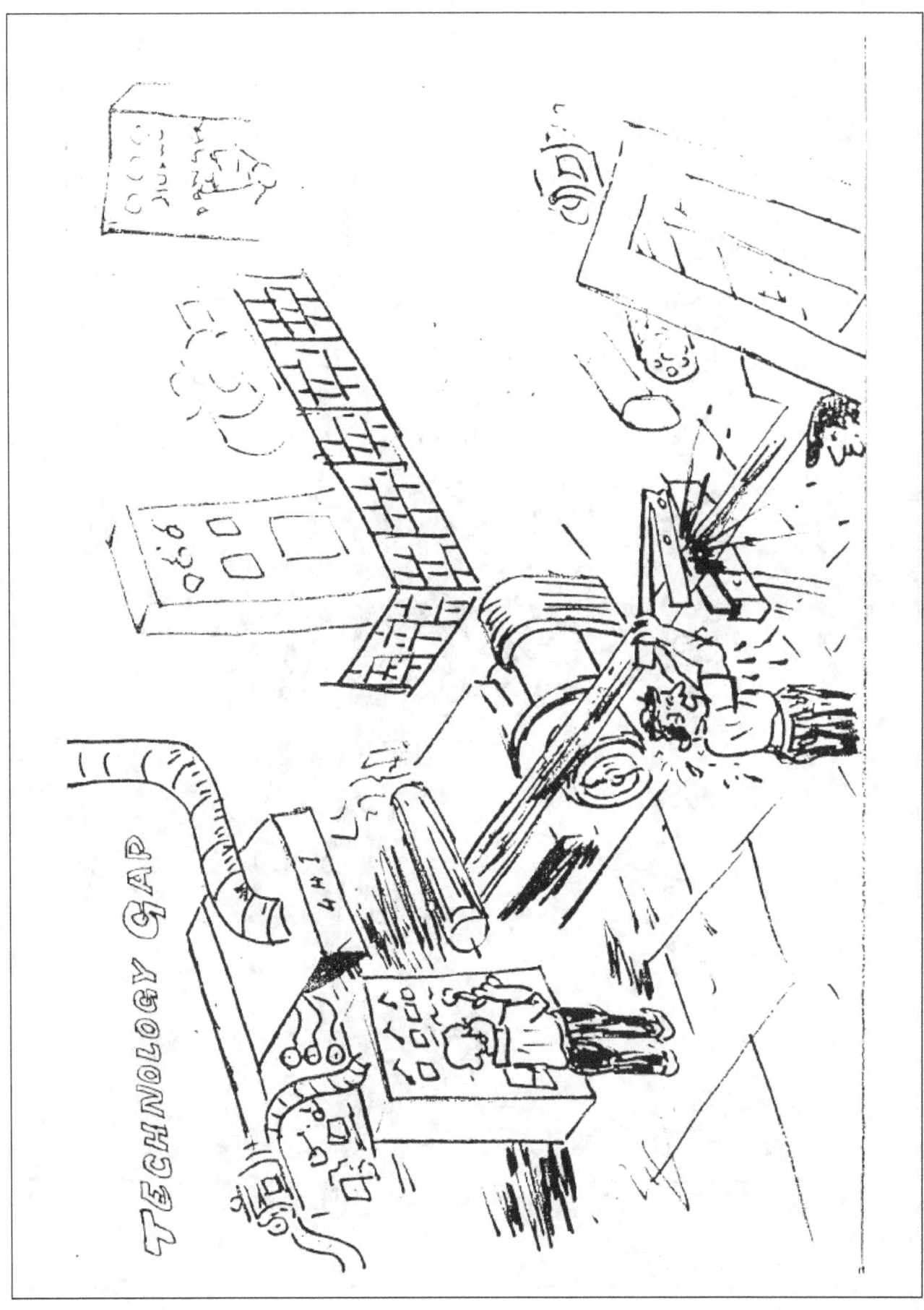

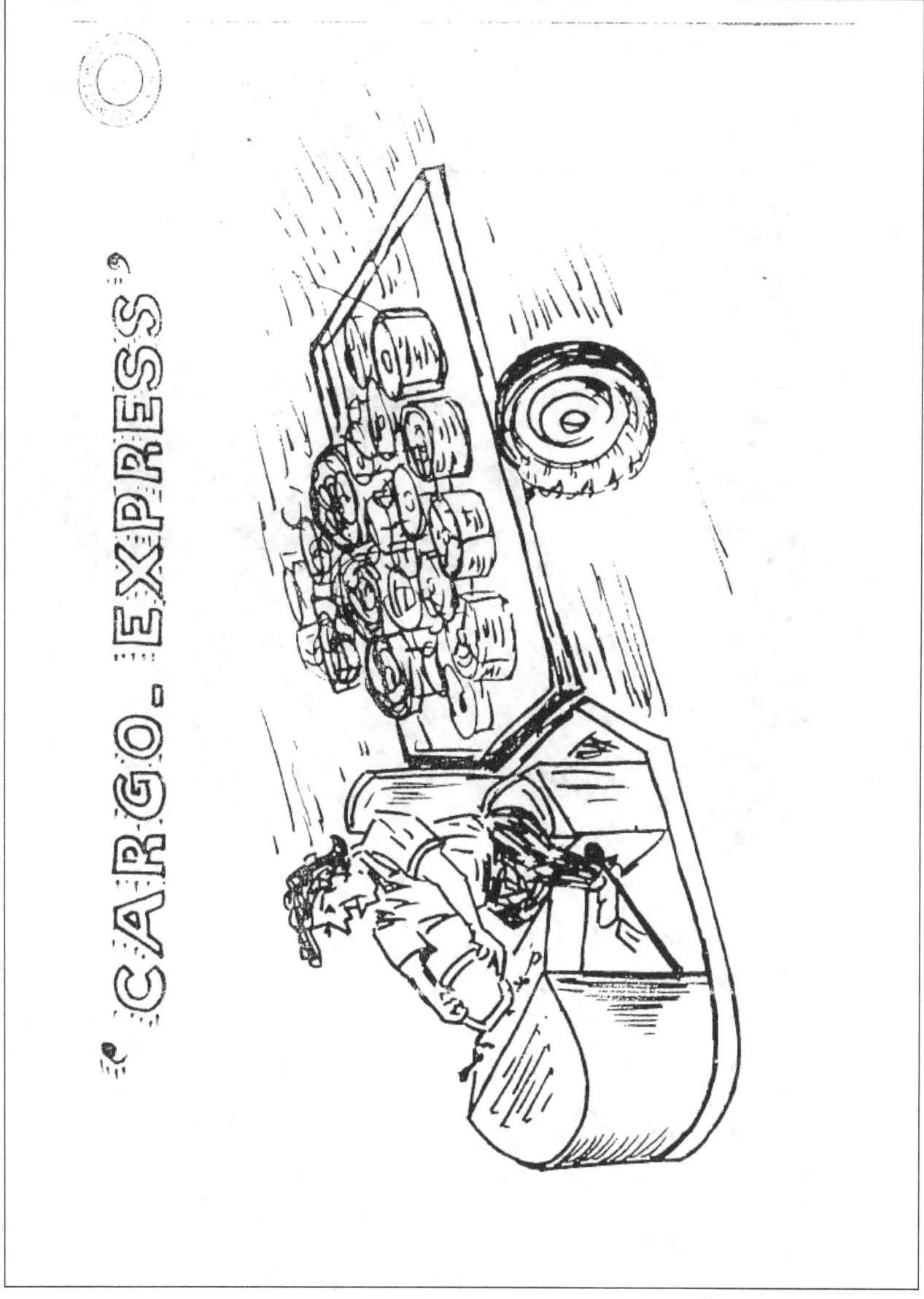

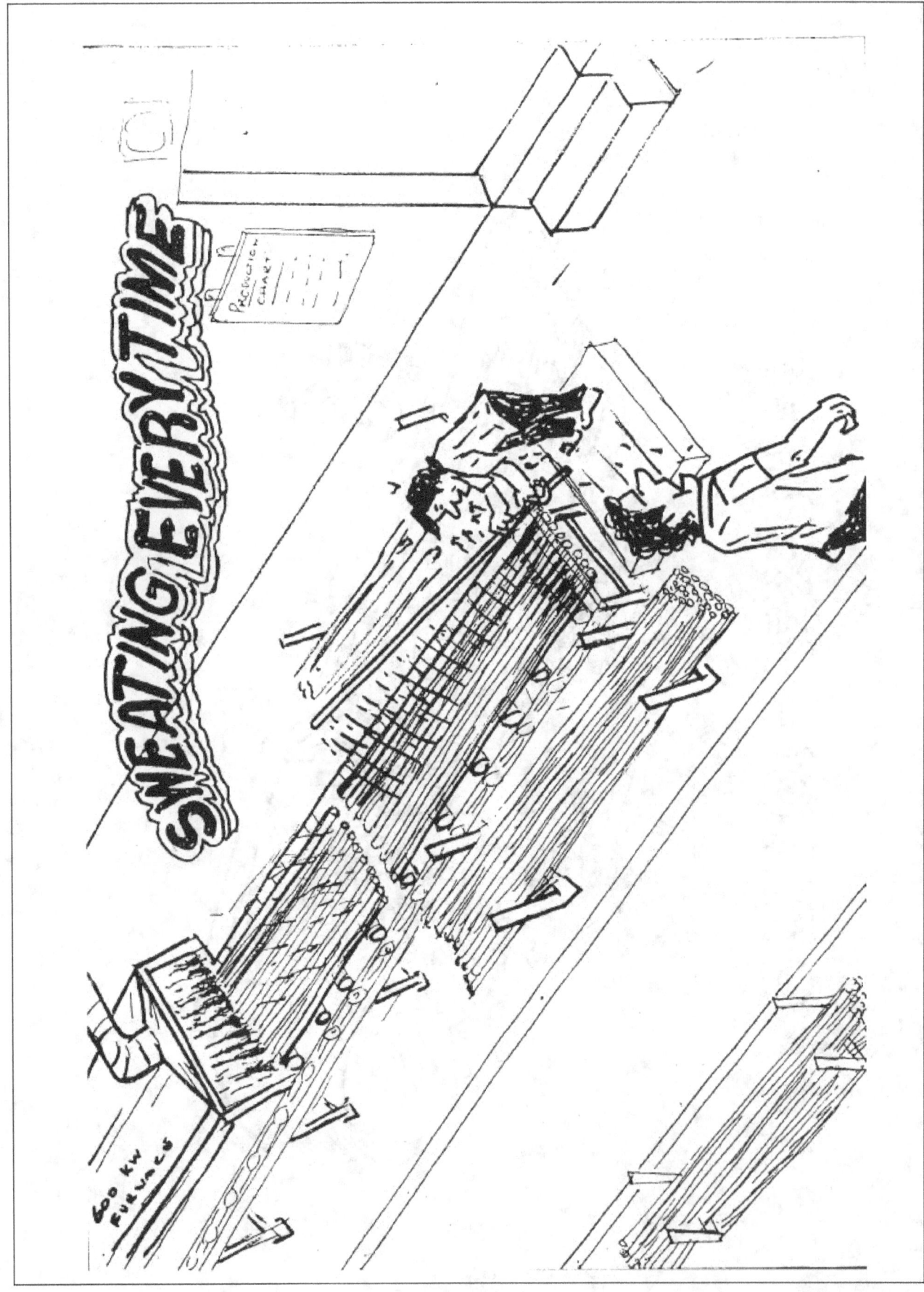

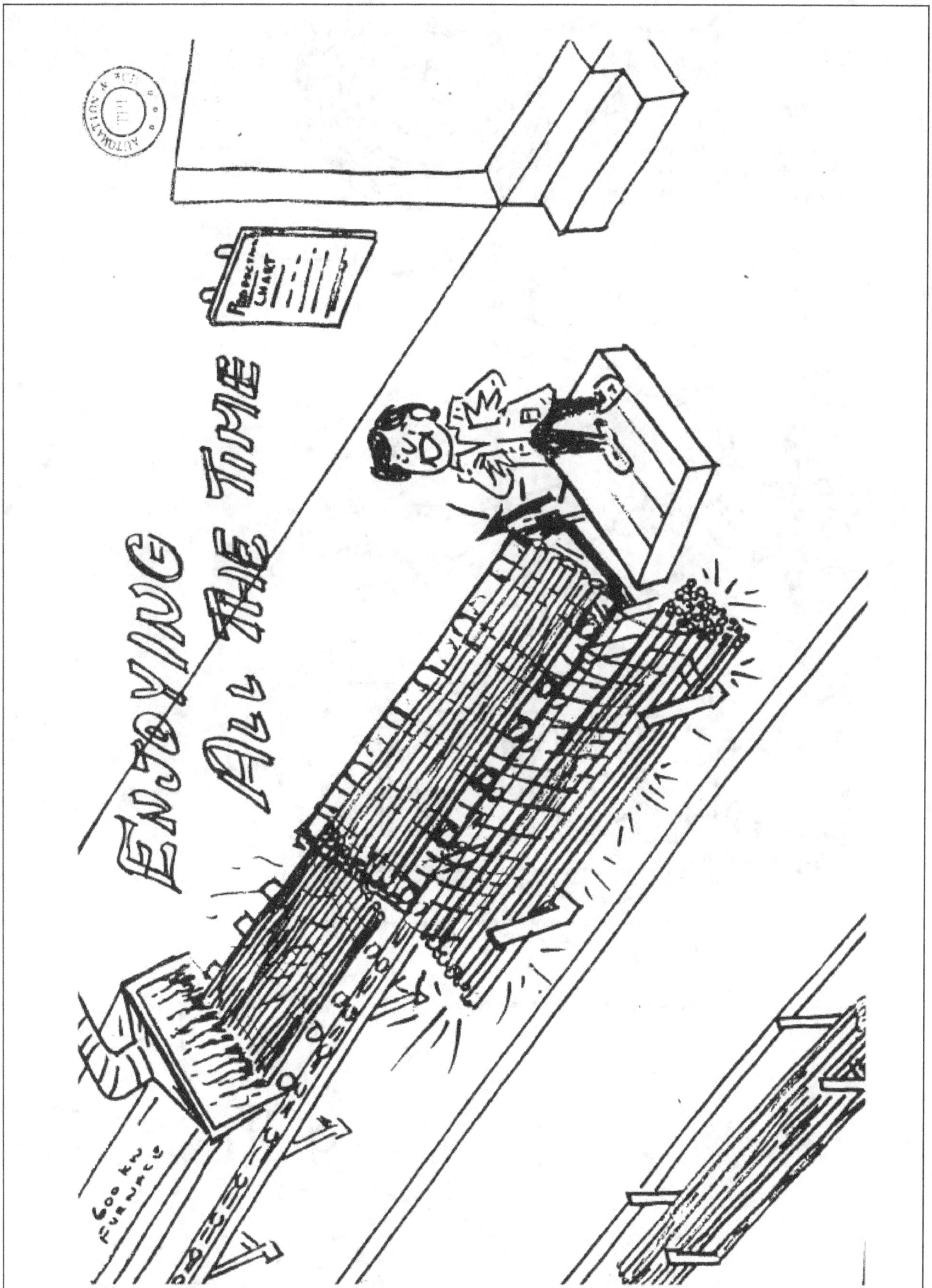

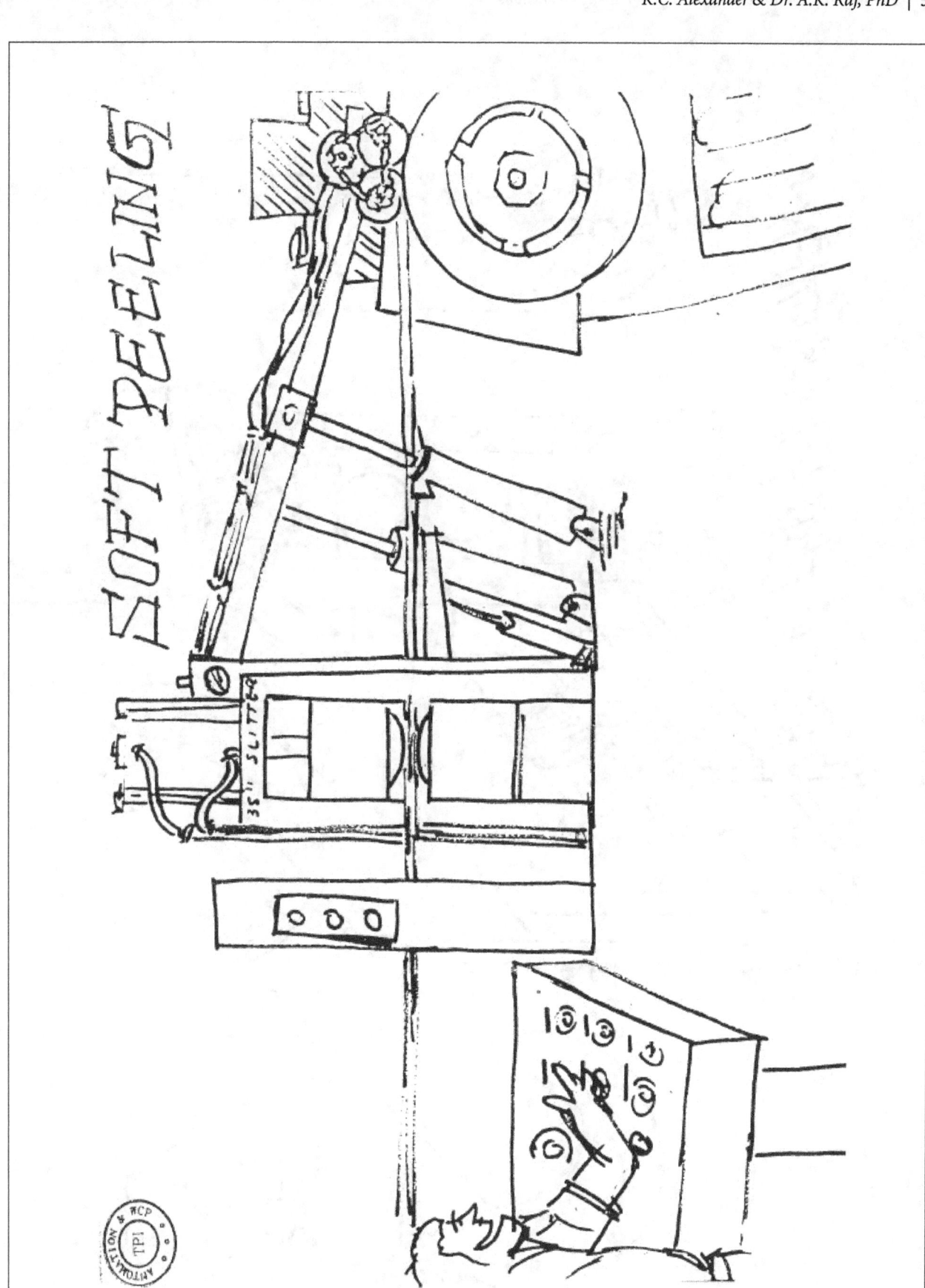

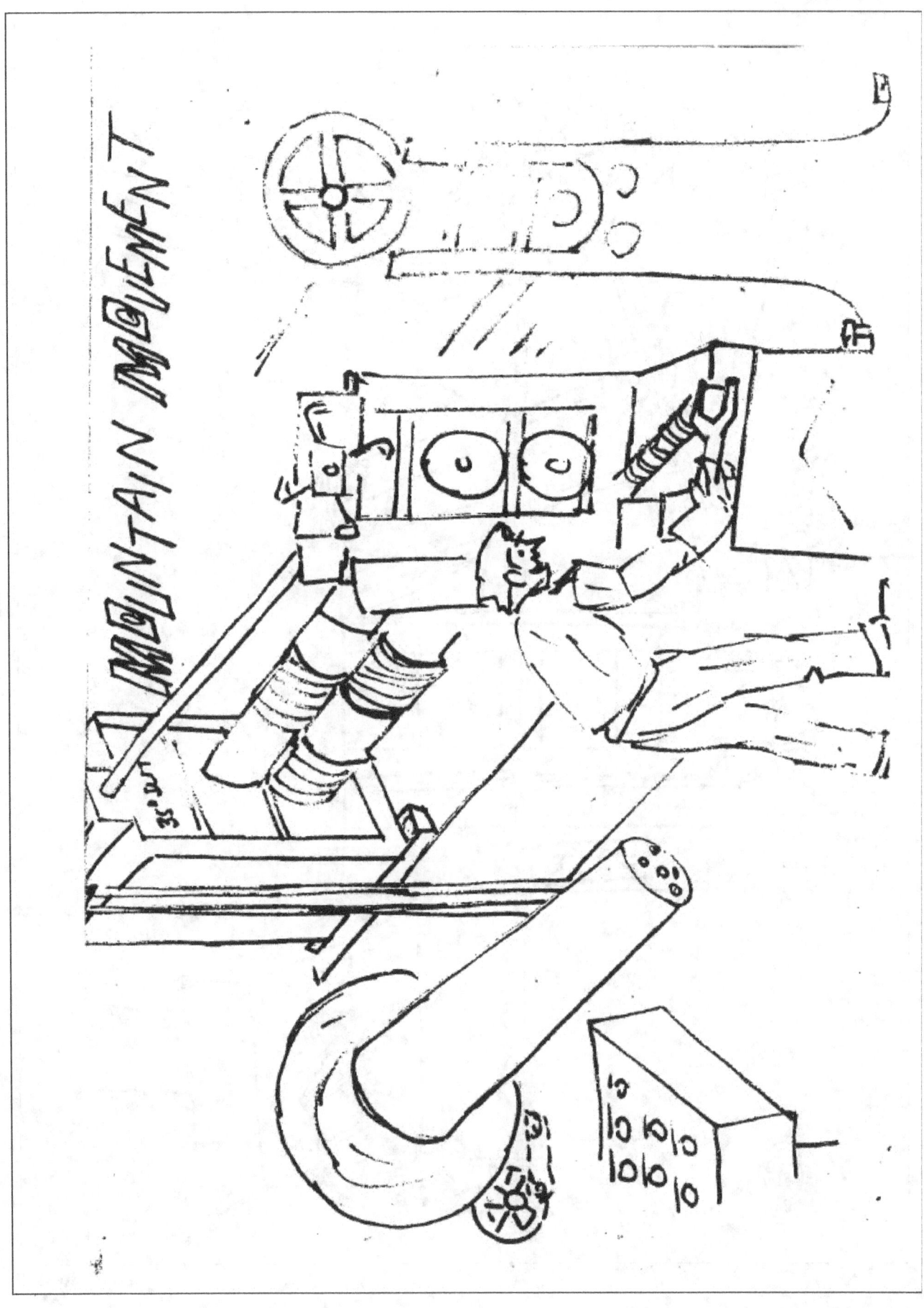

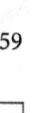

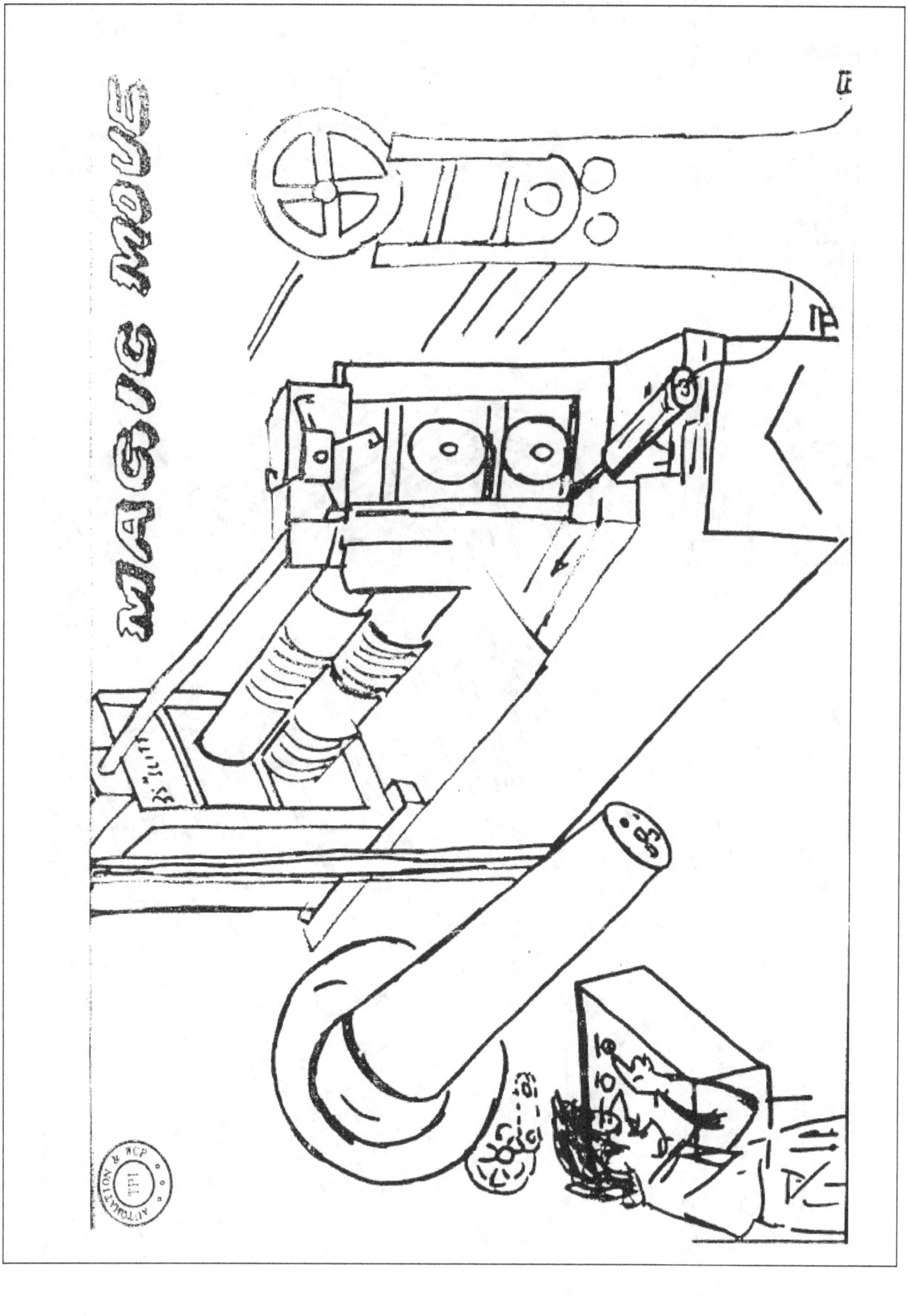

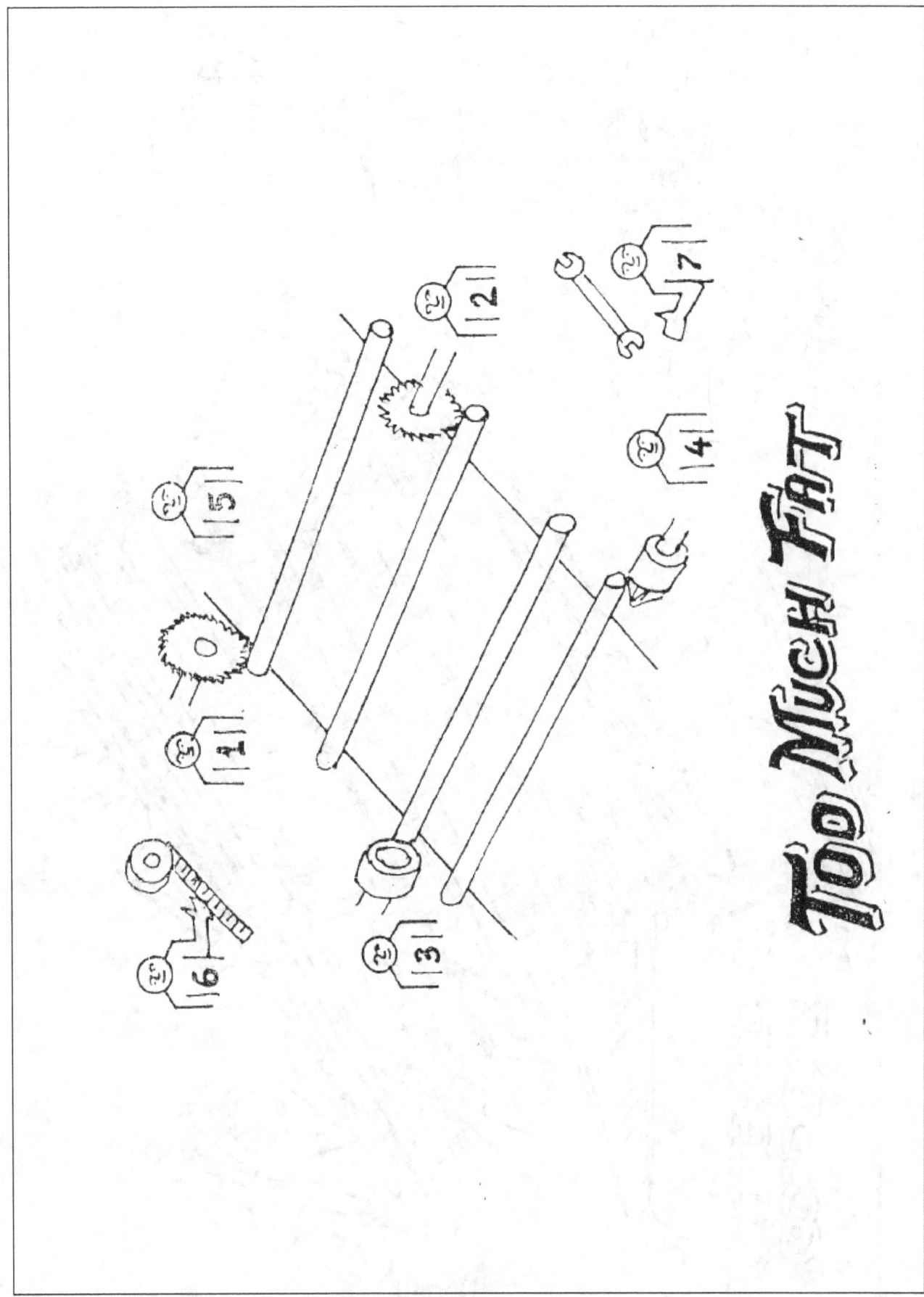

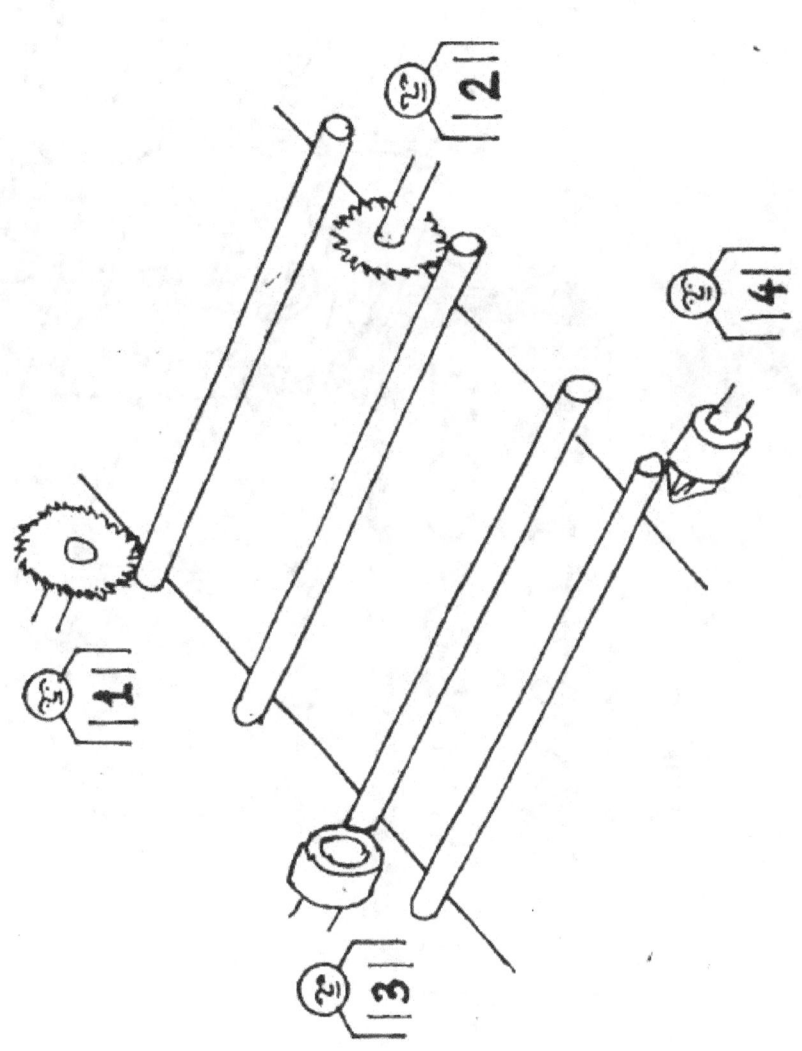

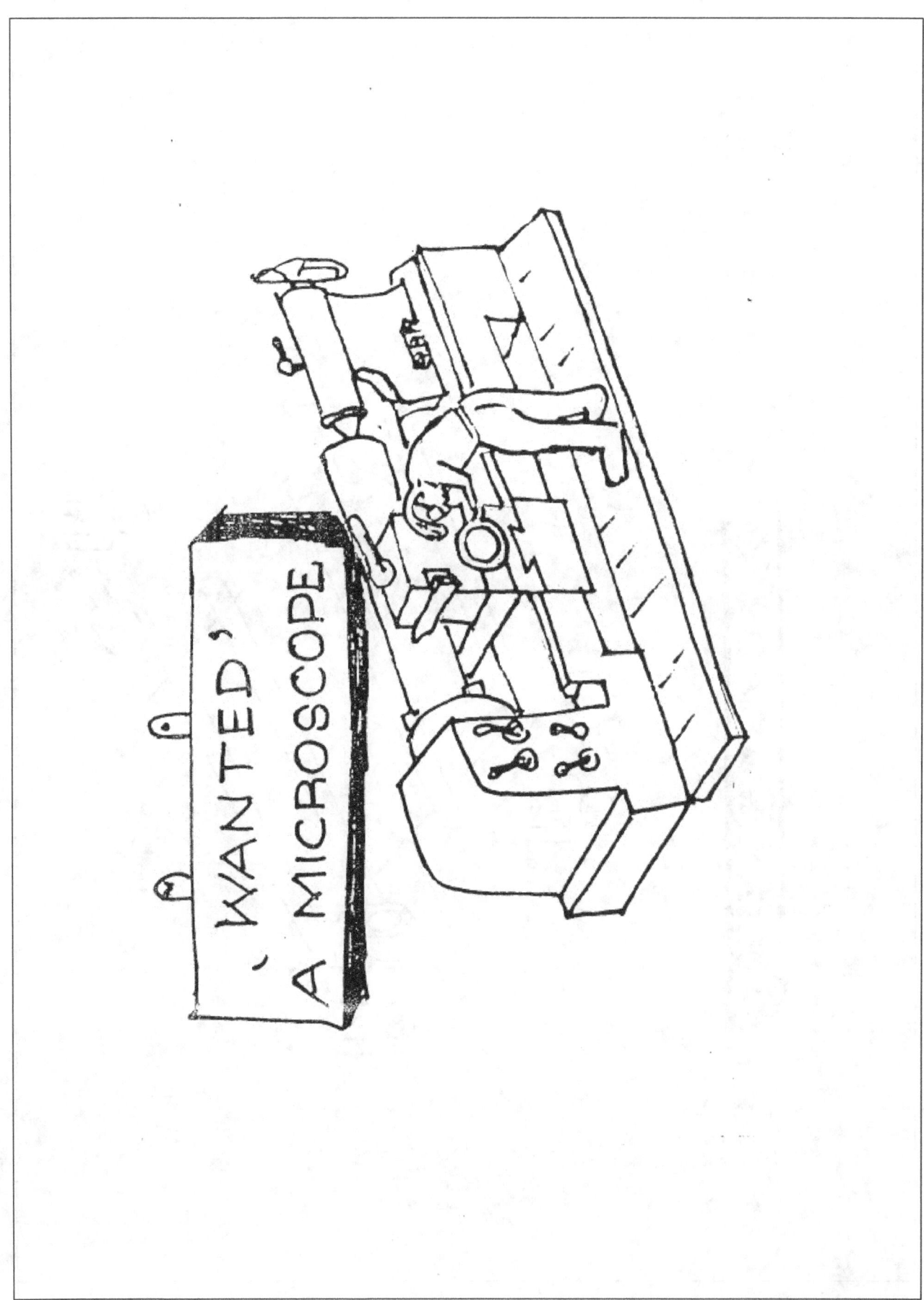

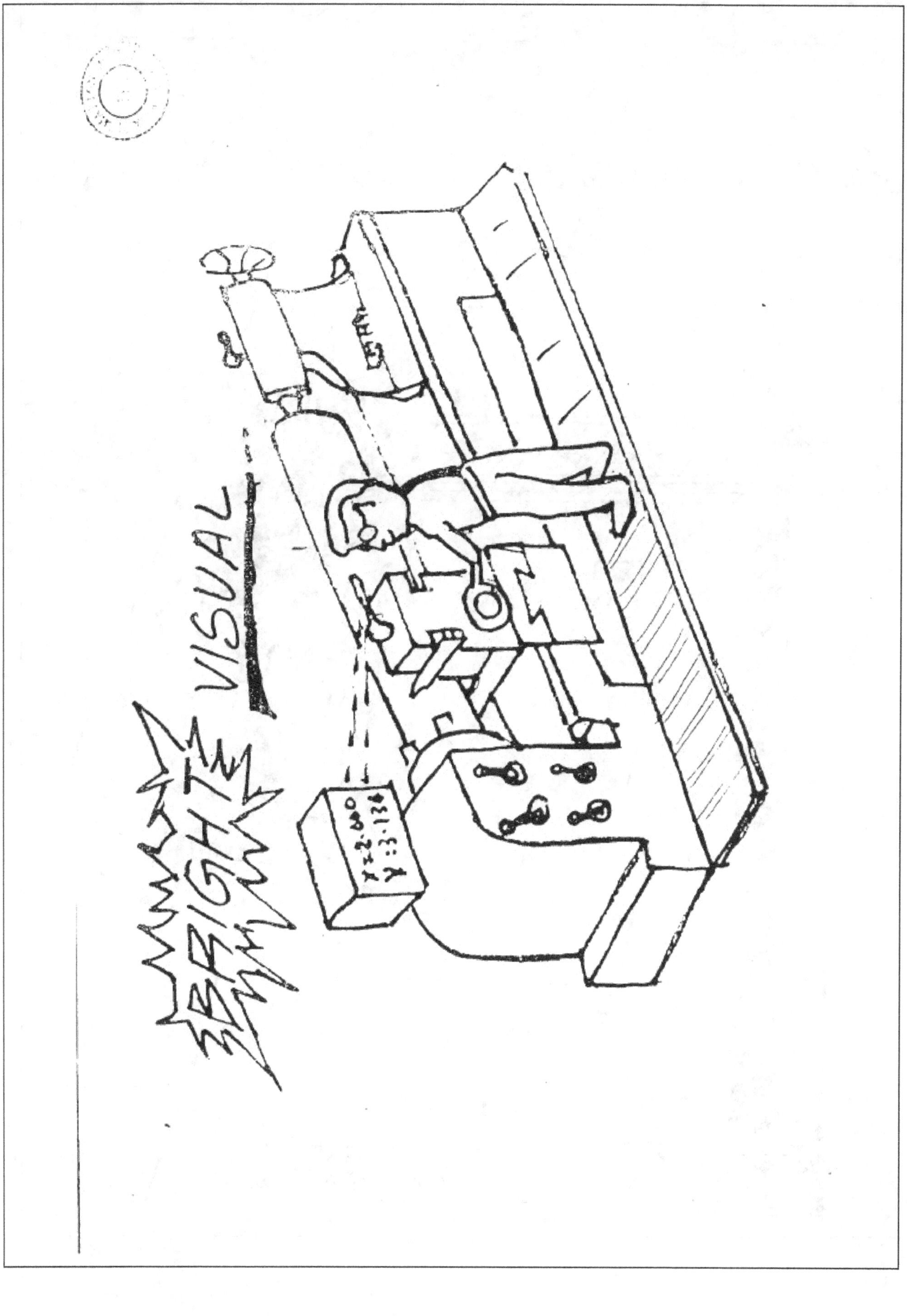

BRIGHT VISUAL

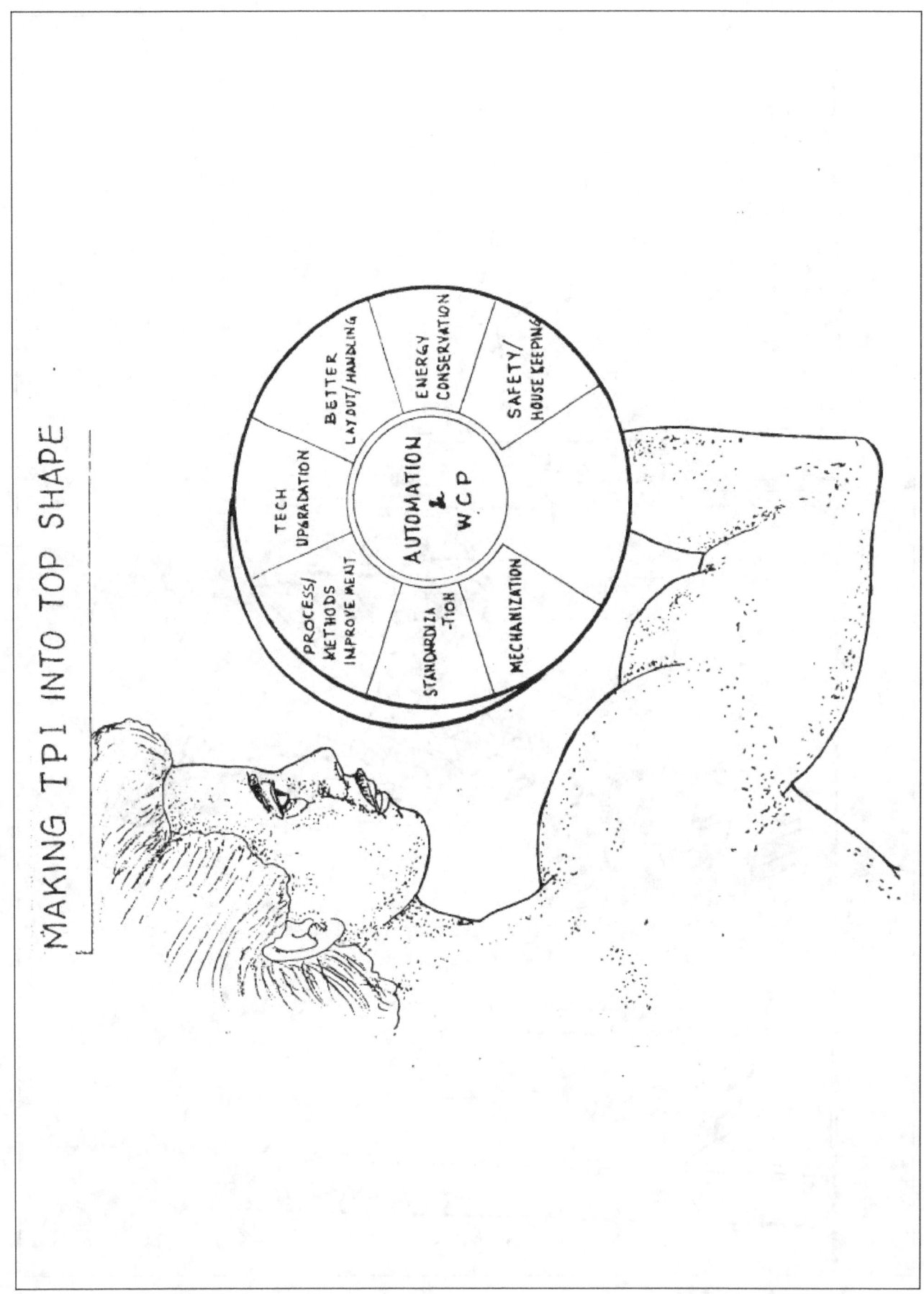

MAKING TPI INTO TOP SHAPE

BETTER LAYOUT/HANDLING

ENERGY CONSERVATION

SAFETY/HOUSE KEEPING

TECH UPGRADATION

AUTOMATION & W.C.P

PROCESS/METHODS IMPROVEMENT

STANDARDIZA-TION

MECHANIZATION

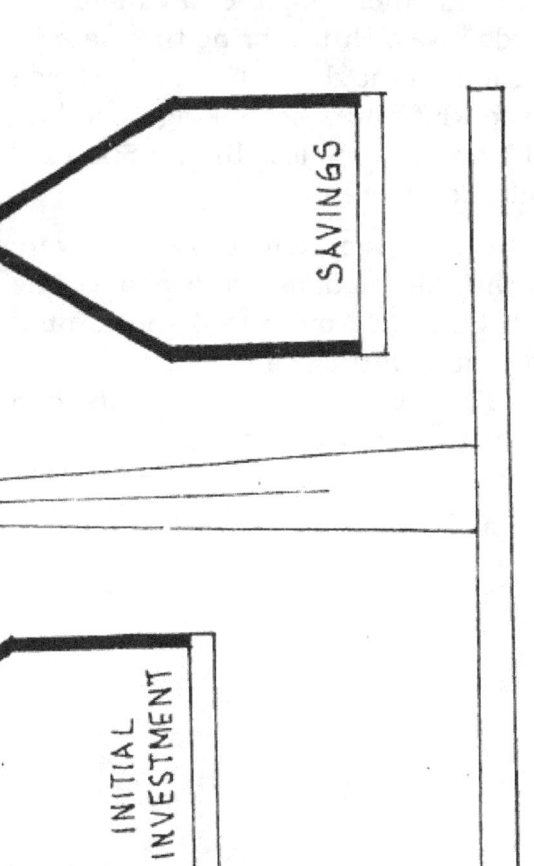

AUTOMATION & WCP BENEFITS

- FATIGUE REDUCTION
- PRODUCTIVITY
- SCRAP REDUCTION
- MAN POWER REDUCTION
- COST REDUCTION
- SAFETY
- HOUSE KEEPING
- ENERGY SAVING

3. Fundamentals of Layout Changes

Introduction and Methodology

One of the most neglected area in most of the manufacturing shops, is that of improper lay out for placing each of the equipment for completion of the total process. This usually happens when there is sudden demand and when expansion takes place in the already congested area of the shop floor. The Project manager to avoid the delay of commissioning the equipment will try to locate in wherever there is some vacant space and ultimately the heat treatment furnace will be in one corner, cleaning cells in another area for proximity for water supplies, and presses in another area and finally the assembly operations can be at farther end adding to crisscross or zigzag movements of the products. The poor supervisors may have to go to different buildings for the sake of follow up of the production of the parts and he may be walking to the tune of 6–8 km on daily basis. In one shop I added the total walking distance and it was about 10 km on each day. In another shop the raw material needed for few presses were stored just about 30 yards away. But to bring the material to press by forklifts, one has to travel about one furlong through existing gang ways and blocked by brick walls constructed log ago. This forklift would be making a total trip of about 30 km a day during the shift which could be reduced to less than 0.5 km a day if the brick walls can be demolished for the forklift movement!!

But the Supervisors need to know on how to make a good study on the lay outs from start to end with all the data and logically. The case study narrated in the next pages will highlight the steps from A to Z and ultimately it will motivate, reignite and trigger his knowledge and enthusiasm to come out with revised proposals for the sake of the organization. The unnecessary movements forced on the products are the silent killers with nonproductive work content for which customer will not be paying any way!

Re-Layout Changes @ Modules – 605, 606 & 607

Concerns/Issues with the present layout manufacturing of Modules 605/606/607

- ❖ Process being carried out in different buildings.
- ❖ Distance travelled is extremely/unimaginably high.
- ❖ Material handling/movement delays too much affecting the daily production at various modules.
- ❖ Component manufacturing machines are positioned here there in different location based on the earlier demand of the products. A few products got out dated but the machines are still there to serve for 8 years as spares (agreed with customer).
- ❖ Assembly done at first floor, other operation done on ground floor with frequent transporting through the lift operation.
- ❖ Movement follows zigzag pattern for few products.
- ❖ No specific area earmarked for Kanban.
- ❖ CNC/Cleaning cell/Vibrator etc. are located far from the module assembly line.
- ❖ No accountability/Responsibility from centralized department of Heat Treatment/CNC/Cleaning cell/Vibrator etc. for the daily assembly output.
- ❖ On the whole it looks that the assembly output is the major requirement of the assembly operators and module owners, but the enablers/support function alone do not play the needed vital role for the Daily quantity and quality achievement, and this is because of the present Manufacturing System following the Centralized department work culture.

Re-layout study conducted by the team members along with Module owners/ CNC/Mfg. Engg/PMD are captured in the following pages.

ABSTRACT SUMMARY OF RE-LAYOUT CHANGES - MODULE # 605, 606, 607

S. No	Description	Existing Method	Proposed Method	Remarks
1	Distance travelled (in km)	100.33	34.47	
2	Space Saved (In Sq ft)	8366	2866	
3	No. of Building Handled	3	1	
4	Unwanted Machines removed	-	15	
5	No of Floor handled	2	1	(1) in Existing Method at 303-Building first floor for Assembly & ground floor for Component Mfg.
				(2) 303 Building-First floor is reserved for future expansion
6	CNC Cell	CLG cell is processed in 3 Cells in 3 Buildings	Re-layout of CNC Cell nearer to the respective module & in one place in same building	
7	Cleaning Cell	CNC cell is processed in 2 areas in 3 buildings	Re-layout of Cleaning Cell as per Modules allocated in the building	
8	Component Mfg.	Machines are located at different places in the same building & some in the different building with no correlation to assembly line	Re-layout of Component Mfg. as per Assembly line process sequence in the same building	
9	Material Handling	Materials are transported in small batch qty through lift for Assembly lines located on the first floor	Material transportation is considerably reduced with Comp. Mfg. & Assy lines are nearby in the same ground floor	

10	Kanban System	(1) Materials are issued/received before the start of the shift (2) Very often some comp. are short & Quantity issue	A humble start has been made with visual Kanban System @ Modules # 601 for one line each from 1st June-13	
11	Flexibility/ Mobility	Assembly & Comp. Mfg. are not in perfect alignment	We propose to have good alignment with Comp. Mfg. with respective assembly (Assy) lines	
12	Mfg. Process Style	More centralized with mass Mfg. System as was followed @ USA motor Mfg. Companies	More of Lean Mfg. system or Toyota Production system with single piece flow getting priority for each assembly lines	
13	Line Balancing	The Line Balancing is being attempted at assembly lines, but not in other areas of operations.	Line Balancing & Expected quantity (qty) at assembly line are to be achieved in other area of comp Mfg./ Cell/HTS etc.	
14	NVA Activity	NVA activities are very high for transportation materials, Process delay & By operating in different buildings & different places	Such NVA activities could be very low after the implementation of proposed Re-Layout	
15	Product Throughput Time	High in the Present system.	Less with modified layout with less distance travelled & other delays	
16	Productivity Improvement	(x) with no correlation & integration with various support functions	It is supposed to achieve (x+25%) along with all Layout/Low volume/Heat treatment proposals	

17	WIP	(x) with far too many places of finished goods (Fg) & stock holding	It is expected to come down by (x-50%) with far less areas of movements, stock locations & multiple building movements.	
18	Team work Culture	(1) Extremely low with support functions not aligned for daily assembly line output. (2) Hardly any support functions know the assembly output of any lines in any shift	With the functional reporting system of all support man power the team work culture can go up considerably high	
19	Response of support functions	Extremely low as of now considering the pressure and urgency at production modules	The functional approach work can improve the response from the support functional lot	
20	5'S Practice	Maintaining is difficult	Maintaining can be better and easy	
21	Accountability of below support functions Comp Mfg. CNC Cell ClLG Vibratory HTS GI HMI Stores	Not directly accountable & responsible for daily Assembly output	All these Functions are to work functionally for the respective Modules & Administratively to the concerned Dept., With this work culture change the accountability/ responsibility of all functions will go high	

22	Morale/ Happiness	Generally very poor among Module supervisors and even support functions such as Materials/ Quality	With much high Team work culture and combined problem solving culture, the end Results can go up and hence the morale & happiness can also go up in the future months	
23	Profitability	Low	Should be much better than the present achievement with all the proposed change Management	

605 MODULE EXISTING LAYOUT FOR – 2 SOP PUMP BODY (PROCESS FLOW)

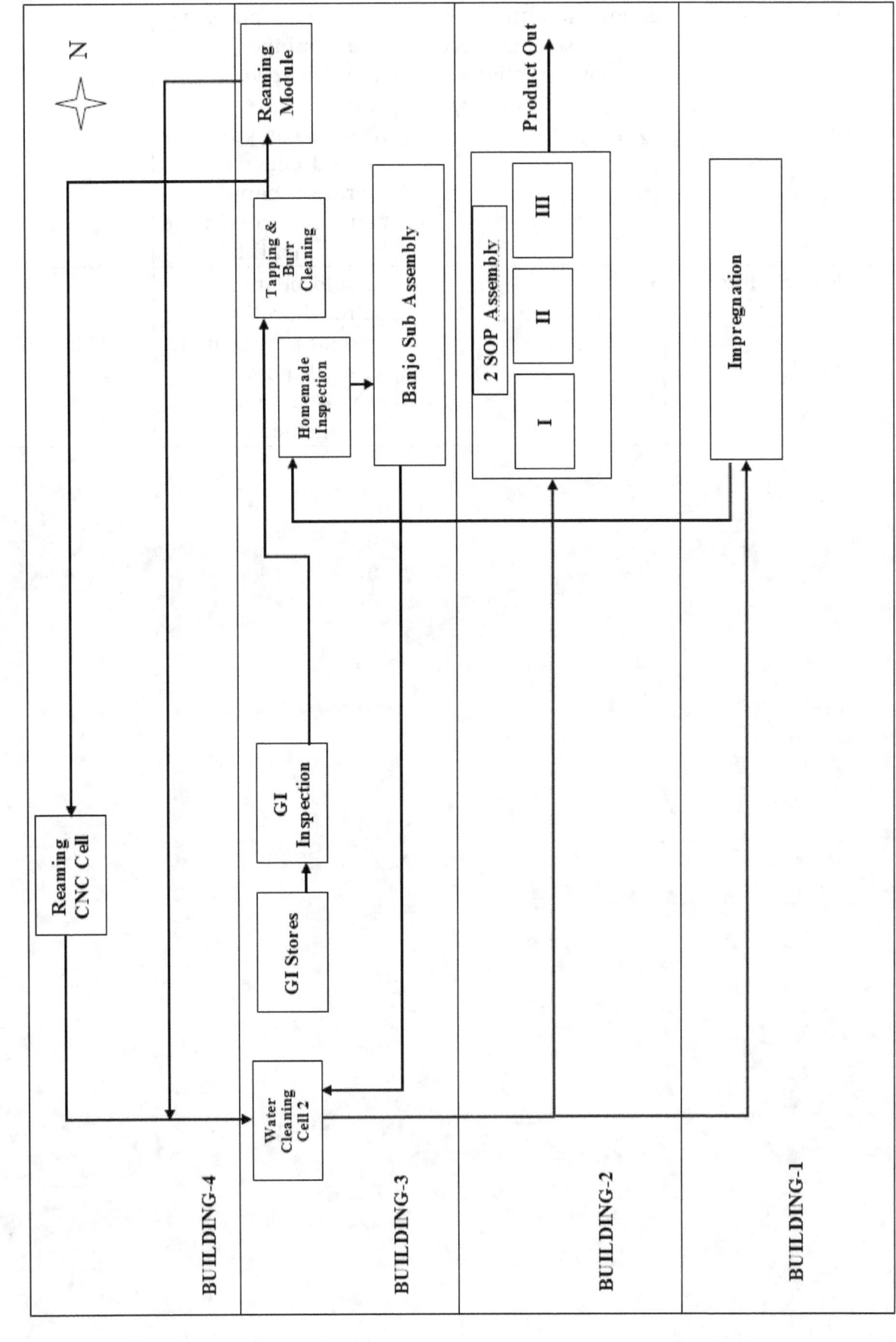

605 MODULE PROPOSED LAYOUT FOR – 2 SOP PUMP BODY (PROCESS FLOW)

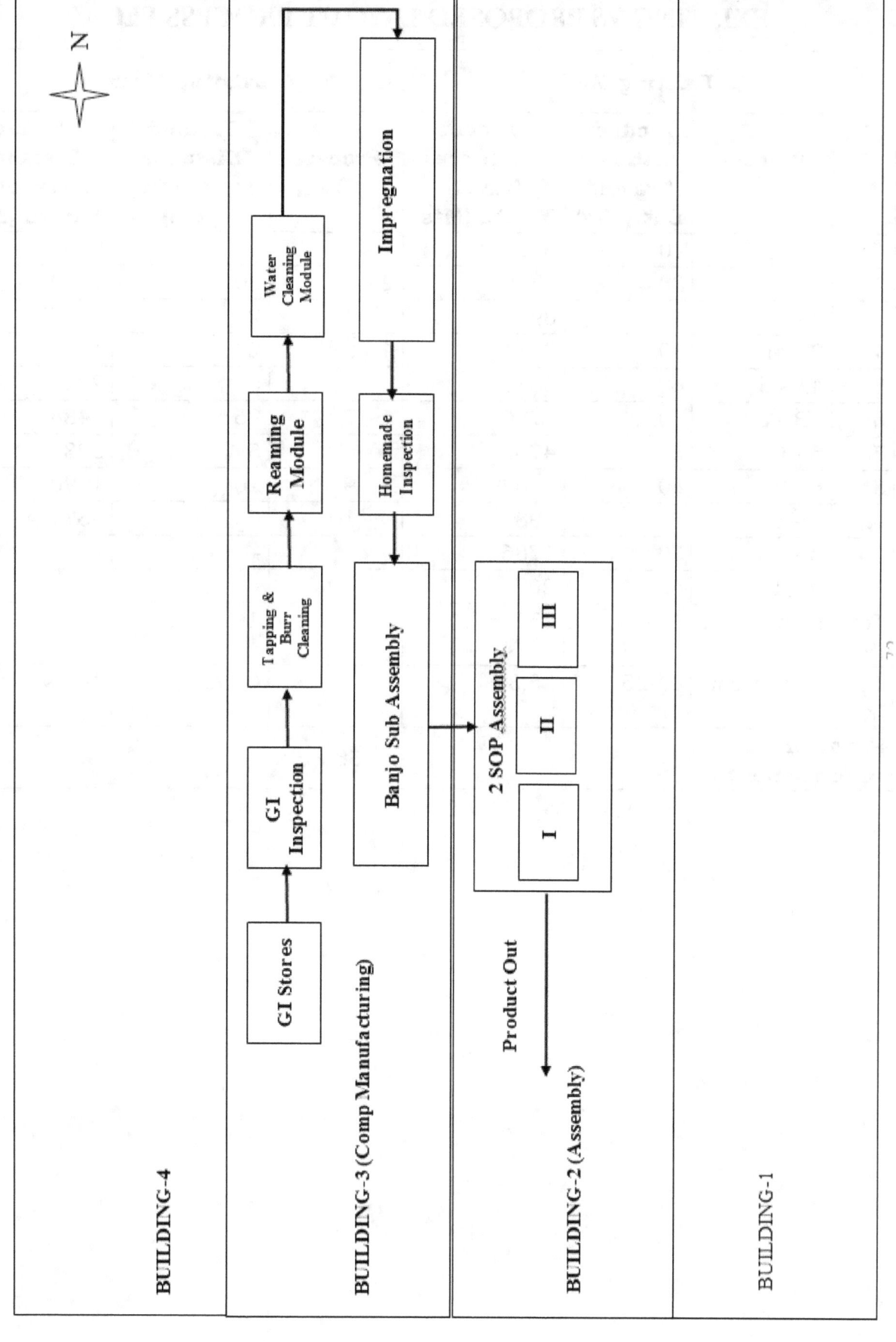

MODULE # 605 PUMP BODY EXIBBSMODULE # 607 PUMP BODY EXISTING VS PROPOSED LAYOUT PROCESS FLOW

S. No	Process No	Existing Method		Process No	Existing Method	
		Product Distance Travel/ Day (Mts)	Product Distance Travel/ Month (Mts)		Product Distance Travel/Day (Mts)	Product Distance Travel/ Month (Mts)
1	1 - 2	10	596	1 - 2	10	595
2	2 - 3	30	1786	2 - 3	30	1786
3	3 - 4A	15	893	3 - 4	2	119
4	3 - 4B	40	2381	4 - 5	20	1190
5	4A - 5	60	3571	5 - 6	5	298
6	4B - 5	30	1786	6 - 7	25	1488
7	5 - 6	80	4762	7 - 8	5	298
8	6 - 7	80	4762	8 - 9	20	1190
9	7 - 8	5	298	9 - 10	60	3571
10	8 - 9	30	1786	-	-	-
11	9 - 10	45	2679	-	-	-
Total Distance in (Mts)		452	25298	-	177	10536
Total Distance in (Km)		0.425	25.3	-	0.177	10.54
Scope of Improvement%		58.35%				

607 MODULE EXISTING LAYOUT FOR – 4 SOP PUMP BODY (PROCESS FLOW)

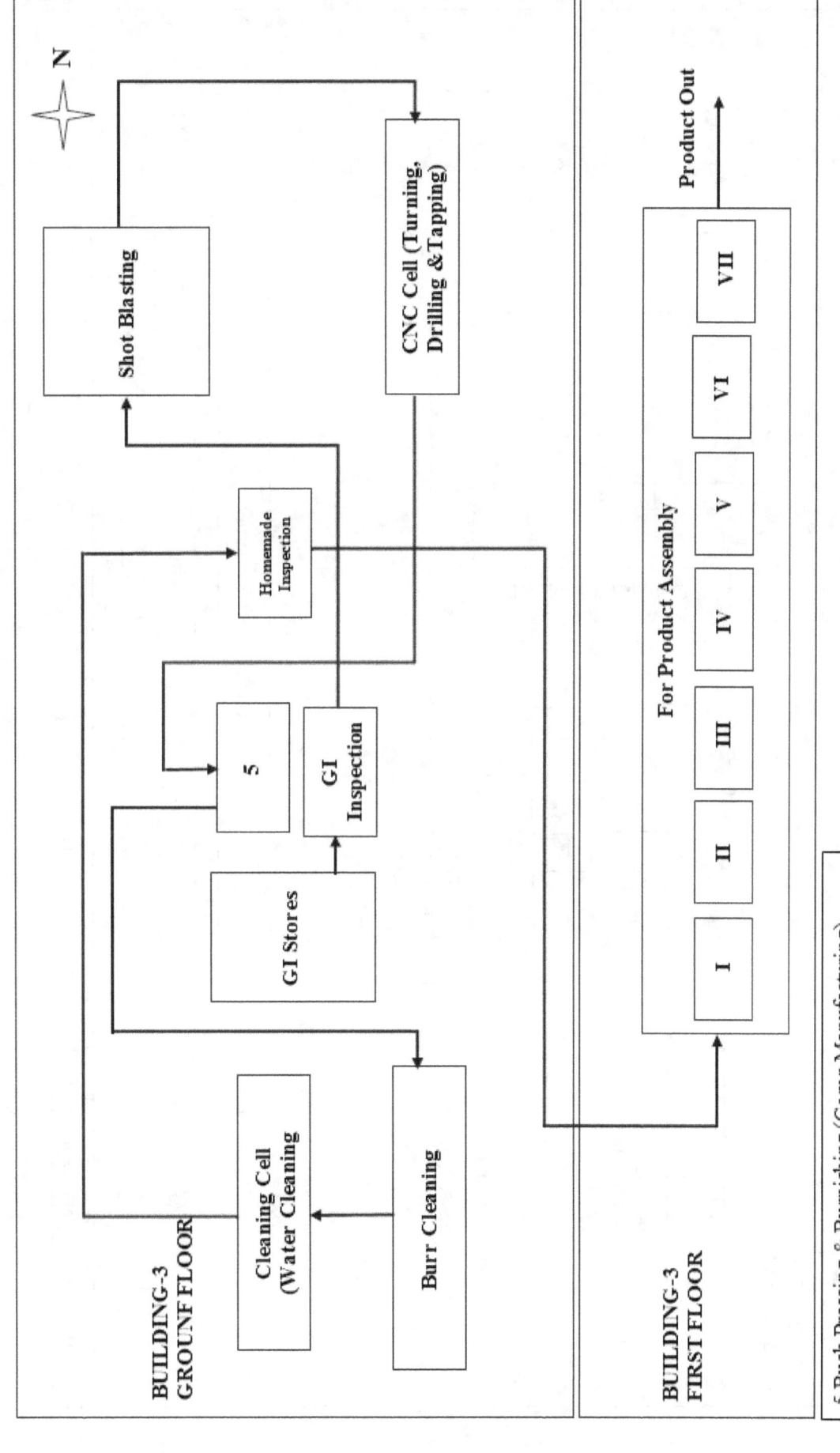

607 MODULE PROPOSED LAYOUT FOR – 4 SOP PUMP BODY (PROCESS FLOW)

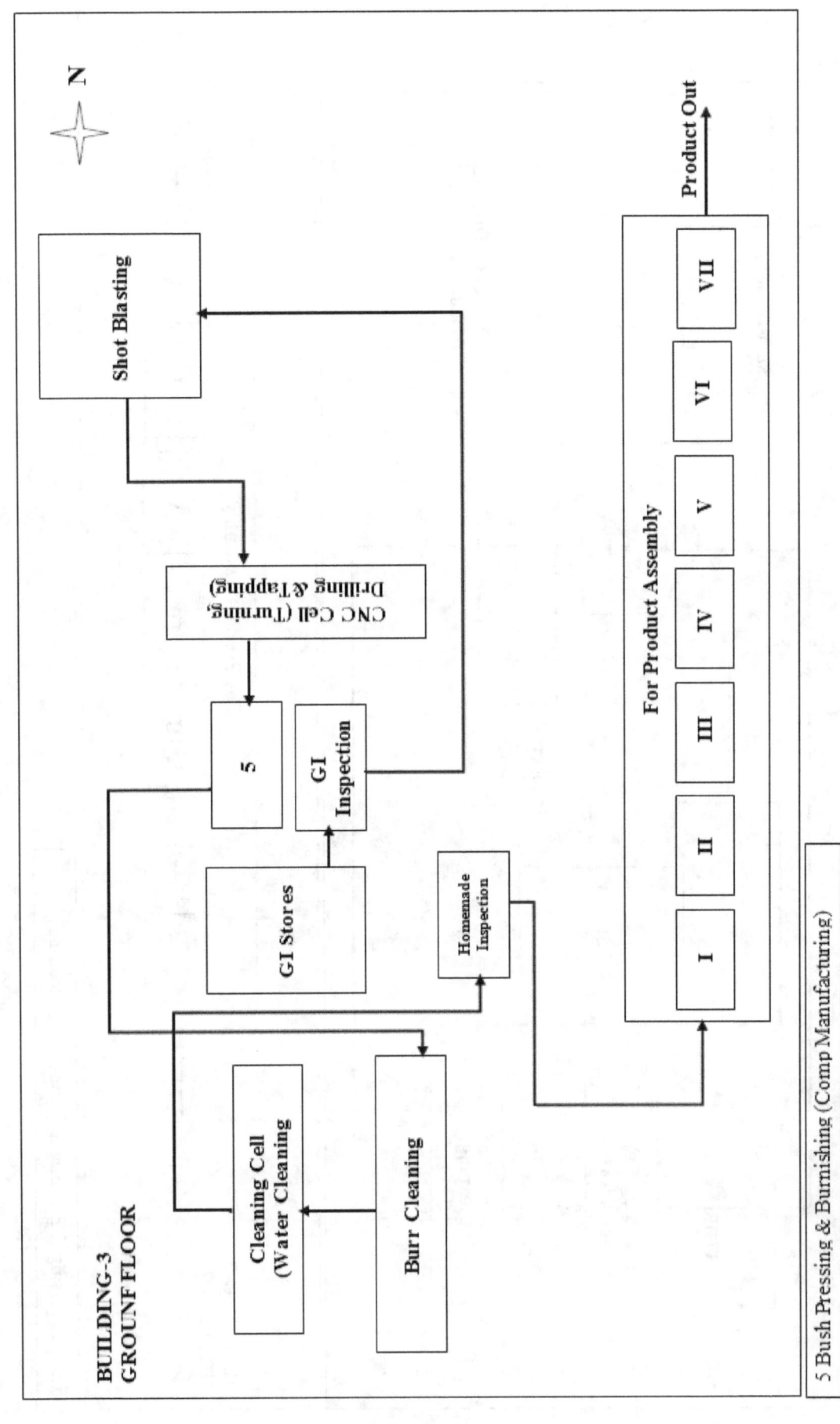

BUILDING-3
GROUNF FLOOR

5 Bush Pressing & Burnishing (Comp Manufacturing)

MODULE # 606 PUMP BODY EXISTING VS PROPOSED LAYOUT PROCESS FLOW

S. No	Existing Method			Existing Method		
	Process No	Product Distance Travel/Day (Mts)	Product Distance Travel/Month (Mts)	Process No	Product Distance Travel/Day (Mts)	Product Distance Travel/Month (Mts)
1	1 - 2	5	175	1 - 2	5	175
2	2 - 3	188	6580	2 - 3	188	6580
3	3 - 4	263	9205	3 - 4	250	8750
4	4 - 5	25	6250	4 - 5	2	500
5	5 - 4	25	6250	5 - 6	15	3750
6	4 - 5	25	6250	6 - 7	4	1000
7	5 - 6	15	3750	7 - 8	5	1250
8	6 - 7	8	2000	8 - 9	4	1000
9	7 - 8	40	10000			
10	8 - 9	69	17250	-	-	-
Total Distance in (Mts)	663	67710		-	473	23005
Total Distance in (Km)	0.663	67.71		-	0.473	23.01
Scope of Improvement%				66.02%		

607 MODULE PRESENT LAYOUT FOR – 4 SOP ROTOR (PROCESS FLOW)

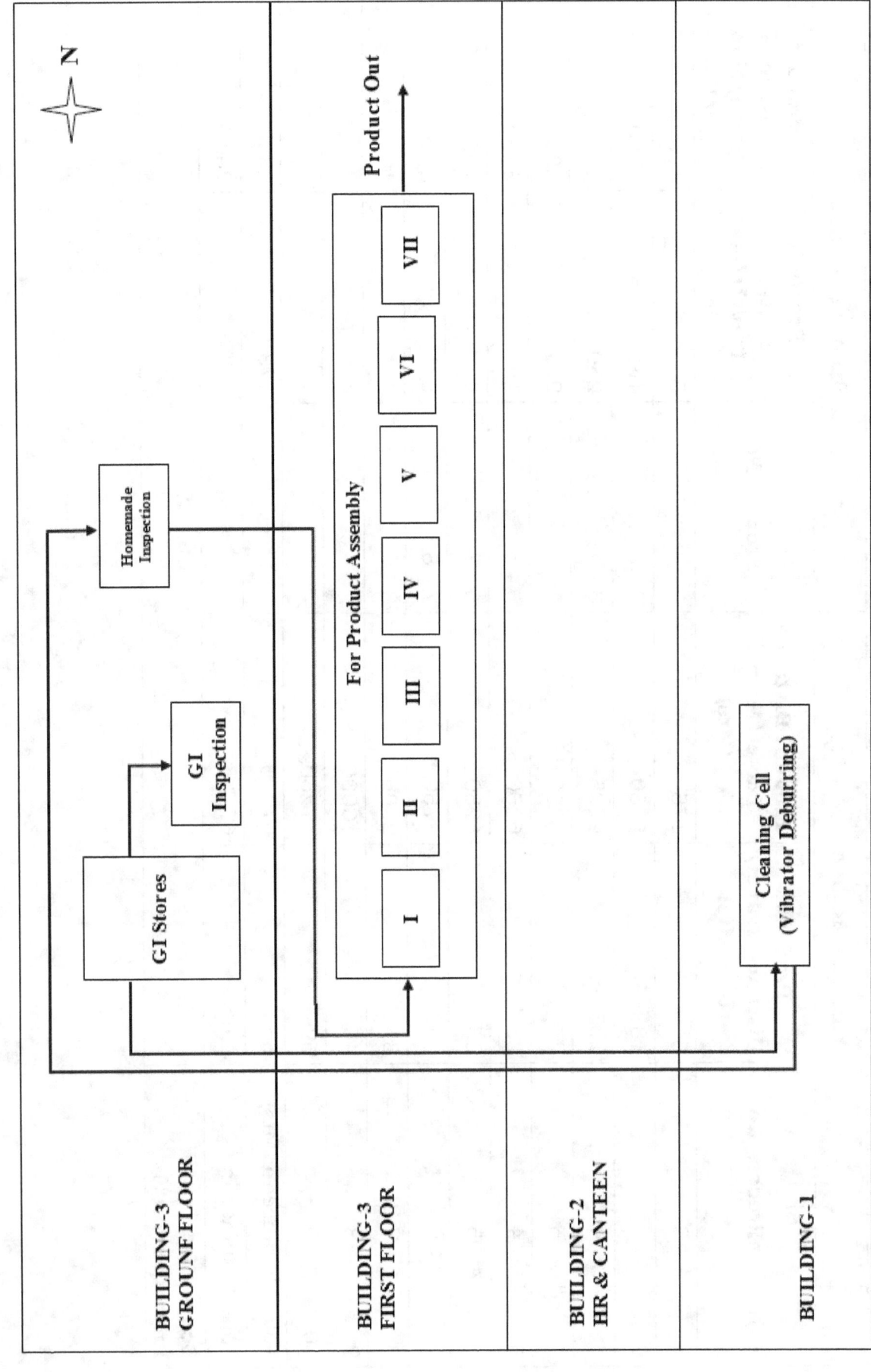

607 MODULE PROPOSED LAYOUT FOR – 4 SOP ROTOR (PROCESS FLOW)

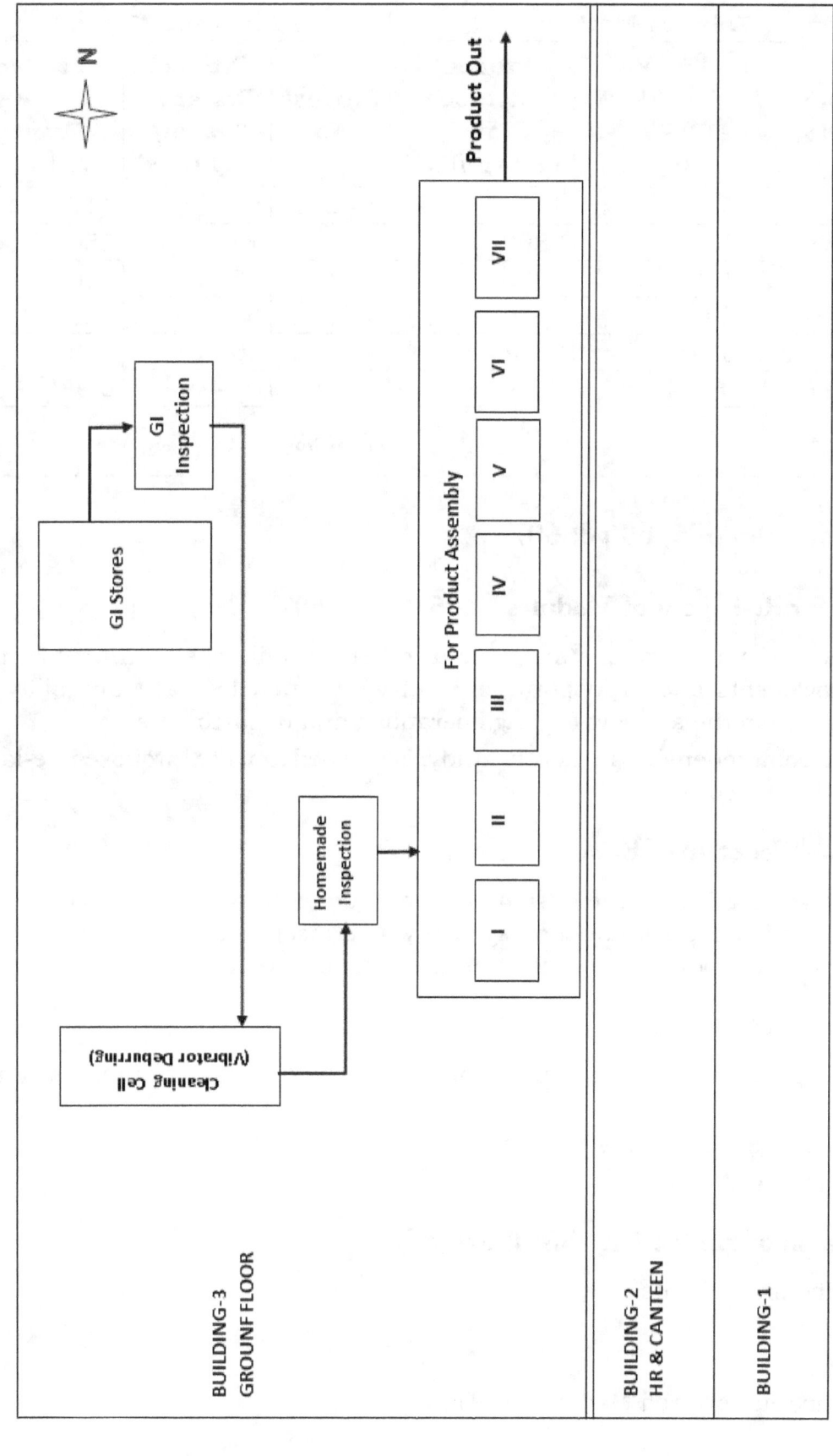

MODULE # 607 PUMP BODY EXISTING VS PROPOSED LAYOUT

S.No	Existing Method			Proposed Method		
	Process No	Product Distance Travel/Day (Mts)	Product Distance Travel/ Month (Mts)	Process No	Product Distance Travel/ Day (Mts)	Product Distance Travel/ Month (Mts)
1	1 - 2	5	117	1 - 2	5	117
2	2 - 3	120	2800	2 - 3	15	350
3	3 - 4	120	2800	3 - 4	15	350
4	4 - 5	69	1610	4 - 5	5	117
Total Distance (Mts)		314	7327	-	40	933
Total Distance (Km)		0.314	7.33	-	0.04	0.93
Scope of Improvement%		87.26%				

Relayout of Modules-605, 606 & 607

Why the need for Re-Layout of Modules – 605, 606 & 607?

❖ Because the various operations are done at different buildings with far too much material movements and Transportation and with much less accountability and responsibility from the support feeding operations and departments.

❖ Therefore a comprehensive in depth study is needed on the proposed re-layout exercise of these modules

Plant Re-Layout/Redesign of Existing Layout

❖ It is the integrating face of the design of a production system. The basic objective of Lay-out is to develop a production system which meets requirement of Assembly volume of various products and quality in the most economical way.

Integrated System of Production

❖ What are the products/quantity/quality of assembly products to be processed @this unit?

❖ The process route of assembly products?

❖ How much to make?

Integrated System of Production Must Provide for

❖ Required Machines/Plants

❖ Line Balancing

❖ Work places

❖ Storage for in/out for each Machine or Plant

❖ WIP

❖ Most economical transportation system of low of assembly products up to finishing
❖ Easy dispatch of assembly products

Severe Constraints of Redesign & Re-layout of Facilities

❖ Financial/Physical restriction of moving the Heat treatment, cleaning cell & shot blasting etc. to different places.

Ideal Layout vs Practical/Feasible Re-layout

❖ We do not recommend an ideal layout which may be totally impracticable for implementation
❖ An Ideal Layout within the Existing Layout is probably as difficult as to locate an ideal bride or groom!
❖ Nor, we do not recommend shifting of Heat treatment, shot blasting process etc.
❖ All the Team members opine and it is a known fact that assembly & comp. Mfg. processing output is much less, because of the long distance travelled and with Mfg. Setup at various building
❖ Most important strategy is to move out unwanted machines & assembly process and make the men achieve and surpass Norm by an efficient result oriented Management Staff Team, who will make things happen.
❖ Certainly we should facilitate easy and faster movement of material between wherever working process & stations available and it is possible.
❖ Our re-layout work is in line with the above serve constraints/practical consideration

What Are the Basic Needs or Salient Expectation of the Re-layout Task?

❖ To meet the changing/emerging Marketing Demand taking into consideration of higher trend of auto parts/export market and considering the competition
❖ Equipment/re-layout should be market oriented than age old exiting Layout of equipment related to market demands of previous year.
❖ Based on market scenario, lowest minimum level of equipment/Plants/Facilities to be provided with no extra additional equipment which only breed inefficiency/ idle waiting time/occupy space/more man power and all those in variably leads to confusion department working.
❖ The latest innovative trend in layout changes is to go for compact accountable product line, known as cellular autonomous production system or cellular model system. Such production systems has been implemented successfully i the last 15 years at TVS group companies, in CUMI units (6 companies @ 6 locations), Rane group companies (4 companies in a 4 different location)/TI Metsec, to name a few companies with spectacular achievement in many areas.

Basic Needs or Salient Expectations of the Re-layout Task

❖ Faster Throughout, Faster delivery.
❖ Greater customer service/satisfaction/quality level.
❖ Clear accountability from start to finish for each range of production module system
❖ Much reduced equipment/man power with better line balancing/flow of material.

❖ Significant reduction in rejection/WIP
❖ Significant reduction in movement of material especially back track
❖ Unimaginable productivity rise ranging from 20% to 40%
❖ Much better bottom line.

Features of a Cell

❖ Make a discrete product stage
❖ Own tools, jigs, fixtures & gauges
❖ Own technical support as well as company support
❖ Ownership of process
❖ Responsibility for delivery, quality & cost.
❖ All Comp. Mfg., CNC, cleaning, vibratory & HTS process personal to functionally report to module.

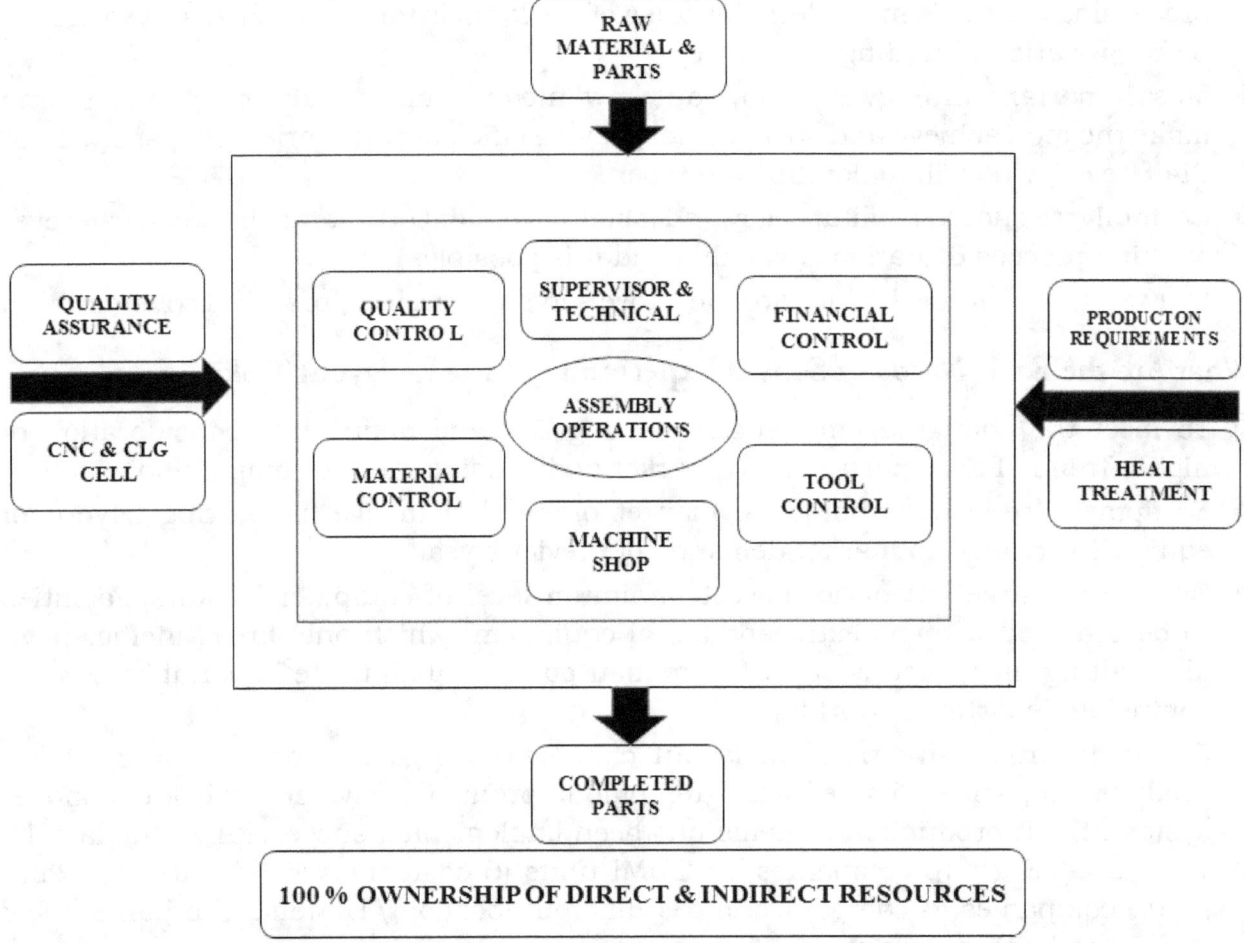

Old Traditional System

In the old Traditional System given the choice, the Modules may be happier with products that are easy to manufacture than the high value products with processing difficulties. This strategy worked so for when we were in monopoly to customer.

New Strategy System

In the New Strategy System Customer is the king and he dictates/drives what he wants & when he wants. The Facilities & priorities to be tuned for this Task. We have to decide or tailor made the plant & operations Management that will ensure high volume products with highest Customer satisfaction level.

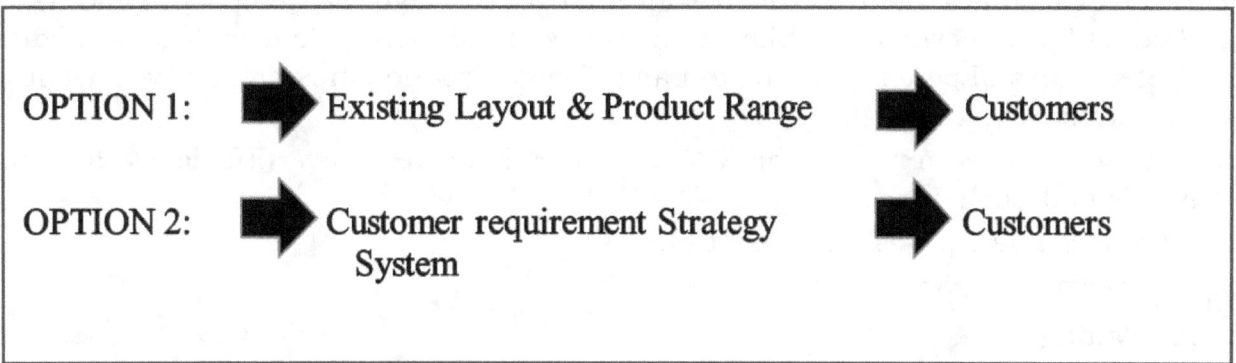

EXISTING VS CELLULAR MANUFACTURING

Sl No	Existing Method	Cellular Method
1	High skill/Expertise	Multi - skilled
2	High variety capability	Customer focus
3	Individuals	Team work
4	High NVA	Low NVA
5	Poor Quality traceability/Ownership	High Quality
6	Long Lead Time	Reduce Lead Time
7	High WIP & Inventory	Reduce WIP & Inventory
8	Poor Schedule adherence	High Schedule adherence

Objectives of a Good Layout

- ❖ Reduced risk to Health & Safety of workmen.
- ❖ Improved morale & worker satisfaction – Less Fatigue
- ❖ Increased Output
- ❖ Fewer Production Delays
- ❖ Savings in floor space (Production, Storage and Service Areas)
- ❖ Reduced Material Handling
- ❖ Greater utilization of Machinery, Manpower and/or service
- ❖ Reduced WIP
- ❖ Shorter Manufacturing Time
- ❖ Reduced Movement/Indirect Men
- ❖ Easier & Better Supervisor
- ❖ Less congestion and confusion
- ❖ Reduced Hazard to Material or its Quality or Mix up

❖ Easier adjustments to changing condition
❖ Miscellaneous other advantages

Let Us Strive for the Best on Attainment of the Above Objectives at Our Main Plant

❖ The Latest innovative trend in Layout changes is to go for Compact Accountable Product Line, known as Cellular Autonomous Production system or Cellular Module System. Or still better could be to name Toyota Production System, if you want to westernize, call Lean Mfg.

❖ Our emphasis is to reduce the NVA Time and Improve all over Efficiency, and our Aim is to become Lean.

❖ What is Lean? Take care and control.

1. Over production
2. Waiting
3. Conveyance
4. Processing
5. Inventory
6. Motion
7. Correction
8. Transferring/Scooping/Manual Loading/Unloading etc.

❖ The team has come out with very many proposal/ideas to control the Non Value Added activities of Assembly areas, particularly by going away from Mass Production System → Product Line, reducing the distance moved, improving Material Handling System and flow.

❖ With the introduction of proposed improvements, waiting delay & movement will be drastically reduced. Further process are enroute on dedicated/Balanced Equipment.

❖ All the above topics are covered elsewhere in the report.

4. Abstract Summary of Major Layout Changes

Power Flex Belt Manufacturing Module

Introduction and methodology

A big industrial and automobile belt manufacturing company along with oil seals located in South India had the inherent problem of doing subsequent operations in different buildings. This very old unit had the fundamental concepts of mass production with all presses in one location, heat treatment furnaces in another location, curing presses centralized in one location and so on with unimaginable movement of materials in crisscross or noodles type of movements Confronted with the need of reducing manufacturing costs and productivity enhancement the top management initiated a study in the year 2005 in all the manufacturing shops. In the following pages one summarized version of one shop is shown with various options for higher volume and lower man power strength with high productivity growth with considerable automation in various shops and operations. It is hoped that such a study actually implemented will motivate supervisors to repeat his success story in his shops.

Current scenario

1. This product holds the major volume out of the total belts produced (30%) in FIL.
2. The cost of REC belts are 30% more than the competitor's price, so not able to book the orders for the required volume. It affects the poly and wrapped belts orders in some common export customers.
3. Lot of WIP accumulation in between operations.
4. The machine utilization is around 65%. The capacity is underutilized due to lower productivity and lower market demand.
5. The cost of production is not competitive in the international market.
6. Equivalent sizes. I.e., Bottom fabric sizes, reverse building sizes, big sizes reduces the overall output by 20%.
7. Loading pattern of big & small sizes combination reduces the overall output by 10%.
8. No norms area i.e. in tyre cord preparation the output is only 50%.
9. The domestic market volume is around 70% of the total production and 10% of the volume is catered to industrial segment.
10. The process is more labour oriented with very low automation.

11. There are around 1000 part numbers in export and 300 part numbers in domestic handled every month.

12. The setup changes in the critical operations.

13. (Building-Curing-Stripping) reduces the output by 25%.

Layout

The Layout plays a major role in improving the free flow of materials from one process to the next process.

Present layout

1. The existing lay out is process centered.

2. The present layout is congested.

3. There is lot of crisis cross movement in the material flow.

4. There is no visibility in the shop floor.

5. Muda of movement of men and material is high.

6. Muri for the operator is high.

PRESENT LAYOUT – POWER FLEX

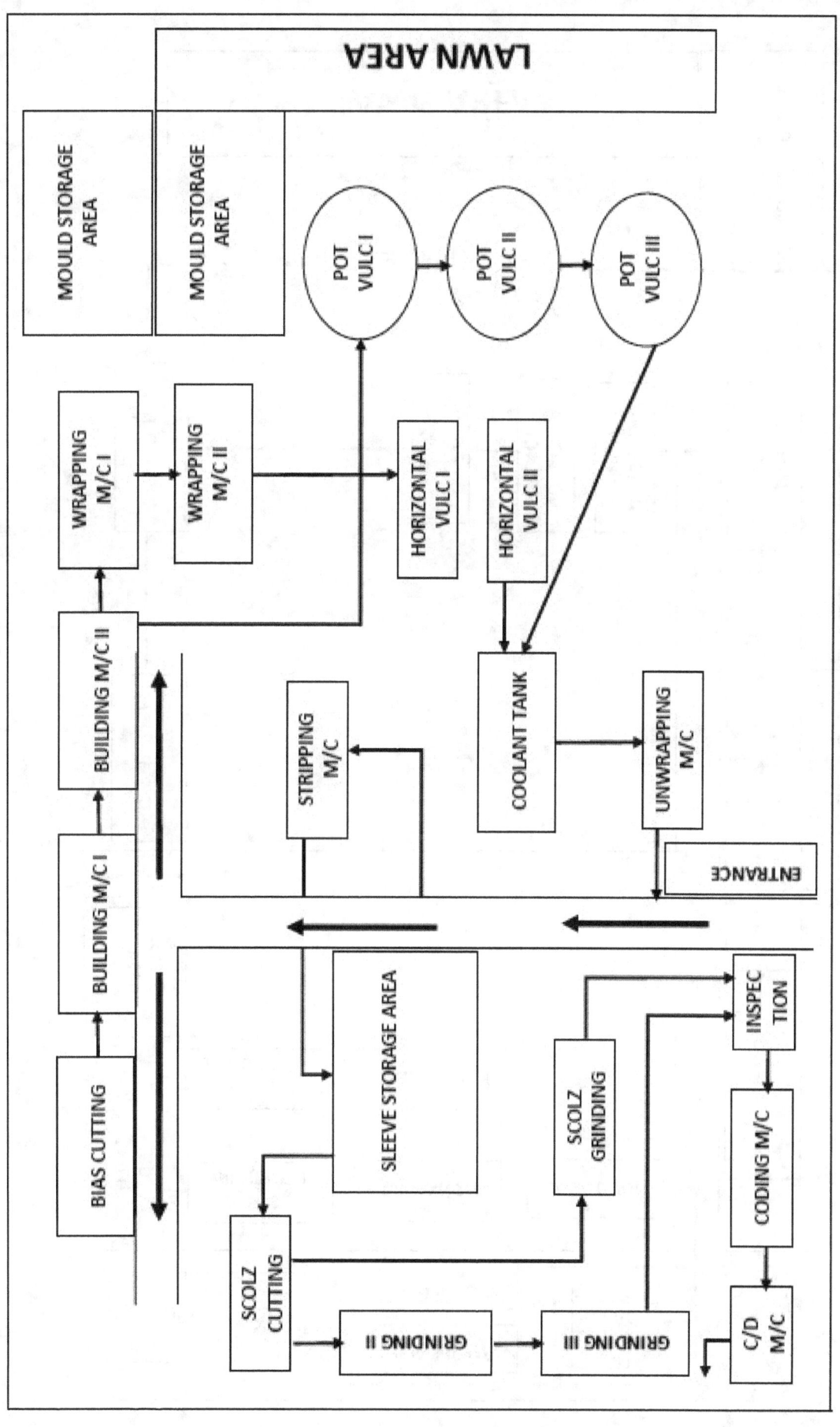

PROPOSED LAYOUT – POWER FLEX

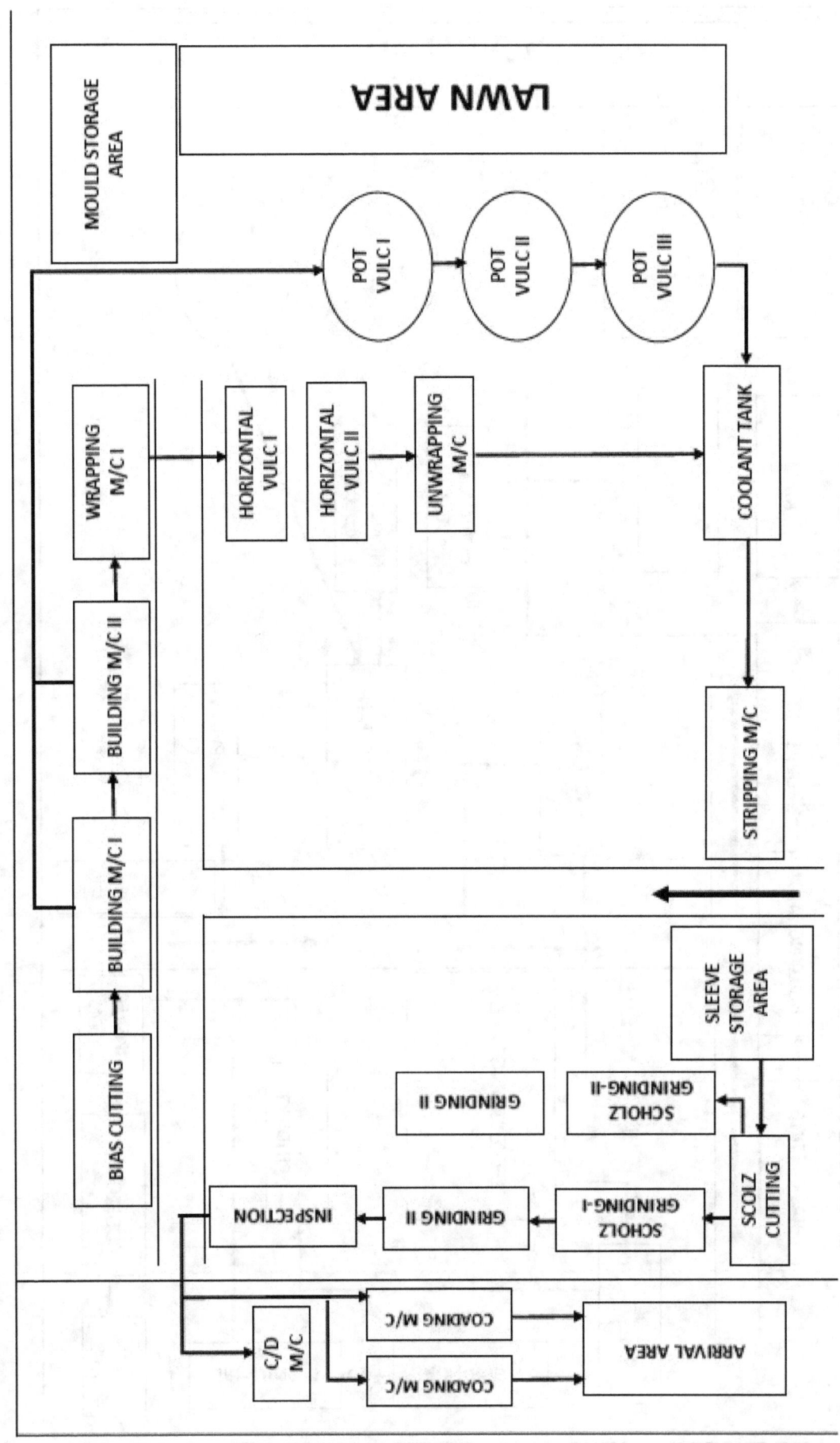

Proposed layout

1. Ensuring free flow of material from one operation to the other operation.
2. Better visibility in shop floor.
3. Reduction in material movement by 50%.
4. Elimination of all MUDA in shop floor.
5. Change from process centered to product centered by grouping the products in to two families – pot & wrapping method.
6. Improvement in the shop floor morale because of improved work environment.
7. Minimum WIP in each work station-From the current Rs: 13 lacs to 3 lacs.
8. Improved deliveries leading to better customer satisfaction.
9. Reduction in delivery leads time from 4 weeks to 2 weeks.
10. Reduction of excess production from 10% to 1%.

Benefits through layout changes & improved material handling

1. The distance travelled before the changes – 170 m.
2. The distance travelled after the changes – 140 m.
3. Operator fatigue reduced.

Material Handling

Present

1. The material is stored in fixed stands.
2. The material is carried by hand in building, curing, cutting & grinding area.
3. The material is stored in floor.
4. The material is kept in metal pallets with difficulty to access.

Proposed

In Building Area

1. Base roll storage to be near the machine in a trolley with pegs.
2. No. of trolleys required – 4.
3. The cured sleeves after curing will be stored in movable stands.
4. No. of mobile stands required – 7.

Cutting

1. The cured sleeves will be stored in movable trolleys.
2. Each trolley will have pegs for storing 10 sleeves as per cutting mandrill (required for 8 hrs production in cutting.)
3. No. of trolleys required – 12 nos.

Grinding Section: (Super Market Concept)

For transporting Ground belts from cutting to grinding to Inspection continuous chain conveyor will be provided.

Coding Area

The transportation of cured belt from inspection area to Coding machines will be done through movable trolleys with pegs.

Cured Sleeves Storage Area

The cured sleeves waiting for maturation/process will be stored in pegs mandrill wise.

The excess belts in shop floor lying as slow moving WIP will be stored in pegs.

AUTOMATION

S. No	Area to Automate	Benefits	Approx Cost in Rs: Lacs	Target
1	Mould Stripping	Man power can be reduced from 12 to 6 per day Mould damages will be avoided Sleeve damages will be avoided	20	Jan'06
2	Mould storage	Easy retrieval system Mould damages will be avoided	2.00	End Dec'05
3	Coding facility in the grinding M/c	At the time of grinding itself coding will be completed Coding rework will be eliminated	2.0	End Jan'06
4	Pot curing-Temperature control system	It's process requirement Quality Improvement; Suspect product will not go to the customer	2.00	End Dec'05

PRODUCTIVITY

S. No	Particulars	Data	Productivity
1	Present volume/month	2 lacs	
2	Present head count	99	2020 pcs/man/month
3	Proposed volume/month	2.0 lacs	
4	Proposed head count	62	3226 pcs/man/month
5	Productivity improvement scope		60%

PRODUCTIVITY – SCOPE - 1

Sno	Particulars	Data	Productivity
1	Present volume/month	2 lacs	
2	Present head count	99	2020 pcs/man/month
3	Proposed volume/month	2.5 lacs	
4	Proposed head count	65	3571 pcs/man/month
5	Productivity improvement scope		77%

PRODUCTIVITY – SCOPE - 2

Sno	Particulars	Data	Productivity
1	Present volume/month	2 lacs	
2	Present head count	99	2020 pcs/man/month
3	Proposed volume/month	3.75 lacs	
4	Proposed head count	79	4412 pcs/man/month
5	Productivity improvement scope		118%

5. Layout Changes in a Module of a Manufacturing Company

Introduction and Methodology

The benefits of changing simple lay out changes with low cost of a module of one big Bicycle manufacturing unit are shown in the next pages. It is recorded with all humility that this writer never bothered to correct the lay out changes despite having walked in the shop for almost 10 years. When I had the opportunity to revisit the shop after retirement with focus, it turned out to be an eye opener with the help of one youngster. All that done was to identify the movement of products from A to Z and then started discussing the desired movement paths without dislocating the costly equipment and by adding few lost presses here and there for each product with the rule that the movement to be always forward and avoid back and forth movements. It took one week end to implement the lay out changes to the satisfaction of all concerned with the initiative of the then works manager. If you have the focus, you can do much better than this example for sure!

Layout changes of a module

1. The present & proposed layout of machineries and process are given in the fallowing pages.
2. In the proposed layout we recommended shifting/relocation of machineries for faster movement of materials keeping in mind the Product line concept for STD/BSA type model.
3. Incidentally the changes will enable to reduce 4 direct men/day, besides reducing through-put time and reducing the non-productive men and setters.

SUMMARY OF MAN POWER REDUCTION

Description	Present Men		Proposed Men		Method & Process changes
	Day	Night	Day	Night	
Non Productive					
General tube movement-FFI	2	2	1	1	Modified layout/tube picking nearer to swaging
General movement-Weld fork	1	1	1		To be done by FFY NP J
Tube movement –pit pot	1	1	1	-	Addition man withdrawn
Fork movement-fork shop	2	2	1	1	Product type layout/flow
Setters				-	
Swaging	1	1	1	1	
Weld fork line	1	-	1	-	
Fork shop	1	1	1	1	
Total men	9	8	7	4	6 men saving

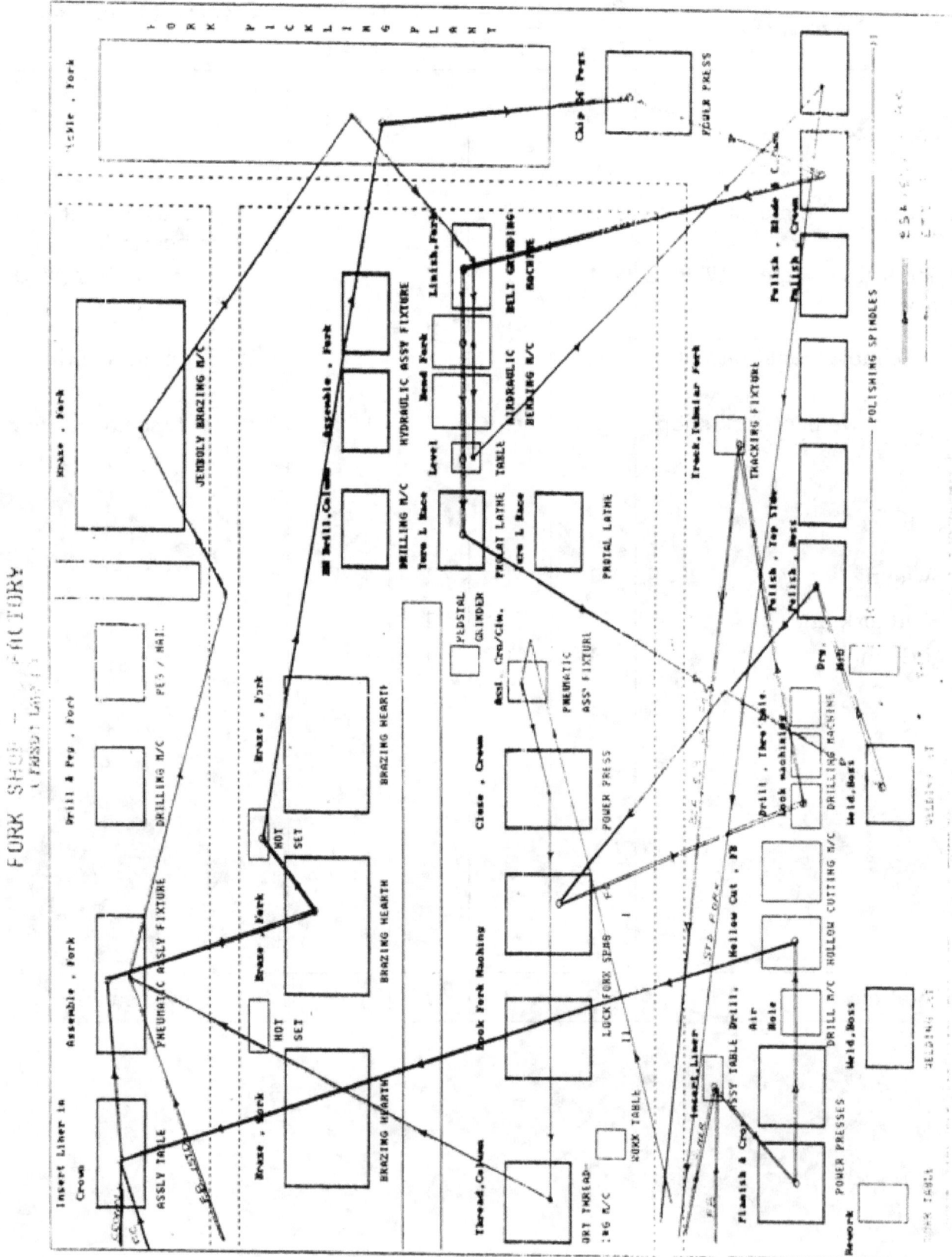

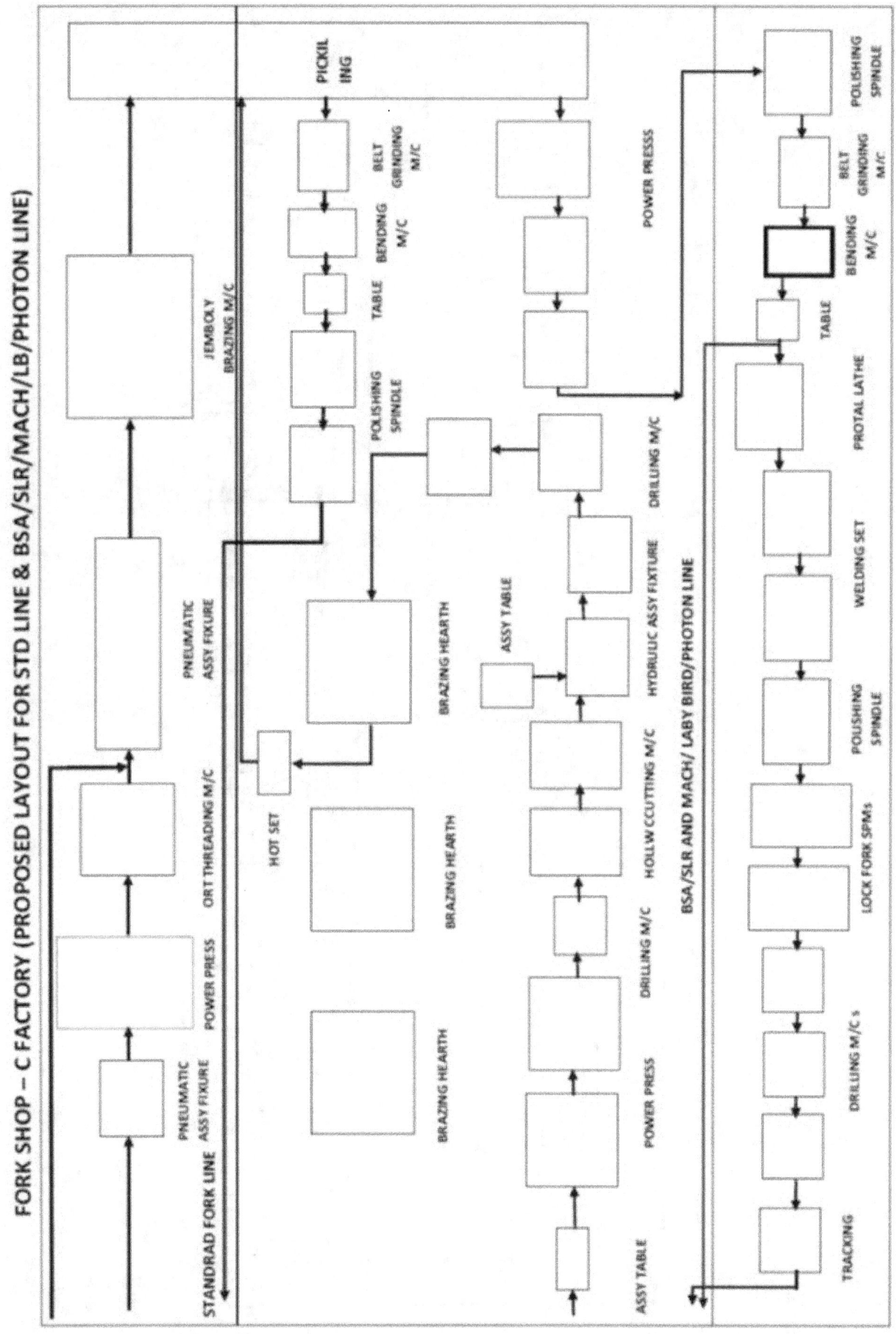

FORK SHOP – C FACTORY (PROPOSED LAYOUT FOR STD LINE & BSA/SLR/MACH/LB/PHOTON LINE)

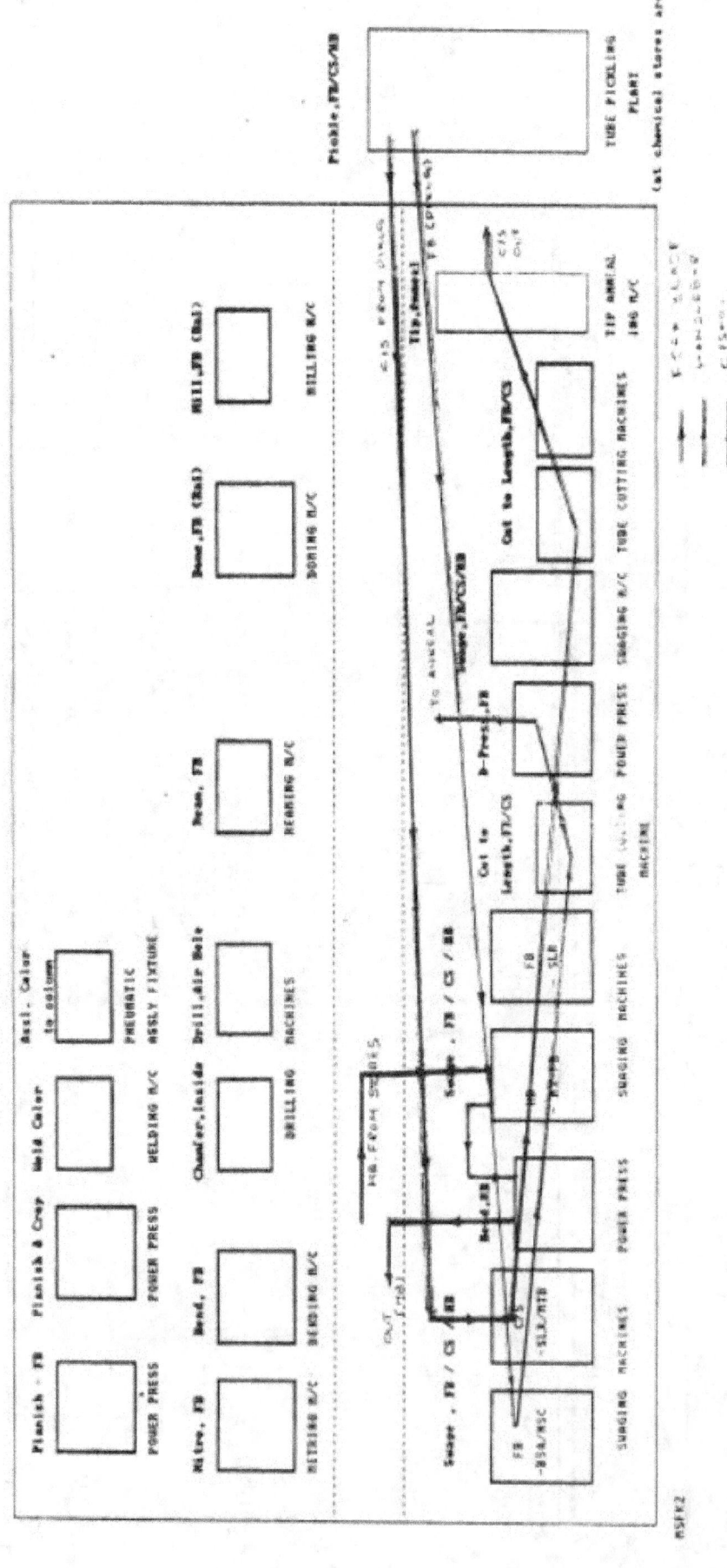

SWAGING SHOP / FORK LINE (HOME WELDED)
(PROPOSED LAYOUT WITH TUBE PICKILING PLANT)

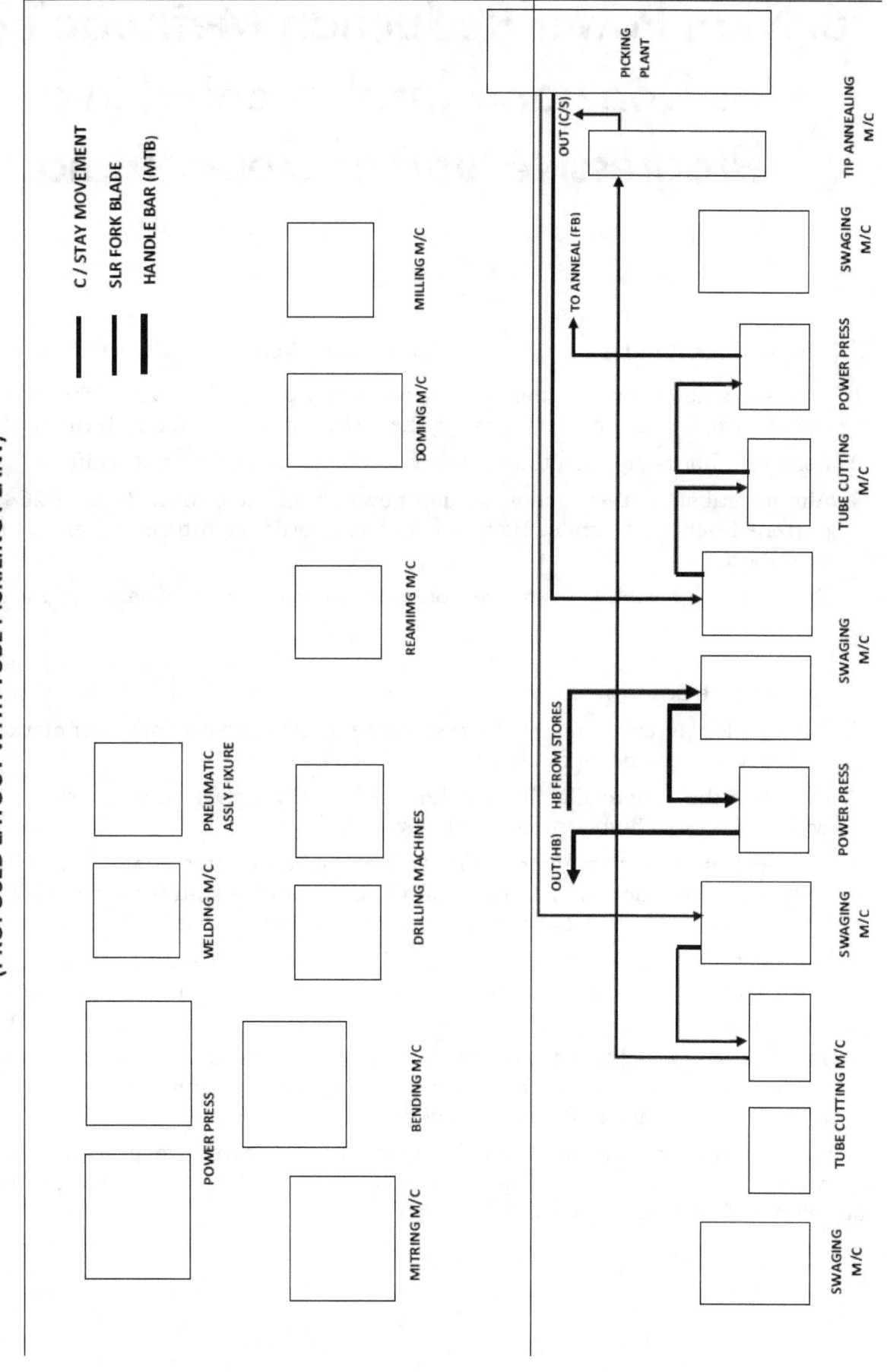

6. Man Power Reduction Methodology as Done and Implemented in a Progressive Unit of Upper India

Objective of Assignment or Study to Be Undertaken in This Unit

1. Find ways and means to increase the present productivity level to the tune of 40 - 50% above the current level through the forth coming LTS (Long Term Settlement).

2. Achieve 8 hours of touch time out put or machine rated output/shift.

3. Aim for substantial reduction of man power from the current level of 268 for the current level of "X" units. Have a lean work force for future higher volume and operations.

4. Bring in total flexibility to ensure workmen to move anywhere based on the ongoing needs.

5. Achieve product ownership from the existing process ownership by breaking or splitting the departmental barriers.

6. Make union and work men to be responsive to the changing needs of market along with new improved work culture.

7. Generate the fund availability for the LTS hike through head count reduction and with substantial higher productivity levels.

8. In order to be competitive in the market, recommend various steps such as substantial reduction of permanent man power strength through a suitable separation scheme or VRS, by which the wage cost per unit to come down by about 25%.

9. Conduct study to decide what jobs need to be done by permanent men and what other jobs can be done by unskilled man power or by non-permanent man power.

10. Do a thorough study to bring down the head count by way of revised higher man machine ratio, improved material handling systems or facilities, enlarged work content job content with higher basic wage or grade, combining the jobs, automation and through significantly higher productivity.

In this report we will only touch up on present restrictive practices, proposed desirable practices and one example of man power reduction methodology, considering the volume of work and space in this report.

Present Restrictive Practices

General

❖ Resistance for moving from one department to other place for working whenever required by supervisors. Adheres to the department or compartment work culture.

❖ Hesitate to do certain jobs, which they feel inferior.

❖ Union members not attending the work spot on time, moving from work spot in between and stopping the work.

❖ Not starting the work on time and not reaching the work spot in time after lunch break.

❖ Stopping the machines before the shift ends.

Machine Shop

❖ Switching of machines during lunch break even when production is critical.

❖ Fixed pattern of job rotation is demanded and general resistance for total flexibility.

Heat Treatment

❖ Stopping the heat treatment plant loading at shift end before shift end time by which the quantity to be heat treated is affected along with higher power consumption.

Assembly

❖ Not handing over the running machines to the next shift operator without affecting the production.

❖ Shift changes without prior approval from the concerned authority.

❖ Some employees not following shift schedule and coming in different shifts without prior permission and intimation.

Proposed Flexibility Changes

❖ Workmen to move from one job to another, one department to another when situation demands.

❖ Touch time working and handing over running machines to next shift operator.

❖ Maintenance men to do production job when maintenance work is not there and vice versa through a participating work culture by breaking the narrow department/compartment work culture.

❖ Quality Inspectors to do production jobs when needed.

❖ Be flexible to work on Sundays/Holidays when situation demands on staggered of basis.

❖ Critical machines to run in lunch breaks.

❖ Self-inspection and corrective actions at respective stations.

❖ Simple maintenance to be done by production operators especially on their machines which they are so much familiar.

❖ Tool room fitters to give the required tooling to the production operator near the machine before it is needed for change overs.

❖ Tool room fitters to do or assist setting jobs of progressive tool by participating approach with the production operators and avoid the need for re settings.

❖ Stores to give the coils in ready to use condition to production operators by participating approach to increase production and productivity

Proposed head count reduction at progressive blanking and piercing

Present man power - 21

Various steps or methodology taken and recommended to reduce the head count by optimum productivity at this section

1. Higher Man Machine Ratio
2. Improved Material Handling System
3. Change in Machine Lay out

1. Higher Man Machine Ratio

The work content of the operators for the Progressive Blanking & Piercing Operations include the following,

❖ Loading of coils

❖ Removing the punched out coils

❖ Collection of Dot scarp

❖ Changing the tool from the machine

❖ Collecting the components

❖ Moving the components to Heat Treatment section

❖ Checking the Quality of the Product

❖ Updating the Records

Time spent by the operator to perform the above present activities

❖ Coil loading time - 36 minutes (12 min x 3 coils)

Weight of the coil - 400 min to 1200 max in Kg

No of coils/shift - 2 to 3

❖ Removing the punched coil - 15 min/shift (5 min x 3 coils)

No of coils/shift - 2 to 3

❖ Collecting of Dot scrap - 18 min/shift

Quantity of scrap collected - 100 to 300 Kg

❖ Changing the tool - 40 min (20 x 2 times)

No of tool removal - 2/shift

Time taken/change - 20 min

❖ Collecting the components - 16 min/shift

Operator intervention required for every 10 to 20 min as follows

Once in 18 min for 63 Ton Press

Once in 10 min for 100 Ton Press

❖ Moving the components to HT - 25 to 46 min/shift

No of times the bins are removed to HT - 5 to 8 times

❖ Check for Quality (Audit)

Check for Quality confirmation - 11 min/shift

❖ Record keeping - 13 min

Entering Quality results in OQC Records

Write information of the product in the route cards

❖ JH time required - 30 min/shift

Time to clean, lubricate, inspect and retighten

Proposed changes for the improved system of manufacturing

❖ Change the method of collecting the components in bins of 20 Kg to a Trolley of approximately 140 Kg of one batch size. This will reduce the attention and physical pressure required by the operator and also reduce the time for collecting the components from 16 min to almost zero min/shift

❖ The component collection conveyors will be oriented in such a way that the component collection and the machine operation will be done from the same place for both the machines. This will facilitate the operator to look after and man two machines/ Presses for Progressive Tool/Blanking Operations.

❖ Tool change time can be reduced to 8 min from 20 min per occurrence by providing the serviced tool near the machine, equipping with self-clamping pneumatic clamps

❖ Mechanized strip cutter to be provided to the machines to reduce time for loading/ cutting the coil on to the machine.

❖ Movable trolleys will be provided to the machine to collect the component thereby eliminating picking and placing the bins on the Trolley every now and then.

❖ By doing this the operator time required for operating two machines will come down to 5 hours and 30 min. There can be a overlap of activities like tool change and loading to the tune of 20 to 40 min in a shift which can be reduced i due course by way of further reducing the time taken for loading and unloading.

2. Improved Material Handling System

❖ Present method of material handling

➢ Monorail hoist to load the coil

➢ Trolley to move 6 component bins

➢ Trolley/monorail hoist to unload the punched coil

➢ Belt conveyor to collect the components from the machine

➢ Tool trolley to bring and give the tool from Tool Room to the machine

❖ Proposed method of material handling

➢ EOT crane on coil loading side of the machine

➢ Monorail for all the machines to unload the punched out coil

➢ Conveyor to collect Dot scrap

➢ Container trolley to collect component for approximately 1 kg of load (2 numbers per machine)

> ➤ Container to collect Dot scrap every day
> ➤ Tool trolley to bring and give the tool from Tool Room to the machine

3. Change in the Machine Layout

This is not covered in this book since layout changes have been already explained

COMPARISON OF PRESENT AND PROPOSED ACTIVITIES

Activity	Present (1 M/c) Time inn Min	Proposed (2 M/c s) Time inn Min
Coil loading time	36	72
Removing the punched coil	15	30
Collecting of Dot scrap	18	8
Collecting the components	16	0
Moving the components to Heat Treatment	46	60
Check for quality (Audit)	11	22
Record keeping	13	26
JH time required	30	60
Total time in minutes	185	278
Total time in hours	3	5
Operator intervention with machines (while running) - frequency	**Every 9 Min**	**Every 30 Min**

Blanking and Piercing Machine shifts required for present Production - 18

Present Man Machine Ratio	-	1:1
Proposed Man Machine Ratio	-	1:2
Present Manpower in Progressive Blanking	-	21 Men
Proposed Manpower in Progressive Blanking	-	10 Men
Head Count Reduction	-	11 Men
Head Count Reduction%	-	50%

It may be mentioned that the man power reduction proposed is just for one machine by way of revised Man: Machine Ratio. Extending this methodology of revised Man: Machine Ratio, lay out changes, better material handling systems, automation, simplifying, various methods improvement etc. this Plant Head was able to reduce the man power strength drastically as shown in summary of Head Count Reduction Chart in the next page. What is shown above is just 4/5 page note from 175 page report.

Reduction of Head Count From 268 to 192

Non Value Added Activities (NVA)

Any factory will have direct man power and indirect man power for various operations. Some may even call productive work men and nonproductive work men because a few of them could be helpers, movement men, men engaged in loading and unloading activities. Say the man power strength of a shop is 100 men by way of 50 direct men and 50 indirect men and they produce 100 parts daily. The productivity is just 1 y PMPD, or Production per Man per Day. If the Indirect strength can come down to 30, then the PMPD is 1.25 (100/50+30), that is 25% more productivity. Therefore all out efforts need to be taken for Head Count Reduction especially in indirect man power strength. Tool Room, Stores activities, loading, unloading activities can be off loaded as done successfully by TII units, Rane Group companies etc. The next important task is to critically examine the worth of all activities of various operations going on in the shop.

Non Value Added Activities %

➤ Most Business Processes are 90% Waste and 10% value added work.
➤ Let us examine the movement of Parts from Machine shop to Assembly Line of a Manufacturing Unit.

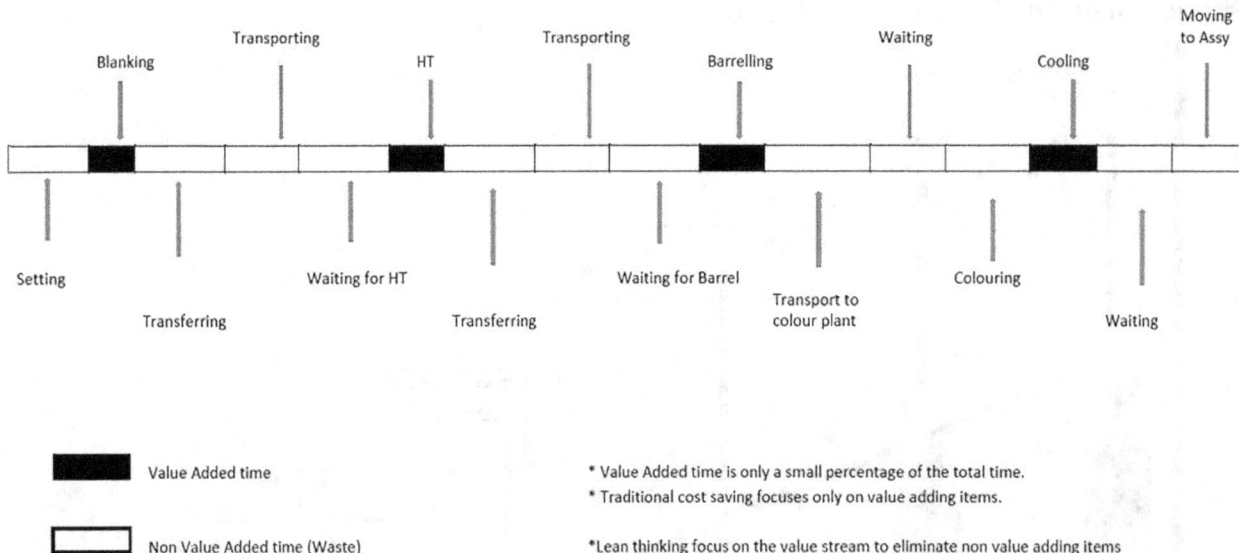

> ➤ Take the typical example of Progressive Tool Blanking at Machine Shop

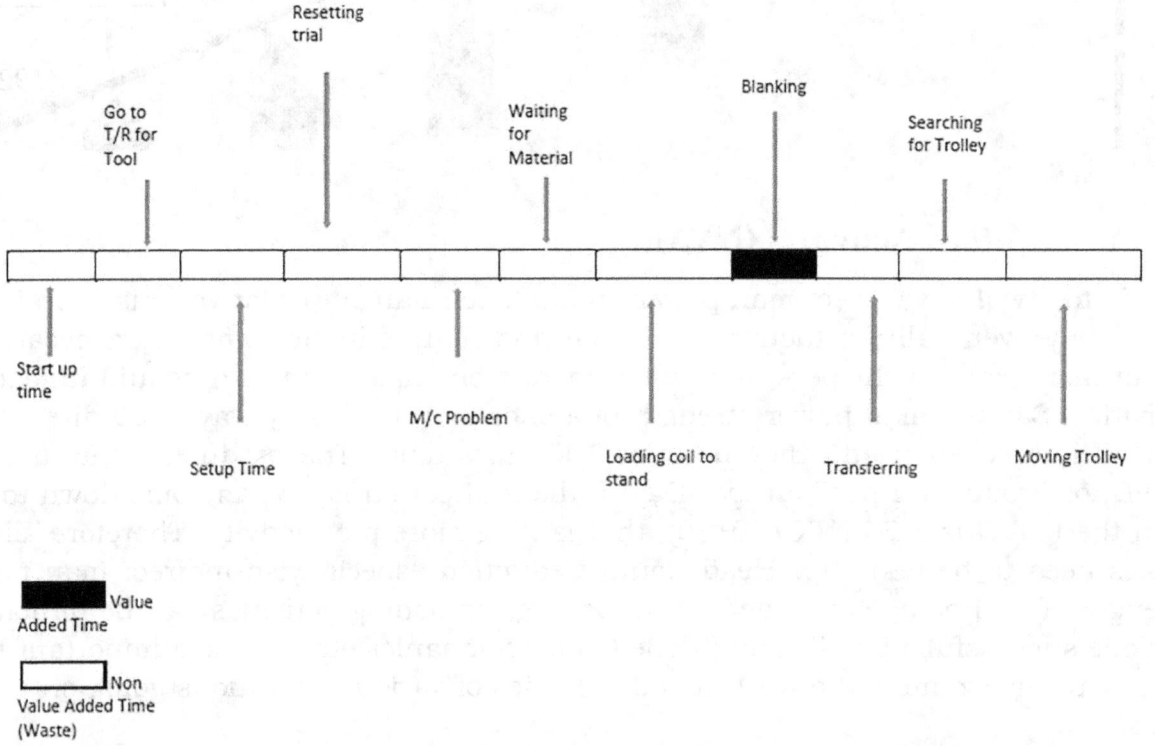

This can open our eyes to understand that Value Added Activities are just about 10 to 25% of the total Activities, the majority falls under Non Value Added Activities. Even in Japan, they say the story is more or less same.

Now, where is the remedy for quantum jump in productivity? Clearly it is by attacking all Non-Value Added Activities to the extent possible.

It is very difficult and thus very challenging too. We cannot eliminate LDL from our Cholesterol blood profile although it is supposed to be bad for health. Likewise we may not be able to totally eliminate all Non-Value Added Activities, but certainly we can eliminate very few, reduce the duration of such undesirable activities if we are determined to look from our third eye. The Set up time is inevitable, but, in Japan they call it SMED, it is so small by time as compared to typical Indian companies so far as the total time taken for Settings in Machines.

Since a reduction of Non Value Added Activities mean directly increase in productivity by better through put time of the product.

Automation, effective material handling systems, lay out changes, elimination of few operations by methods improvement, usage of simple trolleys, hoists and several other facilities are there before us to minimize the Non Value Added Activity duration in the manufacturing shops.

Value Added Focus

Value added is the concept that every activity and element of a system (materials, time, space, and energy) should add value to the output of the system. As such it provides perceptive for determining what needs improvement in manufacturing operations. Generally the tendency is to improve up on Value Added Activities, and same importance is not given for eliminating or reducing various Non Value Added Activities.

Distinguishing necessary non value added activities from the unnecessary wasteful ones is tricky because unnecessary activities in organizations often seem necessary. A good organized purchase activity is necessary. Activities such as inspecting incoming parts for defect or counting materials in inventory also seem necessary. The fact that an activity fulfills should not be confused with its adding value. For inspection and counting alternatives exit that would obviate the need for either of them. For example, by requiring vendors to deliver only zero defect parts, the need for incoming inspection can be eliminated to a great extent. Fixed containers can minimize the individual counting of parts.

- ❖ Value Added time is only a small Percentage of the total time
- ❖ Traditional cost savings focus only on Value adding items
- ❖ Lean thinking focuses on the value stream to eliminate non value adding items
  - ➢ Our emphasis is to reduce the NVA Time and improve all over Efficiency and our aim is to become Lean
  - ➢ What is Lean?
    - • Balanced use of people, Equipment and Material that gives us the Lowest Manufacturing cost.
    - • Low manufacturing cost assumes all waste in eliminated.
  - ➢ What are the common wastes?
    - • Over Production
    - • Waiting
    - • Conveyance
    - • Processing
    - • Inventory
    - • Motion
    - • Correction
    - • Transferring/Scooping/Manual Loading/unloading etc.

➢ The study team may come out with very many proposals and ideas to control the Non value Added Activities of the shop particularly by going away from Mass Production System to Product Line System for reducing the distance moved, improving Material Handling System and flow

In summary, the value added concept says to distinguish value added from non-value added activities. Among the latter activities, seek out the ones that are unnecessary and try to eliminate them. The remaining activities, which are the value added and necessary non value added activities then become the focus for improvement.

Do remember the customers are not willing to pay for your high level of non-value added activities.

For sure you can wear the hat of eliminating or significantly reduce non value added activities in your area of manufacturing operations, if so reading of this topic will serve the purpose of becoming an effective supervisor for productivity and cost improvement also.

7. Simple Productivity Studies of Few Operation of a Manufacturing Unit

Introduction and Methodology

This study done in one of the best companies in Asia deals with simple productivity improvements of few operations of a Manufacturing unit located in South India.

On perusal it may be seen that each and every operation can be modified for better productivity or yield. The sample sheets pertain to a few of operations only This sort of study can be called as Methods improvement of each and every operation with a view to explore change of methods to simplify and speed up the productivity. The lay out changes or far too many materials handling of the whole factory does not come under this purview of the study. The focus is on how to simplify the method and how to reduce the man power deployed which ultimately leads to much higher productivity of that operation.

On seeing the few examples which were very much appreciated by The French Directors of this unit, it may motivate you to get rid of mental blocks or negative thinking that there is no need for any changes even though the plant is set up by foreign collaborators.

Likewise the productivity enhancement through Yield improvement study samples is shown in topic 8 of Yield Improvement of the same manufacturing unit.

It is mentioned that the full report submitted under topic 7 & 8 do have about 175 pages each, whereas given in this report for your perusal are hardly 20 pages.

The unit head is very specially and fondly remembered with gratitude for making use of the study reports for much higher productivity improvement although the plant is considered to be best in Asia for same product manufacturing. He believed in the management principle of "Good is the Enemy of Best." In order to be competent we need to strive for better utilization of machines or plants, better yield improvement and not the least on productivity with head count reduction.

PRODUCTIVITY IMPROVEMENT STUDY AT SPUN LINE PRESENT MAN POWER

Details of operation	Present Man Power
Employees & casuals	
Furnacing & Spinning	6/day
Needling	3/day
Blanket line	9/day
Warehouse keeping & dispatch	1/day
Sub Total	**19/day**
Contract Labour	
Shots recycling System	3/day
Edge trim recycling additional feeding	3/day
Water bin waste clearing	2/day
Rolls shifting	2/day
Water bin waste feeding	5/day
Raw material conveying	2/day (4/4 hrs)
Needle fixing in the needle boards	1/day
Sub Total	**18/day**
Total	**37/day**

PRESENT PRODUCTIVITY (DIRECT & OVER ALL)

Details	1998
Conversion efficiency	73.44%
Total production	1521037 kgs
Direct man hour	
Productive	32680 hrs
	(19men x 8 hrs x 215 days)
Non Productive	8423 hrs
Total production	41103 hrs
Direct productivity	**37.00 Kg/hr**
	(1521037/41103)
Indirect man hours	
Contract - 18 men	
Maintenance - 6men	43000 hrs
Qc - 1men	(25 men x 215 days x8 hrs
Overall man hours	841013 hrs
Overall Productivity	**18.1 Kg/hr**
	(1521037/84103)

METHODS IMPROVEMENT

Process	Machine/ Manual	Existing Method	Existing men/ Day	Proposed Method	Proposed men/Day	Facility required	Responsible department	Investment Lac/Time required	Savings	Implemen-tation
Shots recycling	Manual	Manual pushing the shots collected on the scraping conveyor crusher	3	shots recycling system to convey all the shots generated automatically	Nil	Modification of shots recycling system	Development Department	Rs:0.7/8 weeks	3 Men/ day	3rd Quarter 1999
Water bin waste cleaning	Manual	Removal by means of mechanical winch	2	Motorized Winch and hoist	1	Motorized Winch and hoist	Development Department	Rs:1.5/ 16 weeks	1 Man/ day	1st Quarter 2000
Rolls shifting to warehouse	Manual	Manual moving the cartons to warehouse/ process area	2	using pallets and power driven pallet trucks - one man can	1	Pallets - 100nos; Power driven pallet truck-1	Development Department	Rs:7.0/ 36 weeks	1 Man/ day	4th Quarter 2000
Water bin waste feeding	Manual	Manual collection, drying & feeding	5	Reduction in water bin waste generation by modification of shots recycling system(refer above)		Motorized Winch and hoist	Development Department	Rs:1.5/ 16 weeks	1 Man/ day	1st Quarter 2000

(Contd.)

Process	Machine/ Manual	Existing Method	Existing men/ Day	Proposed Method	Proposed men/Day	Facility required	Process	Investment Lac/ Time required	Savings	Implemen- tation
Raw material conveying	Manual	Manual lifting raw material from ground level pneumatic conveyer vessel level	4 for 4 hours/ day for 8 ton	Using scissor platform for handling	2 for 4 hours/day for 8 ton	Scissor platform	Development Department	Rs:1.0/ 28 weeks	1 Man/ day	4th Quarter 2000
Needle fixing	Manual	Manual removal of broken needles and fixing new needles by contract labors	Contract labors	Using pneumatic press by maintenance crew		Pneumatic Press	Development/ Production Department	Rs:0.5/11 weeks	1 Man/ day	4th Quarter 1999

METHODS IMPROVEMENTS-SUMMARY

S. No	Operation	Methods Improvement	Possible Savings
1	Shots recycling	Modified shots recycling system	3 men/day
2	Edge trim recycling additional level	By reducing needle bulk and bulk Generation	2 men/day
3	Water bin waste cleaning	By using motorized winch and hoist	1 men/day
4	Rolls shifting to warehouse	By using pallets & Power driven pallet Trucks	2 men/day
5	Water bin waste feeding	Reduction in the water bin waste generation by the modification of the shots recycling system	3 men/day
6	Raw material conveying	Use scissor platform for raw material Handling	1 men/day
7	Needle fixing	By using pneumatic press for removing and fixing the needles	1 men/day

PROPOSED MAN POWER BY END -1999

Details of operation	Present Man Power	Proposed Man Power
Employees & casuals		
Furnace & Spinning	6/day	6/day
Needling	3/day	3/day
Blanket line	9/day	9/day
Warehouse keeping & dispatch	1/day	1/day
Sub Total	19/day	19/day
Contract Labour		
Shots recycling System	3/day	-
Edge trim recycling additional feeding	3/day	3/day
Water bin waste clearing	2/day	2/day
Rolls shifting	2/day	2/day
Water bin waste feeding	5/day	5/day
Raw material conveying	2/day (4/4 hrs)	2/day (4/4 hrs)
Needle fixing in the needle boards	1/day	-
Sub Total	**18/day**	**14/day**
Total	**37/day**	**30/day**

PROPOSED PRODUCTIVITY BY END – 1999 DIRECT & OVERALL

Details	End 1999
Conversion efficiency	75.00%
Total Production	1553438 kgs
Direct man hour	
Productive Non Productive Total	32680 hrs (19men x 8 hrs x 215days) 2280 hrs 34960 hrs
Direct Productivity	**44.44 Kg/hr** (1553438/34960)
Indirect man hours Contract-14men Maintenance-6men QC-1man	36120 hrs (21men x 8 hrs x 215days)
Overall man hrs	71080 hrs
Overall productivity	21.85 kg/hr (1553438/71080)

Productivity Improvement	% Increase
Direct Productivity	20.10%
Overall Productivity	20.72%

PROPOSED MAN POWER BY END – 2000

Details of Operation Employees & Casuals	Present Man Power	Proposed Man Power
Furnace & Spinning	6/day	6/day
Needling	3/day	3/day
Blanket line	9/day	9/day
Warehouse keeping & dispatch	1/day	1/day
Sub Total	**19/day**	**19/day**
Contract Labor		
Shots recycling System	3/day	-
Edge trim recycling additional feeding	3/day	3/day
Water bin waste clearing	2/day	1/day
Rolls shifting	2/day	1/day
Water bin waste feeding	5/day	2/day
Raw material conveying	2/day (4/4 hrs)	1/day (2/4 hrs)
Needle fixing in the needle boards	1/day	-
Sub Total	**18/day**	**8/day**
Total	**37/day**	**27/day**

PROPOSED PRODUCTIVITY BY END – 2000 DIRECT & OVERALL

Details	End 2000
Conversion efficiency	77.85%
Total Production	1612469
Direct man hour Productive	32680 hrs (19men x 8 hrs x 215days)
Non Productive	2280 hrs
Total	34960 hrs
Direct Productivity	**46.12 Kg/hr** (1612469/34960)
Indirect man hours Contract-8men	25800 hrs
Maintenance-6men	(15menx8 hrsx215days)
Qc-1man	
Overall man hrs	60760 hrs
Overall productivity	21.85 kg/hr (1553438/60760)

Productivity Improvement	% Increase
Direct Productivity	24.65%
Overall Productivity	46.63%

PROPOSED MAN POWER BY END-2001

Details of Operation	Present Man Power	Proposed Man Power
Employees & casuals		
Furnace & Spinning	6/day	6/day
Needling	3/day	3/day
Blanket line	9/day	9/day
Warehouse keeping & dispatch	1/day	1/day
Sub Total	19/day	19/day
Contract Labour		
Shots recycling System	3/day	-
Edge trim recycling additional feeding	3/day	1/day
Water bin waste clearing	2/day	1/day
Rolls shifting	2/day	-
Water bin waste feeding	5/day	2/day
Raw material conveying	2/day (4/4 hrs)	1/day (2/4 hrs)
Needle fixing in the needle boards	1/day	-
Sub Total	**18/day**	**8/day**
Total	**37/day**	**24/day**

PROPOSED PRODUCTIVITY BY END – 2001 DIRECT & OVERALL

Details	End 2000
Conversion efficiency	80.10%
Total Production	1659072 kgs
Direct man hour Productive	32680 hrs (19men x8 hrs x215days)
Non Productive	2280 hrs
Total	34960 hrs
Direct Productivity	**47.46 Kg/hr** (1659072/34960)
Indirect man hours Contract-5men Maintenance-6men Qc-1man	20640 hrs (12menx8 hrsx215days)
Overall man hrs	55600 hrs
Overall productivity	29.84 kg/hr
	(1659072/55600)

Productivity Improvement	% Increase
Direct Productivity	28.27%
Overall Productivity	64.86%

PROPOSED MAN POWER BY END -1999

Details of Operation	Present 1998	Proposed 1999	Proposed 2000	Proposed 2001
Employees & casuals				
Furnacing & Spinning	6/day	6/day	6/day	6/day
Needling	3/day	3/day	3/day	3/day
Blanket line	9/day	9/day	9/day	9/day
Warehouse keeping & dispatch	1/day	1/day	1/day	1/day
Sub Total	**19/day**	**19/day**	**19/day**	**19/day**
Contract Labour				
Shots recycling System	3/day	-	-	-
Edge trim recycling additional feeding	3/day	3/day	3/day	1/day
Water bin waste clearing	2/day	2/day	1/day	1/day
Rolls shifting	2/day	2/day	2/day	-
Water bin waste feeding	5/day	5/day	2/day	2/day
Raw material conveying	2/day (4/4 hrs)	2/day (2/4 hrs)	1/day (2/4 hrs)	1/day (2/4 hrs)
Needle fixing in the needle boards	1/day	-	-	-
Sub Total	**18/day**	**14/day**	**8/day**	**5/day**
Total	**37/day**	**33/day**	**27/day**	**24/day**

SUMMARY OF METHODS IMPROVEMENT

S. No	Description	Potential Saving	Implementation By	Productivity Improvement%	Investment in lacs
1	Shots Recycling	3 Men/Day	3rd Quarter 1999		0.7
2	Needle Fixing	1 Men/Day	4th Quarter 1999		0.5
Subtotal - 4 Men/Day				**20.72**	**1.2**
3	Water bin waste cleaning	1 Men/Day	1st Quarter 2000		1.5
4	Water bin waste Feeding	3 Men/Day	3rd Quarter 1999		-
5	Raw material Conveying	1 Men/Day	4th Quarter 2000		1
6	Rolls Moving	1 Men/Day	4th Quarter 2000		7
Subtotal - 6 Men/Day				**46.63**	**9.5**

(Contd.)

7	Rolls Moving	1 Men/Day	4th Quarter 2001		
8	Edge trim recycling	2 Men/Day	4th Quarter 2001		
Subtotal - 3 Men/Day				**64.86**	
Total - 13 Men/Day End 2001				**64.86**	**10.7**

SUMMARY OF PRODUCTIVITY IMPROVEMENT

Details	Present		Proposed	
	1998	**1999**	**2000**	**2001**
Direct men/day	19	19	19	19
Over all men/day	25	21	15	12
Direct productivity (kg/hr)	37	44.44	46.12	47.46
Overall productivity (kg/hr)	18.1	21.85	26.54	29.84

Productivity Improvement	% Increase		
	1999	**2000**	**2001**
Direct productivity (kg/hr)	20.1	24.65	28.27
Overall productivity (kg/hr)	20.72	46.63	64.86

8. Productivity Enhancement through Yield Improvement

STAGE   WISE YIELD

PRESENT LEVEL - (1998)

Stage	Yield at this Stage	Cumulative yield upto this stage
Conveying	99.75	99.75
Batching & Mixing	99.5	99.25
Furnace Feeding	99.75	99
Furnace Wood dust collector	99.75	98.75
Ignition Loss	99.7	98.45
Furnace scrap	99.29	97.75
Spinning (Waterbin waste)	90.28	88.25
Spinning Room Shots	99.43	87.75
Taprate measurment	99.82	87.59
Shots recycling	94.81	83.04
Unrecycled Shots	93.98	78.04
Collection Chamber	98.72	77.04
Bulk Fiber	96.57	74.4
Bulk Waste	99.19	73.8
Needled Bulk	99.73	73.6
Blanket Waste	99.86	73.5
Annealedofcut	96.83	70.8
Unplanned strips	92.97	65.82
Ok Blanket & Strips	**100**	**65.82**

Over all Yield - 65.82%

Process Improvements

1. Spinner Guard/Safety Screen.
2. Modified Shots Recycling System.
3. On Line Fiber Weighing System.
4. Spinning Monitor Camera Multiplexer.
5. Furnace Power Monitoring System.
6. Blanket Cutting System.
7. Modified Spinner Unit for Higher Speed.
8. Auto Weighing System in Blanket Line.

Spinner Changing

Machine	:	Spinner
Existing Method	:	Spinner changing work carried out during non-fabrisation time only
Proposed Method	:	Improve conversion efficiency by reducing on fabrisation time taken for spinner related works
Facility required	:	Spinner guard, spinner partition (safety screen)
Responsible Dept (s)	:	Development/Production Department
Investment/time required	:	Rs: 0.25 lacs/4 weeks
Savings	:	In conversion efficency1.18% - 24.3 tones/year- Rs: 7.3 lacs/year
Implementation	:	4th Quarter1999

Shots Recycling

Existing Method	:	Existing system not working properly and recycles only 40% of the shots generated
Proposed Method	:	Modified shots recycling system to convey all the shots generation into the furnace.
Facility required	:	Modified shots recycling system.
Responsible Dept (s)	:	Development/Production Department.
Investment/time required	:	Rs: 0.70 lacs/6 weeks
Savings	:	Shots recycling will improve from 4.55% to 12%. Manpower reduction for recycling 3men/day.
Implementation	:	3rd Quarter1999

ON LINE FIBER WEIGHING SYSTEM

Existing Method	: Every one hour furnace tap rate is checked manually and the conveyor speed adjusted accordingly.
	Fibre fleese height checked visually for any Variation and then the conveyor speed Adjusted accordingly.
Proposed Method	: On line fibre weighing system.
Responsible Dept(s)	: Development / Production Department.
Investment / time required	: Rs 3.0 lacs / 30 weeks
Saving	: Rejects will reduce from 2.96% to 1.48%. In conversion efficiency - 1.48% In tons - 30.5 T/ year In Rs. 3 lacs / year.
Implementaion	: 4th Quarter 1999

FIBRISATION ADJUSTMENT

Existing Method	: Manual
Proposed Method	: Additional CCTV camera with multi player to locate the stream position failing on the Spinner Unit.
Facility required	: CCTV camera & mutliplayer
Responsible Dept(s)	: Development / Production Department.
Investment / time required	: Rs 1.0 lacs / 9 weeks
Savings	: Fibrisation will be uniform & maximum fibre. Shots percentage will be less. Shots patches will be reduced. **Fibrisation yield will be improved from 85 to 88%**
Implementaion	: 4th Quarter 1999

FURNACE POWER MONITORING	
Existing Method	: Every hour furnace operator manually monitor and Record the parameters to control the process
Proposed Method	: Auto Furance power, monitoring system and printout of all power & cooling circuit parameters to avoid manual recording every hour
Facility required	: Furnace power monitoring system
Responsible Dept(s)	: Development / Production Department.
Investment / time required	: Rs 0.5 lacs / 9 weeks
Savings	We can use one man from furnace to check product quality and process development works. Shot content testing and tensile strength testing can be done by the production people
Implementaion	: 4th Quarter 1999

STAGE WISE YIELD PRESENT LEVEL (1999)

Stage	Yield up to this Stage	Cumulative Yield up to this Stage	Recommendation
Conveying	99.75	99.75	
Batching & Fixing	99.75	99.25	
Furnace Feeding	99.75	99	
Furnace Wood dust collector	99.75	98.75	
Ignition Loss	99.7	98.45	
Furnace scrap	99.29	97.75	
Spinning (Water bin waste)	92.84	90.75	Online spinner replacement
Spinning Room Shots	99.45	90.25	
Tap rate measurement	100	90.25	
Shots recycling	94.96	85.7	
Un-Recycled Shots	95.33	81.7	Modified shots Recycling system.

(Contd.)

Stage	Yield up to this Stage	Cumulative Yield up to this Stage	Recommendation
Collection Chamber	99.39	81.2	
Bulk Fiber	99.38	80.7	
Bulk Waste	99.75	80.5	
Needled Bulk	100	80.5	
Blanket Waste	99.88	80.4	
Annealed output	97.51	78.4	
Unplanned strips	96.17	75.4	
Ok Blanket& Strips	**100**	**75.4**	
Overall Yield 75.40%			

BLANKET CUTTING SYSTEM	
Existing Method	: After needing one set of cutting system to cut the blanket in required width.
Proposed Method	: One more set of cutting system to be provided in the process line, it can be used during cutter changing time and blanket width changing time or any break down time without disturbing the process line
Facility required	: Blanket cutting system
Responsible Dept(s)	: Development / Production Department.
Investment / time required	: Rs 1.5 lacs / 17 weeks
Savings	: In conversion efficency : 0.4%, In tons : 8 tons / year, In Rs 0.80 Lacs / year
Implementaion	: 4th Quarter 2000

SPINNING PROCESS	
Machine	: Spinner
Existing Method	: Molten material fiberised with spinning wheel operating at 9000 - 10500 rpm
Proposed Method	: Spinning to be done at 11500 - 12500 rpm
Facility required	: Spinner unit capable to operate upto 13000 rpm
Responsible Dept(s)	: Development / Production Department
Investment / time required	: Rs 8 lacs/ 56 weeks
Savings	: Reduction in rejects due to shots and shots patches. Fibrisation yield will be improved from 85 - 88%
Implementaion	: 4th Quarter 2000

INSPECTION & PACKING	
Existing Method	: Manual recording
Proposed Method	: By providing auto weighing system we can avoid all manual work in the blanket line. System itself can check for density, length, thickness then printout a sticker with all details of the roll.
Facility required	: Auto weighing system
Responsible Dept(s)	: Development / Production Department.
Investment / time required	: Rs 6.5 Lacs Phase-1 Rs. 1.00 Lacs - Year 1999, Phase- 2 Rs. 2.00 Lacs - Year 2000 Phase - 3 Rs. 3.50 Lacs - Year 2001
Savings	: -Manual error will be eliminated. -at any time we can check for fibrisation yield over weight to control the process. - one man can be used for keeping the rolls in ware house.
Implementaion	: 4th Quarter 2001

* System will be implemented along with thickness monitoring system. Possibility of sticker printing incorporating with Thickness Monitoring to be assessed.

STAGE WISE YIELD PROPOSED LEVEL (2000)

Stage	Yield at this Stage	Cumulative Yield up to this stage	Recommendation
Conveying	99.75	99.75	
Batching & mixing	99.5	99.25	
Furnace Feeding	99.75	99	
Furnace hood dust collector	99.75	98.75	
Ignition Loss	99.7	98.45	
Furnace scrap	99.29	97.75	
Spinning(Water bin waste)	92.84	91.79	
Spinning Room Shots	99.45	91.49	

(Contd.)

Tap rate measurement	100	91.49	
Shots recycling	94.96	86.94	
Un-recycled Shots	95.33	83.94	
Collection Chamber	99.39	83.44	
Bulk Fiber	99.38	83.44	Additional blanket Cutting system
Bulk Waste	99.75	83.24	
Needled Bulk	100	83.24	
Blanket Waste	99.88	83.14	
Annealed output	97.51	81.64	
Unplanned strips	96.17	79.14	High speed spinner unit
Ok Blanket & Strips	**100**	**79.14**	
Over all Yield 79.14%			

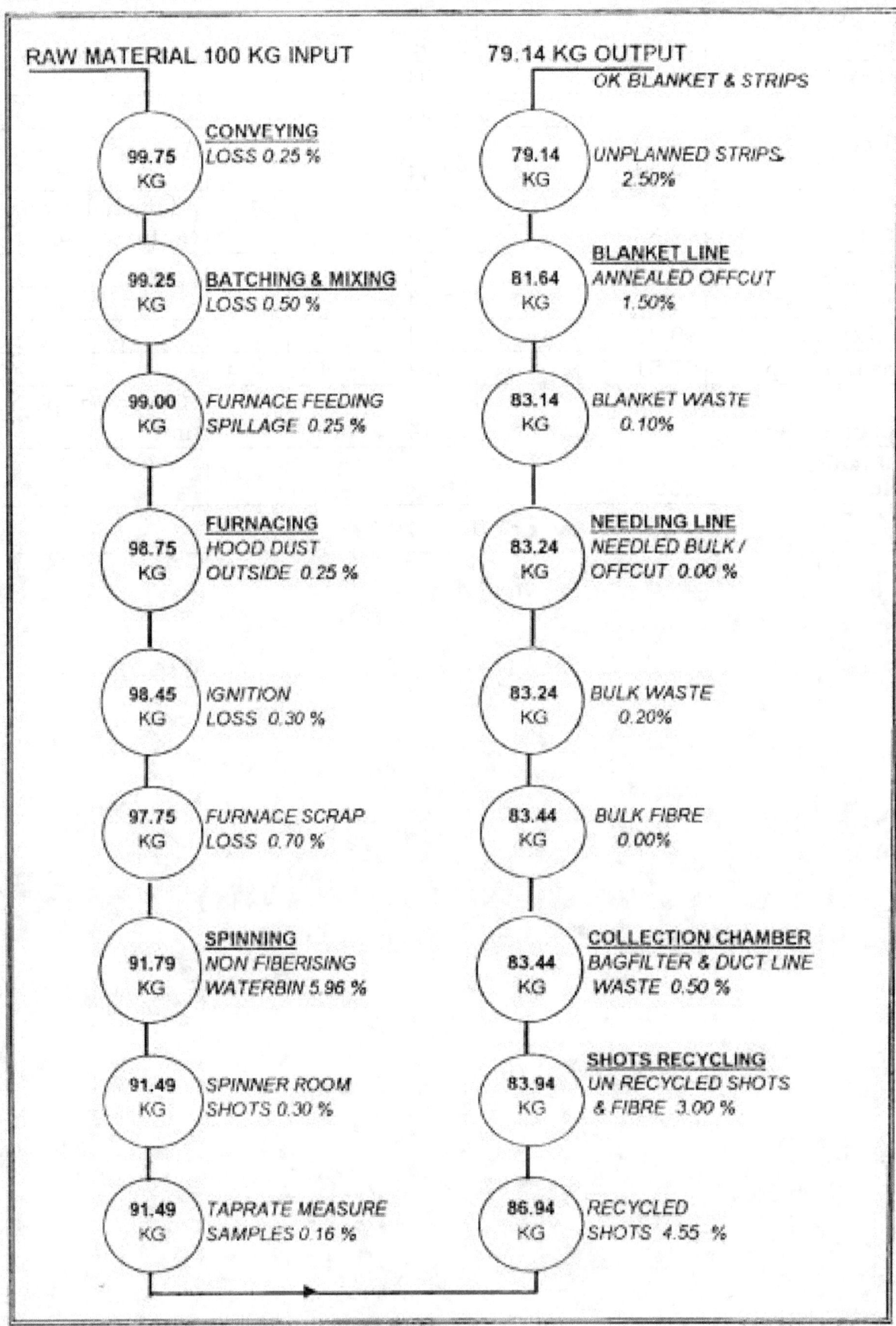

RAW MATERIAL 100 KG INPUT

CONVEYING
99.75 KG — LOSS 0.25 %

BATCHING & MIXING
99.25 KG — LOSS 0.50 %

99.00 KG — FURNACE FEEDING SPILLAGE 0.25 %

FURNACING
98.75 KG — HOOD DUST OUTSIDE 0.25 %

98.45 KG — IGNITION LOSS 0.30 %

97.75 KG — FURNACE SCRAP LOSS 0.70 %

SPINNING
91.79 KG — NON FIBERISING WATERBIN 5.96 %

91.49 KG — SPINNER ROOM SHOTS 0.30 %

91.49 KG — TAPRATE MEASURE SAMPLES 0.16 %

79.14 KG OUTPUT
OK BLANKET & STRIPS

79.14 KG — UNPLANNED STRIPS 2.50%

BLANKET LINE
81.64 KG — ANNEALED OFFCUT 1.50%

83.14 KG — BLANKET WASTE 0.10%

NEEDLING LINE
83.24 KG — NEEDLED BULK / OFFCUT 0.00 %

83.24 KG — BULK WASTE 0.20%

83.44 KG — BULK FIBRE 0.00%

COLLECTION CHAMBER
83.44 KG — BAGFILTER & DUCT LINE WASTE 0.50 %

SHOTS RECYCLING
83.94 KG — UN RECYCLED SHOTS & FIBRE 3.00 %

86.94 KG — RECYCLED SHOTS 4.55 %

STAGEWISE YIELD PROPOSED LEVEL (2001)

Stage	Yield at this Stage	Cumulative Yield up to this stage
Conveying	99.75	99.75
Batching & mixing	99.5	99.25
Furnace Feeding	99.75	99
Furnace hood dust collector	99.75	98.75
Ignition Loss	99.7	98.45
Furnace scrap	99.29	97.75
Spinning(Water bin waste)	94.97	92.83
Spinning Room Shots	99.68	92.53
Tap rate measurement	100	92.53
Shots recycling	95.08	87.98
Un-recycled Shots	97.73	85.98
Collection Chamber	99.42	85.48
Bulk Fiber	100	85.48
Bulk Waste	99.77	85.28
Needled Bulk	100	85.28
Blanket Waste	99.88	85.18
Annealed of cut	98.83	84.18
Unplanned strips	97.62	82.18
Ok Blanket & Strips	100	82.18
Overall Yield 82.18%		

FLOW CHART FOR THE YEAR 2001.

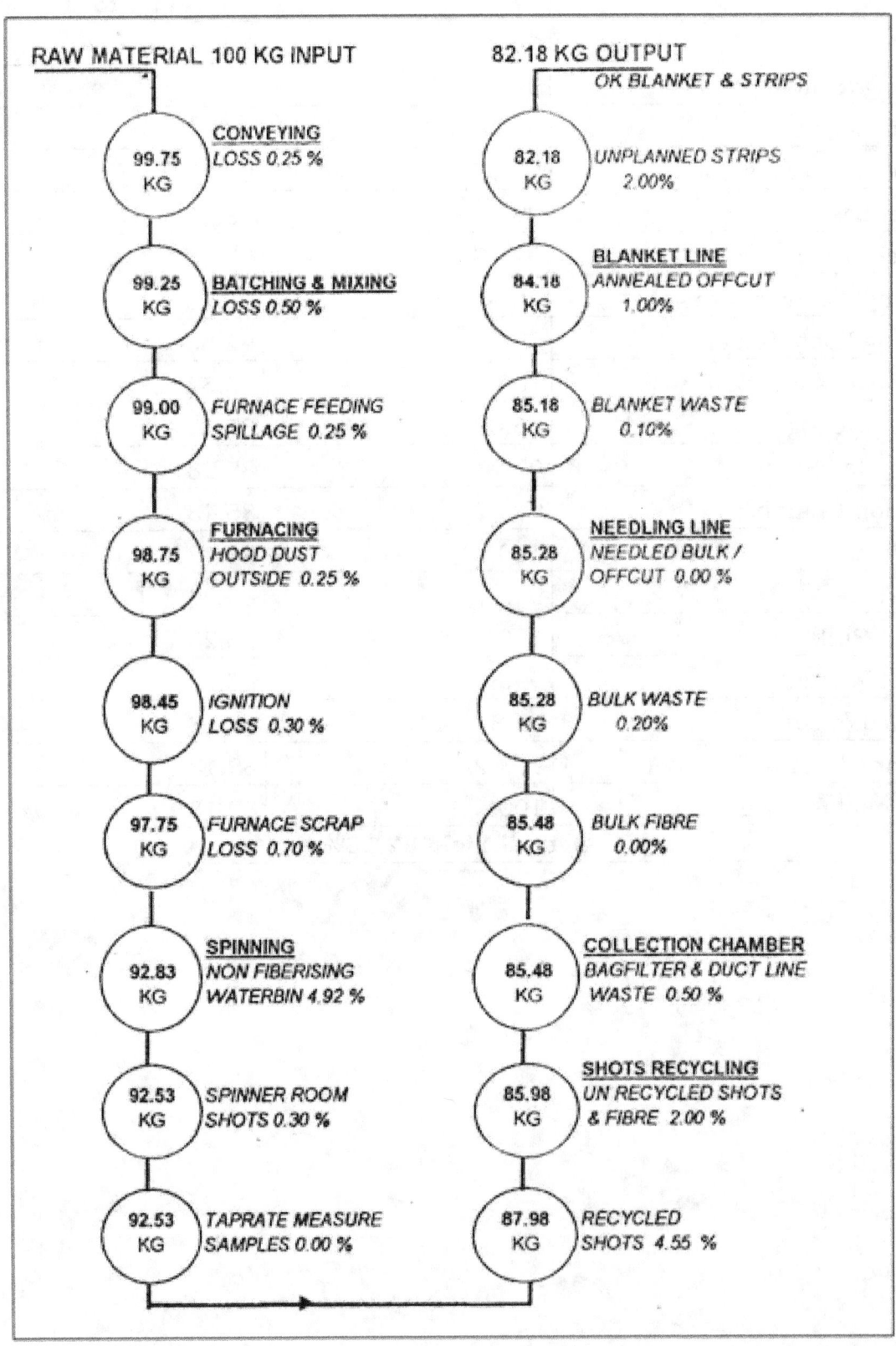

PROPOSED REDUCTION OF VARIOUS LOSSES

Stage	Present	Proposed			Recommendation
	1998	1999	2000	2001	
Conveying	0.25	0.25	0.25	0.25	
Batching & mixing	0.5	0.5	0.5	0.5	
Furnace Feeding	0.25	0.25	0.25	0.25	
Furnace hood dust collector	0.25	0.25	0.25	0.25	
Ignition Loss	0.3	0.3	0.3	0.3	
Furnace scrap	0.7	0.7	0.7	0.7	
Spinning (Water bin waste)	9.5	7	5.96	4.92	
Spinning Room Shots	0.5	0.5	0.3	0.3	Online spinner replacements
Tap rate measurement	0.16	0	0	0	Recycling of tap samples
Shots recycling	4.55	4.55	4.55	4.55	
Shots (un recycled)	5	4	3	2	Modified shots recycling system
Collection Chamber	1	0.5	0.5	0.5	Recycling of 50% waste fiber
Bulk Fibber	2.64	0.5	0	0	Additional blanket cutting system
Bulk Waste	0.6	0.2	0.2	0.2	
Needled Bulk	0.2	0	0	0	
Blanket Waste	0.1	0.1	0.1	0.1	
Annealed output	2.7	2	1.5	1	Online fiber weighing system, high Speed spinner unit. Additional Camera For stream positioning.
Un planned strips	4.98	3	2.5	2	
Ok Blanket & Strips	**65.82**	**75.4**	**79.14**	82.18	
Increase in yield Improvement (%)		**14.55**	**20.24**	**24.86**	

SUMMARY OF YIELD IMPROVEMENT

Stage Wise					
Stage	**Present**	**Proposed**			**Recommendation**
	1998	**1999**	**2000**	**2001**	
Conveying	99.75	99.75	99.75	99.75	
Batching & mixing	99.25	99.25	99.25	99.25	
Furnace Feeding	99	99	99	99	
Furnace hood dust collector	98.75	98.75	98.75	98.75	
Ignition Loss	98.45	98.45	98.45	98.45	
Furnace scrap	97.75	97.75	97.75	97.75	
Spinning(Water bin waste)	88.25	90.75	91.79	92.83	
Spinning Room Shots	87.75	90.25	91.49	92.53	Online spinner replacements
Tap rate measurement	87.59	90.25	91.49	92.53	Recycling of tap samples
Shots recycling	83.04	85.7	86.94	87.98	
Shots(un-recycled)	78.04	81.7	83.94	85.98	Modified shots recycling system
Collection Chamber	77.04	81.2	83.44	85.48	Recycling of 50% waste fiber
Bulk Fiber	74.4	80.7	83.44	85.48	Additional blanket cutting system
Bulk Waste	73.8	80.5	83.24	85.28	
Needled Bulk	73.6	80.5	83.24	85.28	
Blanket Waste	73.5	80.4	83.14	85.18	
Annealed of cut	70.8	78.4	81.64	84.18	Online fiber weighing system, high Speed spinner unit. Additional Camera For stream positioning.
Unplanned strips	65.82	75.4	79.14	82.18	
Ok Blanket &Strips	**65.82**	**75.4**	**79.14**	**82.18**	
Increase in yield Improvement (%)		**14.55**	**20.24**	**24.86**	

SUMMARY OF YIELD IMPROVEMENT

S.No	Stage	Present Yield (%)	Present Yield (%)	Recommendation
1	Spinning	90.28	94.97	Online spinner Replacement by Providing spinner guard
2	Shots recycling	93.98	97.73	Modified shots Recycling system to Coney all shots generated
3	Bulk fiber	96.57	100	Online blanket cutter Changed by additional Blanket cutting system.
4	Annealed output	96.33	98.83	Online fiber weighing System. High speed Spinner unit. Additional Camera for stream positing
5	Unplanned strips rolls	92.97	97.62	

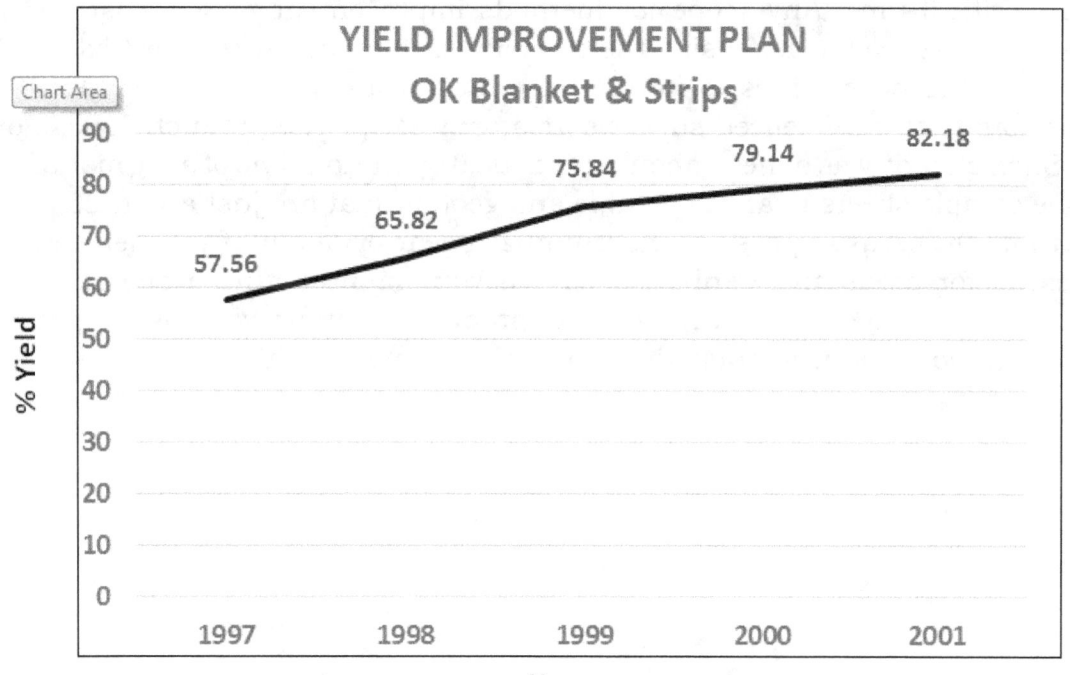

Year	1997	1998	1999	2000	2001
Yield (%)	57.56	65.82	75.84	79.14	82.18

9. Process Improvement Studies of Few Assembly Operation

Introduction and Methodology

There can be a few assembly operations in a manufacturing unit. Say there are about 5 operators assigned for each of the operation to be done in machine or jigs and fixtures or inspection check facilities. Can each cycle time of operation of this assembly product be same? Far from realities. Like the 5 fingers of our hand are different by length, shape and purpose, the individual operations also take different time to complete the unit operation. The question comes up, which one can be taken as most critical from output point of view? Obviously it is the one which takes more time relatively.

Thus the first step for improving the output and possibly reducing the crew size is to list all operation and the cycle time with man power allotted. Then start attacking the most critical time. Any scope for methods improvement by low cost automation concepts? Any scope for increasing the capacity of the machine or jigs/fixtures? What are all the other possibilities to improve the output at this critical operation? It will surprise you when experienced supervisors start wearing the productivity cap on their heads. Such a study was done in about 150 critical operation time of a big manufacturing unit. The sample sheets in an acceptable and good format are just about 25 pertaining to this unit. On perusal, possibly the unutilized gear or talent of yourself can come to your rescue for productivity enhancement in your manufacturing operations. If this unit supervisors can come up with ideas of productivity improvement ranging from 30 to 100%, ask yourself how much you can achieve in your unit?

Process Improvement Detail Sheet

			Page	16	of	140
			Date		1-Aug-13	
			Rev No		0	

Product Code	64020700000P	Module	601
Product Description	2s Oil pump assy	Cell Code	NEW

Sl No	Description	UOM	Present / Existing Status (Before Improvement)	Proposed (After Improvement)
1	Critical Time	Secs	72.00	48.00
2	Output/Shift	Nos	400	600
3	Manpower / Shift	Nos	3	2
4	PMPD	Nos	133	300
5	Method changes	---	1) Driven and driving gear thickness inspection by manual 2) Driven and driving gear outer diameter inspection by manual 3) Rotation checking by manual	1) Driven and driving gear thickness inspection by equipment and G and NG auto indication 2) Driven and driving gear outer diameter inspection by equipment and G and NG auto indication 3) Rotation inspection by equipment method
	Benefits and End Result			
	Output Incr / Shift	Nos		200
	Manpower saving	Nos		1
	% Impvt in PMPD	%		125.00
	Quality Impvt	---		-
6	Investment Required (PI put tick mark)	Minor ----	Major ✓	

Project Proposed by	Name	Ramasamy K
	Dept	Module 601

Responsible Person	1, 2 & 3 - Kumaravelu M 4 - Gopinath C
Dept	1, 2 & 3 - BU 3 - QE 4) BU 3 - Mfg Engg

Time Frame	1, 2 & 3 - 30-Nov-2013 4 - 15-Nov-2013

Process Improvement Detail Sheet

		Page	17	of	140
		Date			1-Aug-13
		Rev No			0

Product Code	E44400000000	Module	602
Product Description	4s Oil pump assy	Cell Code	1111

Sl No	Description	UOM	Present / Existing Status (Before Improvement)	Proposed (After Improvement)
1	Critical Time	Secs	389.19	612.77
2	Output/Shift	Nos	74	47
3	Manpower / Shift	Nos	3	1
4	PMPD	Nos	25	47
5	Method changes	---	1) Pneumatic controlled pressure setting unit leads to cycle time variation during pressure setting - (Average : 240 sec) 2) Variation in G and NG indication due to variation in temperature	1) Pressure control unit replaced to Servo control to reduce the variation in pressure setting (Average : 140 sec) 2) Chiller unit to be provided to reduce the variation in temperature
6	Benefits and End Result			
	Output Incr / Shift	Nos		---
	Manpower saving	Nos		2
	% Impvt in PMPD	%		90.54
	Quality Impvt	---		-

Project	Name	Ramasamy K
Proposed by	Dept	Module 601

Investment Required (PI put tick mark)	Minor
	Major

Responsible Person	1) Chandramohan R 2) Gopinath C	Time Frame	15-Nov-13
Dept	1) PMD 2) MFG.ENGG		

Process Improvement Detail Sheet

		Page	21	of	140

Product Code	D422/D44350	Module	603	Date	8-Aug-13
Product Description	Hydraulic Cylinder Assy	Cell Code	1261	Rev No	0

Sl No	Description	UOM	Present / Existing Status (Before Improvement)	Proposed (After Improvement)
1	Critical Time	Secs	240	240
2	Output/Shift	Nos	120	120
3	Manpower / Shift	Nos	2	1
4	PMPD	Nos	60	120
5	Method changes	---	Riveting operation of Stay and Clamp casing assy is carried out manually with two operators [One operator for riveting and other for holding the components]	One operator is reduced by providing the fixture for holding the components. Riveting operation will be carriedout with single operator. Trial is under progress.
6	Benefits and End Result			
	Output Incr / Shift	Nos		-
	Manpower saving	Nos		1
	% Impvt in PMPD	%		100
	Quality Impvt	---		-

Investment Required (PI put tick mark)	Minor	---	Project Proposed by	Name	Varadharajan MV	Time Frame	Implemented
	Major	---		Dept	Module 603		

Responsible Person		Ragupathy M
Dept		BU - 3 ME

Process Improvement Detail Sheet

				Page	29	of	140
Product Code	D23200000000	**Module**	603		**Date**		8-Aug-13
Product Description	Alarm oil bye pass assy	**Cell Code**	1271		**Rev No**		0

SI No	Description	UOM	Present / Existing Status (Before Improvement)	Proposed (After Improvement)
1	Critical Time	Secs	21.6	14.4
2	Output/Shift	Nos	1333	2000
3	Manpower / Shift	Nos	1	1
4	PMPD	Nos	1333	2000
5	Method changes	—	Three passes is being carried out in valve grinding process	Grinding passes to be reduced from three to two. Grinding stock to be reduced and ECN to be released.
6	Benefits and End Result	Output Incr / Shift	Nos		667
		Manpower saving	Nos		1
		% Impvt in PMPD	%		50.04
		Quality Impvt	—		

Investment Required (PI put tick mark)	Minor	—
	Major	—

	Name	Varadharajan MV
Project Proposed by	Dept	Module 603

Responsible Person	Jayaprakashan N
Dept	PDE - Pumps

Time Frame	31-Aug-13

Process Improvement Detail Sheet

				Page	35	of	140
Product Code	D36700000000	**Module**	603	**Date**			8-Aug-13
Product Description	Pressure relief Valve	**Cell Code**	1039	**Rev No**			0

SI No	Description	UOM	Present / Existing Status (Before Improvement)	Proposed (After Improvement)
1	Critical Time	Secs	760	685.71
2	Output/Shift	Nos	30	42
3	Manpower / Shift	Nos	1	1
4	PMPD	Nos	30	42
5	Method changes	—	1.Table and pneumatic press set-up for crimping is located in valve assy(Building 603). 2.Analog pressure gauge in testing rig.	1.Seperate table and pneumatic press set-up for crimping provided near test rig(Building 601). 2.Analog pressure gauge replaced with digital.
6	Benefits and End Result	Output Incr / Shift	Nos	12
		Manpower saving	Nos	-
		% Impvt in PMPD	%	40
		Quality Impvt	---	-

Project Proposed by	Name	Varadharajan MV
	Dept	Module 603

Investment Required (PI put tick mark)	Minor	---
	Major	---

	Time Frame	Implemented
Responsible Person		Ragupathy M
Dept		BU - 3 ME

Process Improvement Detail Sheet

Page	57	of	140
Date			7-Aug-13
Rev No			0

Product Code	D48100000000
Product Description	4S OP

Module	605
Cell Code	1131

Sl No	Description	UOM	Present / Existing Status (Before Improvement)	Proposed (After Improvement)
1	Critical Time	Secs	720	360
2	Output/Shift	Nos	36	72
3	Manpower / Shift	Nos	2	2
4	PMPD	Nos	18	36
5	Method changes	---	1.Incoming parts received are not getting directly accepted. 2.No repeatability observed in the Flow testing stage - Difference calculation between the PRV opening between various pressures (Given as spec. in drawing) is not getting directly captured in Flow equipment.(Manual intervention required) 3.Opertors working at very high temperature.Due to this more fatigue ,product handling with heat is very difficult. More test rig breakdowns occur due to rubber components getting toughened at high temp.	1.Incoming parts (Pump body, Inner & Outer Rotor, Bolt PRV, Plunger PRV & Cover) component quality to be improved to avoid selective assy in the assy line 2.Flow in terms of litres to be arrived for all the RPM Vs PRV opg.Pressure to improve the yield by having G & NG signals in the Flow test rig. 3. The Oil temperature for testing from 120 Deg to Normal Room temperature to reduce operator fatigue & suffocations. By this the temperature to reduce operator fatigue & suffocations. By this the periodic breakdowns for replacing Oil seals & O rings can be brought down to improve the Test rig availability.

Benefits and End Result	Output Incr / Shift	Nos		36
	Manpower saving	Nos		-
	% Impvt in PMPD	%		100.00
	Quality Impvt	---		-

Investment Required (PI put tick mark)	Minor	---
	Major	---

Project	Name	Anguraj S
Proposed by	Dept	BU 3 Module 605

Responsible Person	1 -Senthilkumar.G 2&3 -Navaneethkrishnan A
Dept	1 - BU3 -Matls 2 - BU3 - PDE

Time Frame

Process Improvement Detail Sheet

Page	61	of 140
Date		7-Aug-13
Rev No		0

| Product Code | D18400150000 | Module | 605 |
| Product Description | Fly weight | Cell Code | 1353 |

SI No	Description	UOM	Present / Existing Status (Before Improvement)	Proposed (After Improvement)
1	Critical Time	Secs	31	9
2	Output/Shift	Nos	932	3250
3	Manpower / Shift	Nos	1	1
4	PMPD	Nos	932	3250
5	Method changes	---	Product stacked and Packing done for 6 Nos and heat sealed.	50Nos directly packed in one cover and heat sealed.(No stacking done)

6	Benefits and End Result			
	Output Incr / Shift	Nos		2318
	Manpower saving	Nos		-
	% Impvt in PMPD	%		248.71
	Quality Impvt	---		-

Investment Required (PI put tick mark)	Minor	
	Major	

Project Proposed by	Name	Anguraj S
	Dept	BU 3 Module 605

Responsible Person	Jayaprakashan
Dept	BU3 - PDE

Time Frame	Completed

Process Improvement Detail Sheet

			Page	62	of	140
Product Code	D18400150000	**Module**	605	**Date**		7-Aug-13
Product Description	Demagnetizing	**Cell Code**	1353	**Rev No**		0

Sl No	Description	UOM	Present / Existing Status (Before Improvement)	Proposed (After Improvement)
1	Critical Time	Secs	18	10
2	Output/Shift	Nos	1620	3000
3	Manpower / Shift	Nos	1	1
4	PMPD	Nos	1620	3000
5	Method changes	---	Travelling distance is high as the process done at SCMS building (No demagnetizer available)	Separate demagnatizer equipment required to reduce the man movement. Investment of 0.065 Mn estimated by Mfg.Engg.
6	Benefits and End Result			
	Output Incr / Shift	Nos		1380
	Manpower saving	Nos		-
	% Impvt in PMPD	%		85.19
	Quality Impvt	---		-

Investment Required (PI put tick mark)	Minor	
	Major	

Project Proposed by	Name	Anguraj S
	Dept	BU 3 Module 605

	Time Frame	End of Sep 2013
Responsible Person	Gopinath	
Dept	BU3 - ME	

Process Improvement Detail Sheet

		Page	83	of	140
Product Code	E273700000000	Module	607	Date	9-Aug-13
Product Description	4S-OIL PUMP ASSY	Cell Code	1106	Rev No	0

Sl No	Description	UOM	Present / Existing Status (Before Improvement)	Proposed (After Improvement)
1	Critical Time	Secs	60.00	45.00
2	Output/Shift	Nos	360	540
3	Manpower / Shift	Nos	1	1
4	PMPD	Nos	360	540
5	Method changes	--	Reaming process done in SPM SM0075 at the cycle time of 60 secs	By optimisation of feed rate in SPM SM0075 the cycle time reduced to 45 secs in reaming process (SM75)

6	Benefits and End Result	Output Incr / Shift	Nos	180
		Manpower saving	Nos	--
		% Impvt in PMPD	%	50
		Quality Impvt	--	-

| Investment Required (PI put tick mark) | Minor | |
| | Major | |

| Project Proposed by | Name | Mathias C |
| | Dept | BU3 - Module 607 |

Responsible Person	Time Frame	Compeletd
		Ragupathy M
	Dept	BU - 3 ME

Process Improvement Detail Sheet

		Module	CNC CELL		Page	89	of	140
Product Code	E44720000000				Date			01.08.2013
Product Description	Oil pump Assy	Cell Code	1151A		Rev No			0

Sl No	Description	UOM	Present / Existing Status (Before Improvement)	Proposed (After Improvement)
1	Critical Time	Secs	294	163
2	Output/Shift	Nos	98	177
3	Manpower / Shift	Nos	1	1
4	PMPD	Nos	98	177
5	Method changes	---	Pump body : 1. Steel shank boring tools used. 2. Manual method of clamping used.	Pump body : 1. Carbide boring tools and optimising the cutting speed for reducing the cycle time. 2. Hydraulic chuck planned for reducing loading and unloading time.
6	Benefits and End Result	Output Incr / Shift	Nos	79 Nos
		Manpower saving	Nos	-
		% Impvt in PMPD	%	81%
		Quality Impvt	---	-

Investment Required (PI put tick mark)	Minor	---
	Major	✓

Project	Name	BU 3 - prodn
Proposed by	Dept	CNC Cell

	Time Frame	Sep -2013
Responsible Person	K.Palanisamy / M.Vijayakumar	
Dept	CNC Cell / ME	

Process Improvement Detail Sheet

			Page	90	of	140

Product Code	E53920000000	Module	CNC CELL	Date	01.08.2013
Product Description	Oil pump Assy	Cell Code	1733	Rev No	0

Sl No	Description	UOM	Present / Existing Status (Before Improvement)	Proposed (After Improvement)
1	Critical Time	Secs	134	91
2	Output/Shift	Nos	215	315
3	Manpower / Shift	Nos	1	1
4	PMPD	Nos	215	315
5	Method changes	---	Pump body : 1. Single component fixture used 2. M10 Bolt clamping for component holding.	Pump body : 1. 2 Nos Multi component fixture used. Clamping made rigid with M16 Bolt and Cutting speed optimisation for M18 x1.5 thread plug bore. 2.
6	Benefits and End Result	Output Incr / Shift	Nos	100 Nos
		Manpower saving	Nos	
		% Impvt in PMPD	%	47%
		Quality Impvt	---	

		Project	Name	BU 3 - Prodn
Investment Required (PI put tick mark)	Minor	✓	Proposed by	Dept	CNC Cell
	Major	.....			

	Time Frame	Implimented
Responsible Person		K.Palanisamy
Dept		CNC Cell

Process Improvement Detail Sheet

			Page	91	of	140
Product Code	E46800000000	Module	CNC CELL	Date		01.08.2013
Product Description	4s Oil pump assy	Cell Code	1481	Rev No		0

SI No	Description	UOM	Present / Existing Status (Before Improvement)	Proposed (After Improvement)
1	Critical Time	Secs	248	161
2	Output/Shift	Nos	116	179
3	Manpower / Shift	Nos	1	1
4	PMPD	Nos	116	179
5	Method changes	---	Pump body : ISO ordinary Boring tool used for facing and boring operation done	Pump body : Carbide boring bars for Facing & Boring operation in Pump body.
6	Benefits and End Result	Output Incr / Shift	Nos		63 Nos
		Manpower saving	Nos		
		% Impvt in PMPD	%		54%
		Quality Impvt	---		---

Investment Required (PI put tick mark)	Minor	---
	Major	✓

Project	Name	BU 3 - Prodn
Proposed by	Dept	CNC Cell

Responsible Person	K.Palanisamy	Time Frame	Sep.-2013
Dept	CNC Cell		

Process Improvement Detail Sheet

		Page	92	of	140

Product Code	E53920000000	Module	CNC CELL	Date	01.08.2013
Product Description	Oil pump assy	Cell Code	1735	Rev No	0

Sl No	Description	UOM	Present / Existing Status (Before Improvement)	Proposed (After Improvement)
1	Critical Time	Secs	294	206
2	Output/Shift	Nos	98	140
3	Manpower / Shift	Nos	1	1
4	PMPD	Nos	98	140
5	Method changes	—	Pump Body- Dia 13 & Dia 9 Reaming 1) 2 Nos - Multi component fixture used for production. 2) By using Dia 13.5 Carbide Reamer.	Pump Body- Dia 13 & Dia 9 Reaming 1) 4 nos. - Multi component fixture introduced. 2) By using Dia 13.5 PCD Reamer cutting parameter increased & cycle time reduced.

Benefits and End Result	Output Incr / Shift	Nos		42 Nos
	Manpower saving	Nos		-
	% Impvt in PMPD	%		43%
	Quality Impvt	—		-

Investment Required (PI put tick mark)	Minor	.....		
	Major	✓		

Project Proposed by	Name		BU 3 - Prodn
	Dept		CNC Cell

Time Frame	Implemented.

Responsible Person	K.Palanisamy
Dept	CNC Cell

Process Improvement Detail Sheet

			Page	93	of	140
Product Code	E44720000000	Module	CNC CELL		Date	01.08.2013
Product Description	Oil pump Assy	Cell Code	1152A		Rev No	0

Sl No	Description	UOM	Present / Existing Status (Before Improvement)	Proposed (After Improvement)
1	Critical Time	Secs	738	335
2	Output/Shift	Nos	39	86
3	Manpower / Shift	Nos	1	1
4	PMPD	Nos	39	86
5	Method changes	---	Pump Body - Reaming operations 1 & 2. Single component fixture used.	Pump Body - Reaming operations 1 & 2. Hydraulic fixtures with Multi component - 4 Nos. for M44720 Pump body shaft bore & dowel hole process.

		UOM		
Benefits and End Result	Output Incr / Shift	Nos		47 Nos
	Manpower saving	Nos		-
	% Impvt in PMPD	%		121%
	Quality Impvt	---		
6				

Investment Required (PI put tick mark)	Minor	---
	Major	✓

Project Proposed by	Name	BU 3 - Prodn
	Dept	CNC Cell

Responsible Person	M.Vijaykumar / K.Palanisamy	Time Frame	Sep -2013
Dept	ME / CNC Cell		

Process Improvement Detail Sheet

			Page	94	of	140

Product Code	E44720000000	Module	CNC CELL		Date	01.08.2013
Product Description	Oil pump	Cell Code	1152 C /1474		Rev No	0

SI No	Description	UOM	Present / Existing Status (Before Improvement)	Proposed (After Improvement)
1	Critical Time	Secs	472 / 757	223 / 338
2	Output/Shift	Nos	61 / 39	129 / 85
3	Manpower / Shift	Nos	1+1	1+1
4	PMPD	Nos	61 / 39	129 / 85
5	Method changes	---	Cover Cooling milling operations 1. Manual clamping done 2.Seperate fixture used for ML01 & ML02 process in Cover cooling. Total Output - 2 Nos./ Fix.	Cover Cooling milling operations 1. Hydraulic clamping planned 2. Same fixture of ML01 is planned for ML02 process in the Hydraulic fixture with 2Nos. component holding for both the process in the same fixture - Total Output - 4 Nos. / fix
6	Benefits and End Result	Output Incr / Shift	Nos	68 Nos / 46 Nos
		Manpower saving	Nos	-
		% Impvt in PMPD	%	89.70% and 84.7 %
		Quality Impvt	---	

Investment Required (PI put tick mark)	Minor	----
	Major	✓

Project	Name	BU 3 - Prodn		Responsible Person	M.Vijaykumar / K.Palanisamy
Proposed by	Dept	CNC Cell		Dept	ME / CNC Cell

	Time Frame	Sep -2013

Process Improvement Detail Sheet

				Page	94	of	140
Product Code	E44720000000	Module	CNC CELL	Date			01.08.2013
Product Description	Oil pump	Cell Code	1152 C /1474	Rev No			0

Sl No	Description	UOM	Present / Existing Status (Before Improvement)	Proposed (After Improvement)
1	Critical Time	Secs	472 / 757	223 / 338
2	Output/Shift	Nos	61 / 39	129 / 85
3	Manpower / Shift	Nos	1 + 1	1 + 1
4	PMPD	Nos	61 / 39	129 / 85
			Cover Cooling milling operations	Cover Cooling milling operations
5	Method changes	—	1. Manual clamping done 2.Seperate fixture used for ML01 & ML02 process in Cover cooling. Total Output - 2 Nos./ Fix.	1. Hydraulic clamping planned Same fixture of ML01 is planned for ML02 process in the Hydraulic fixture with 2Nos. component holding for both the process in the same fixture - Total Output - 4 Nos. / fix 2.
6	Benefits and End Result	Output Incr / Shift	Nos	68 Nos / 46 Nos
		Manpower saving	Nos	-
		% Impvt in PMPD	%	89.70% and 84.7 %
		Quality Impvt	—	-

Investment Required (PI put tick mark)	Minor	....
	Major	✓

Project Proposed by	Name	BU 3 - Prodn
	Dept	CNC Cell

Responsible Person		M.Vijaykumar / K.Palanisamy	Time Frame	Sep -2013
Dept		ME / CNC Cell		

Process Improvement Detail Sheet

		Page	102	of	140
	Module	CNC CELL	Date		01.08.2013

Product Code	E53920000000			Cell Code	1736	Rev No	0
Product Description	Oil pump Assy						

Sl No	Description	UOM	Present / Existing Status (Before Improvement)	Proposed (After Improvement)
1	Critical Time	Secs	133.95	80.45
2	Output/Shift	Nos	215	358
3	Manpower / Shift	Nos	1	1
4	PMPD	Nos	215	358
5	Method changes	—	Pump body - Rear Milling : 1) Single station fixture used. 2) Solid carbide End mill used.	Pump body - Rear Milling : 1) 2 Nos. - Multi component Fixture planned. 2) Insert type end mill used and Cutting speed optimized to reduce the cycle time.
6	Benefits and End Result	Output Incr / Shift	Nos		143 Nos
		Manpower saving	Nos		-
		% Impvt in PMPD	%		67%
		Quality Impvt	---		---

Investment Required (PI put tick mark)	Minor	---	Project Proposed by	Name	BU 3 - Prodn
	Major	---		Dept	CNC Cell

Responsible Person	K.Palanisamy	Time Frame	Implemented
Dept	CNC Cell		

Process Improvement Detail Sheet

				Page	107	of	140
Product Code	24690001RE01	**Module**	CNC CELL	**Date**			01.08.2013
Product Description	Recovery Pump Body	**Cell Code**	1152D	**Rev No**			0

Sl No	Description	UOM	Present / Existing Status (Before Improvement)	Proposed (After Improvement)
1	Critical Time	Secs	310	225
2	Output/Shift	Nos	93	128
3	Manpower / Shift	Nos	1	1
4	PMPD	Nos	93	128
5	Method changes	---	Dia 10 & Dia 7.5 Reaming 1.3 Nos multi component fixture used for production. 2.Individual clamping for each component. 3. Carbide reamer for Dia 10 & 7.5 mm used.	Dia 10 & Dia 7.5 Reaming 1.Reducing cycle time by non cut time elimination and reducing loading and unloading time through 4 nos multi components in the fixture. 2.Improving clamping methods for clamping two components with a single clamp. 3. Dia 10 & Dia 7.5 PCD Reamer will be introduced for increasing the cutting parameters and reducing the cycle time
6	Benefits and End Result	Output Incr / Shift	Nos		35 Nos
		Manpower saving	Nos		-
		% Impvt in PMPD	%		38%
		Quality Impvt	---		-

Investment Required (PI put tick mark)	Minor	....
	Major	✓

Project	Name	BU 3 - Prodn
Proposed by	Dept	CNC Cell

	Time Frame	Sep -2013
Responsible Person	M.Vijaykumar / K.Palanisamy	
Dept	ME / CNC Cell	

Process Improvement Detail Sheet

			Page	108	of	140
Product Code	25390001TU01	Module	CNC CELL		Date	1-Aug-13
Product Description	Pump body	Cell Code	1728		Rev No	0

SI No	Description	UOM	Present / Existing Status (Before Improvement)	Proposed (After Improvement)
1	Critical Time	Secs	212	79
2	Output/Shift	Nos	136	365
3	Manpower / Shift	Nos	1	1
4	PMPD	Nos	136	365
5	Method changes	---	1) Manual method of clamping. 2) M539 2001TU01 - Dia 40.576 Rotor boring operation - LA 61 machine 3) Machine located in 302 Building.	1) Hydraulic clamping fixture method introduced. 2) Cutting Speed optimisation. 3) Re-layout changes proposal for CNC Cell @ 303 Building.
6	Benefits and End Result	Output Incr / Shift	Nos	229 Nos
		Manpower saving	Nos	-
		% Impvt in PMPD	%	168%
		Quality Impvt	---	---

Investment Required (PI put tick mark)	Minor	----
	Major	✓

Project	Name	BU 3 - Prodn
	Dept	CNC Cell
Proposed by		

Responsible Person	K.PALANISAMY / M.VIJAYKUMAR
Dept	CNC / ME

Time Frame	August -13

Process Improvement Detail Sheet

Page	109	of	140

Product Code	24470001TU01	Module	CNC CELL	Date	01.08.2013
Product Description	Pump Body	Cell Code	1151A	Rev No	0

SI No	Description	UOM	Present / Existing Status (Before Improvement)	Proposed (After Improvement)
1	Critical Time	Secs	294	163
2	Output/Shift	Nos	98	177
3	Manpower / Shift	Nos	1	1
4	PMPD	Nos	98	177
5	Method changes	---	1. Cutting tools - Steel shank boring tools 2.Manual method of clamping used. 3.Using Carbide plug gauges and Dial caliper for measuring the component.	1.Reducing cycle time by increasing cutting speed by introducing carbide shank boring tools. 2. Hydraulic chuck planned for reducing loading and unloading time. 3. Multi Gauging system for E447, E444 components geomentrical tolerance inspection purpose.

6	Benefits and End Result	Output Incr / Shift	Nos		79 Nos
		Manpower saving	Nos		
		% Impvt in PMPD	%		81%
		Quality Impvt	---		

Investment Required (PI put tick mark)	Minor	---
	Major	✓

Project Proposed by	Name	BU 3 - prodn	Time Frame	Sep -2013
	Dept	CNC Cell		

Responsible Person	Kumaravel / K.Palanisamy
Dept	QE / CNC Cell

Process Improvement Detail Sheet

			Page	114	of	140
Product Code	253920010000 - Bush body Water cleaning	**Module**	CLG CELL	**Date**		01.08.2013
Product Description	E539200000000 4S OP	**Cell Code**	1506	**Rev No**		0

SI No	Description	UOM	Present / Existing Status (Before Improvement)	Proposed (After Improvement)
1	Critical Time	Secs	64	43
2	Output/Shift	Nos	450	675
3	Manpower / Shift	Nos	1	1
4	PMPD	Nos	450	675
5	Method changes	---	Batch qty. with existing fixture - 24 Nos.	M539 Pump body dia 16 bush bore cleaning fixture modification to 30 Nos.

6	Benefits and End Result			
	Output Incr / Shift	Nos		225 Nos
	Manpower saving	Nos		-
	% Impvt in PMPD	%		50%
	Quality Impvt	---		-

Investment Required (PI put tick mark)	Minor	....
	Major	✓

Project Proposed by	Name	BU3 - Prodn
	Dept	CNC Cell

	Responsible Person	Gopinath / K.Palanisamy
Time Frame	Sep -2013	
	Dept	Mfg Engg / CNC Cell

Process Improvement Detail Sheet

Page	5	of	140
Date			1-Aug-13
Rev No			0

Product Code	D362000000000	Module	601
Product Description	2s Oil pump assy	Cell Code	1003

SI No	Description	UOM	Present / Existing Status (Before Improvement)	Proposed (After Improvement)
1	Critical Time	Secs	240.00	240.00
2	Output/Shift	Nos	120	120
3	Manpower / Shift	Nos	5	3
4	PMPD	Nos	24	40
5	Method changes	---	Flow testing of oil pump had been checked with volume of 0.5 CC	Flow testing process has been checked with volume of 0.4 CC. Hence the critical process flow testing average cycle time reduced and process clubbed with better manning pattern

6	Benefits and End Result	Output Incr / Shift	Nos	-
		Manpower saving	Nos	2
		% Impvt in PMPD	%	66.67
		Quality Impvt	---	-

Investment Required (PI put tick mark)	Minor	---
	Major	---

Project Proposed by	Name	Ramasamy K
	Dept	Module 601

Responsible Person	Dwakarnath Babu R Gopinath C
Dept	BU 3 QE BU 3 - Mfg Engg
Time Frame	Completed

10. A Brief Summary of Productivity Enhancement Study of a Manufacturing Unit

Introduction and Methodology

This unit which belongs to a big group company had about 12 Casual labours for various unskilled and movement or helping jobs during the year 1998. When the demand spurt came up, the shop supervisors started adding 1 or 2 Casual labour for increased output on critical machines. The main permanent operators exploited the same and started applying pressure on supervisors for more helping hands. Very soon the total Casual labour strength went up, to about 167 men on daily basis. Getting such a lot of men were rather difficult and the manager of contract labour supply became very powerful and indispensable. On many days they used to stop supply of men for their petty demands. This prompted the group VP - HR to wake up and he asked for a thorough study to find ways and means to reduce the strength and improve the productivity at this shop. This was the genesis of this study focus at this unit.

It was not easy and all possible techniques mentioned in this report such as automation, material handling method changes, lay out changes, simplifications, methods improvements, elimination of co-worker with suitable changes etc. had to be done to meet the demand as laid down by VP- HR.

It may be of surprise to note that the study team recommended a reduction of 143 casual labour strength without diminishing the output of the unit.

A few sample sheets in summary form of just one shop or module alone is captured in the next few pages. Perusal of the same should ignite and kindle the fire on productivity enhancement in your shop, hopefully! It is most important to record all findings and recommendations for meaningful discussions with top management and even with union team for implementation and the report should never become just paper tiger and on the book only.

| METHOD CHANGE | ELIMINATION OF CO-WORKERS | ADDING HANDLING FACILITY | AUTOMATION |

Note:

Above changes are considered for computing 'B' Column in Standard Time chart and for reworking the required manpower.

SUMMARY OF MANPOWER REDUCTION THROUG METHOD CHANGES/CAPS/INVESTMENT

Department	Proposed Investment (Rs: Lac)	Proposed Reduction of Manpower	Estimated Time Frame
Vetrified Moulding	61.9	71	5 Months
Vetrified Finishing	28.15	29	4 Months
Organic	4	18	3 Months
IG/Bond Plant/Stores/Shipping	3	18	3 Months
Other Indirect		6	
Total	**97.05**	**14**	**About 5–6 month**

Details of Method changes, Manpower reduction and Investments needed are given in the following pages.

Justifications

➤ Over a period of time a unit in South India had become like an overcrowded bus with far too many contract men engaged for assisting production activities.

➤ It is an overdue exercise to trim the flab and make the Manufacturing wing lean.

➤ At the present context this exercise cannot bed one without necessary Method changes/Automation/Handling facilities/Elimination of Co-workers etc.

➤ Obviously it calls for additional facilities and investments

➤ Postponement of the additional investment is not giving to help a unit in South India at least for the following major reasons only:

 a. Reduction of substantial manpower will not take place.

 b. At later point, cost of investment will only go up.

 c. There will not be substantial productivity growth.

➤ It may not be difficult to justify the investment of approximately Rs.1 crore for the saving of 143 contract men and the corresponding cost.

➤ Very many companies look upon the saving of men as most important.

➤ Treating them as the future employees, following will be the labor saving on account of 143 men reduction.

 a. Average cost per employee/month = Rs.11824

 b. Potential saving for143men/annum = Rs.11824 × 143 × 12

   = Rs. 2.03 crores.

➤ Following will be the labour saving if we take the average cost of the plant labour strength.

 a. Average labor cost/month = Rs. 6000/

 b. Potential saving for men/annum = Rs. 6000x143x12

   = Rs. 1.03 crores.

➤ The recurring saving of Rs.1.03 crore per annum is so attractive that it cannot be ignored for one time investment of about Rs.1 crore.

MANPOWER REDUCTION AREAS AND RECOMMENDED INVESTMENT

VITRIFIED MOULDING

PROCESS	PRESENT METHOD	No of men	PROPOSED METHOD	No of men	NEW FACILITY REQUIRED	Reduction (No. of men)	Investment time frame
Liquid dextrin preparation	Mixing in 40kg mixer by contract men (1x2 shift)	2	Using 80kg mixer	1	New mixer, Weighing scale, storage space for powder dextrin	1	Rs.3 lac/ 1 month
Weighing	Part of the grains are taken from bags and bond is 50kgs bags. Profit: 1 Employee + 1contract men	6	All grains in silos, Bond: 1. in 25kgs bag 2. 1 Ton storage bins	3		3	Rs.4 lacs/ 4 months

PROCESS	PRESENT METHOD	No of men	PROPOSED METHOD	No of men	NEW FACILITY REQUIRED	Reduction (No. of men)	Investment time frame
Mix Sieving and feeding	Mix is fed in to the press chute by contract men (9press by 8persons) Job involves-Mix unloading, transfer, sieving and charging	27	1. Mixers at existing locations and using mix dispenser for each press. (2 persons / shift) Note: 150T- sieving to be done by mixing operator, Moulding operator., Moulding operator to charge the mix into mouldg m/c 2. Dedicated mixers closer to press (1 person per shift)	6	1. Mix dispenser-9nos 1. Relocation of mixer 2. Additional 1 100kg mixer 3. Mix dispenser-9nos	21 (can be considered when layouts are changed)	Rs.12 lacs/ 45 days

PROCESS	PRESENT METHOD	No of men	PROPOSED METHOD	No of men	NEW FACILITY REQUIRED	Reduction (No. of men))	Investment time frame
Moulding	850, 300, 250, 225 I, II, Komage, 200T presses have 2 person each	42	1 person per press doing production with self inspection NOTE: 2 persons for moulding wheels size strating from dia 350 thick 50 in 850T & 300T	21	1. Auto weighing system for 300T and 850T press. 2. Wheel handling facility for the above presses	21	Rs. 12 lacs/ 4months

Press	Per shift	Per Day
350T	2	6
250T	2	6
225T 1	2	6
225T II	2	6
200T	2	6
Komage	2	6
850T	2	6
Total		42

Press	Per shift	Per day
350T	1	3
250T	1	3
225T 1	1	3
225T II	1	3
200T	1	3
Komage	1	3
850T	1	3
Total		21

PROCESS	PRESENT METHOD	No of men	PROPOSED METHOD	No of men	NEW FACILITY REQUIRED	Reduction (No. of men)	Investment time frame
814 moulding	Moulded with four stations in conventional press.(320 pieces per stn) I & II shift-4stn + 1 weigh, IIIshift –3stn +1weigh Qty= 4 x320nos =1280nos in I & II shift 3x320 nos=960nos in III shift 3520nos/da	14	Mechanical auto press with twin cavities 4000 nos per shift	1	New press Mix dispenser Coveyor system to feed the m/c	13	Rs.25 lacs/ 5months
Green loss wheel crushing	Green loss wheels are crushed manually for reuse by 5Contractmen in 3shift (2+2+1)	5	Green loss wheel crushing with a crushing mc	3	Crushing M/c	2	Rs. 1.5 lacs/1month

PROCESS	PRESENT METHOD	No of men	PROPOSED METHOD	No of men	NEW FACILITY REQUIRED	Reduction (No. of men)	Investment time frame
Monochite sieving	2 contract men per shift used for sieving	6	Conveyor system to feed the m/c	3	Conveyor system to feed the m/c	3	Rs 0.8 lacs/ 1month
Kiln	Tiles/Post manually cleaned 2C x 3 shift	6	Tiles to be cleaned with pneumatic chisel	3	Pneumatic chisel	3	Rs 0.1 lacs/ 15 days
Ball wheel	Helping in handling the ball wheel at Shaving, disking and Peen blast m/c 3 C men per day	3	Handling the wheel with hoist at all the stations	0	Hoist at Peenblast, disking m/c	3	Rs 2 lacs/ 2 months

PROCESS	PRESENT METHOD	No of men	PROPOSED METHOD	No of men	NEW FACILITY REQUIRED	Reduction (No. of men)	Investment time frame
Skid arrangement	2 Operator with 2 Contract workmen sort and arrange the wares from kiln in skids and move it to finishing. Contract men help in transferring the skids.	4	Transferring the skids with battery operated truck	2	Battery operated truck	2	Rs 1.5 lacs/ 1 month
VITRIFIED MOULDING TOTAL						72	Rs 61.9 lacs / 5months

MANPOWER REDUCTION AREAS AND RECOMMENDED INVESTMENT VITRIFIED MOULDING

Process	Presentmethod	No of Men	Proposed Method	No of Men	Newfacility Required	Reduction (No of Men)	Investment/ Time Frame
Steel grit sieving	Sieved by 2 contract men per shift (3shift)	6	Building enough stock in1and2shift	5		1	
Redeme	2 workmen operating them/c (2shift)	4	To be opened by1 Person after providing Wheel handling system	2	Wheel handling system	2	Rs. 3 lac/4 months
Hand edger	2 hand edgers are manned by 3workmen In day(1+1,0.5+0.5) Edging using resinoid blocks1workmen Inspects the periphery	4	Auto edging facility And man in the edger doing the periphery inspection simultaneously	3	Auto edging facility With diamond drum (as in resinoid) with Between centers spindle	1	Rs. 2.5lacs/ 3months
OOB and powder application inspection	OOB inspection and Correction done in different stations Centerless/crank 4opr, 2CL 5 20" 9Opr, 6CL &2C.	6 17	Simultaneously checking &balancing In the same station, Centerless &crank With wheel handling facility 5 20"OOB inspection & correction in same station	3 12	Wheel handling system for OOB Inspection and stacking the pallet. Simultaneous OOB inspection and balancing system 3 units	3 5	Rs. 0.15Lacs/ 15days Rs. 2Lacs/2 months

Process	Present method	No of Men	Proposed Method	No of Men	Newfacility Required	Reduction (No of Men)	Investment/ Time Frame
500 center-less and Crank wheel arbor painting	Done by 2 contract men x2shift	4	Wheel handling System and pin Rotating facility to be provided 1 person can do the job	2	Wheel handling System and pin Rotating facility to be provided	2	Rs. 0.5lacs/ 2months
Export wheels processing	3 contract workmen Doing the blowing, arbor painting and OOB correction	3	Demand disc for Disking and between Centre lathes for edging to eliminate rework and increase output per shift(will release manpower)	1		2	
814/109 blocks packing	109 block is screen printed manually by 2 Contract men doing cleaning, primary packing, secondary packing the 814and 109blocks.	12	Auto cleaning, stenciling and primary packing of the blocks	2	Auto cleaning, stenciling and primary packing m/c	`10	Rs. 20 lacs/4 months

PROCESS	PRESENT METHOD	No of men	PROPOSED METHOD	No of men	NEW FACILITY REQUIRED	Reduction (No. of men)	Investment time frame
Packing	1 contractor unloads packed carton from the roller in each shift	3	Packing operator himself has to stack the carton in the end of the roller. Shipping will be take the cartons on getting finished vouchers	0		3	
VITRIFIED FINISHING TOTAL						29	Rs 28.45 lacs / 4months

MANPOWER REDUCTION AREAS AND RECOMMENDED INVESTMENT

ORGANIC

PROCESS	PRESENT METHOD	No of men	PROPOSED METHOD	No of men	NEW FACILITY REQUIRED	Reduction (No. of men)	Investment time frame
Blending	2 workmen doing the process	2	1 workman to do the process	1		1	Nil
Bergin press moulding	3 person required-1.mix weighing, & charging 2.adding TWL, fabric, bush 3. Removing wheel and pilling in batts	6	Auto weighing system (2 person to run)	4	Auto weighing system	2	Rs 2 lac / 3months

PROCESS	PRESENT METHOD	No of men	PROPOSED METHOD	No of men	NEW FACILITY REQUIRED	Reduction (No. of men)	Investment time frame
New Matermini press	3 persons operate each station. (total 2stnx2shift) stn-1 –O-2,C-1.stn-2-O-2,C1	12	2 persons can operate Stn 1-O-2,Stn 2-O-2	8		4	
450T press	1person manned for 2 mold pressing (3shift operation)	3	1person operating with 4 mould simultaneously- 75% increase in qty (2shift opts)	2		1	

PROCESS	PRESENT METHOD	No of men	PROPOSED METHOD	No of men	NEW FACILITY REQUIRED	Reduction (No. of men))	Investment time frame
Oven	Oven is running automatically based on program. An operator also records the temp periodically.	3	The auto recording system to be checked for calibration and reliability and technical to approve the system reading itself. This is to be audited by shift electrician	0	Alarm system to indicate if any abnormality or cycle completion	3	Rs 0.5 lacs / 15 days
Arbor open out	4 person (1cl+lc,1c) does the arbor opening of 7mm thick DC wheels	4	Arbor open out to be reduced by redesigning of bush and pin size	2		2	

PROCESS	PRESENT METHOD	No of men	PROPOSED METHOD	No of men	NEW FACILITY REQUIRED	Reduction (No. of men))	Investment time frame
Grain sieving in Razor blade	Done by 1 contract man each shift (3 shift)	3	To be done in sono screen by the Mixing operator	0		3	
			ORGANIC TOTAL			18	Rs 4 lacs/ 3 months

MANPOWER REDUCTION AREAS AND RECOMMENDED INVESTMENT

OTHERS

PROCESS	PRESENT METHOD	No of men	PROPOSED METHOD	No of men	NEW FACILITY REQUIRED	Reduction (No. of men)	Investment time frame
Lorry loading	Contract men doing the job	5	Transporter to take care of lorry loading also	0	Nil	5	Nil
Stores	General and RM stores are in different locations maintained with 2 employees and 2 contract workmen (for issues to department)	4	Stores issues have to be collected by the concerned department	2		2	

PROCESS	PRESENT METHOD	No of men	PROPOSED METHOD	No of men	NEW FACILITY REQUIRED	Reduction (No. of men)	Investment time frame
IG	Wheel cleaning, Stenciling, kiln loading, unloading, arbor painting (6contract men x 2 shift)	12	Stabilization of the main processes like Moulding (leads to higher output per shift), Moulds standardization (eliminates arbor painting and wheel cleaning)	3	Nil	9	
Bond plant	Sieving, weighing, packing and stacking of bond in 50kgs	2	Sieving directly into 1Ton storage bins	1	2T hoist for handling the bins(20nos)	1	Rs 3 lac/ 3months

PROCESS	PRESENT METHOD	No of men	PROPOSED METHOD	No of men	NEW FACILITY REQUIRED	Reduction (No. of men)	Investment time frame
Bond plant Lump breaking	Presently clay lump breaking done manually by 1 man each in 2 shifts	2	Clay can be crushed with Shredder m/c in shift	1		1	
				OTHERS TOTAL		18	Rs 3 lac/ 3months

11. Productivity Enhancement Through Setup Time Reduction

Setup Reduction-Methodology

Benefits of setup of time reduction

Example

Setup	: 4 hrs
Units process time	: 1 minute
Batch size	: 100 Units

$$\frac{4 \times 60 + 100}{100}$$

Units operation time   : 3.4 mts/unit

In batch size 1000 units

$$\frac{4 \times 60 + 1000}{1000}$$

Unit of operation time   : 1.24 mts/unit

If you have to produce at 1.24 mts which lot size 100 units, what should be the setup time?

X + 1.24 (100) – 100 = 24 mts

This is, find ways and means of reducing setup time from 4 hrs to just 24 mts.

As an example of the benefits of reduced setup time, consider the following example: 40 hours operation produces five different parts, each different with parts, each with weekly demand for 240 units and a processing time of 1 minutes per unit. If the setup time to changeover between parts is 4 hours, then half the week end (20 hours) is spent of changeovers. During a 5 day week, each day must be wholly devoted to producing the different part 4 hrs for setup, 4 hrs for production. Now suppose the setup procedure is simplified and standardized, and the time is reduced to 24 minutes. It is then possible each day to produce 1 day's demand 48 units, of every part. Total setup time each day is (24) = 120 minutes and total processing time 5 (24) = 120 minutes, total processing time is 5 (48) (1 min/unit) 240 minutes. Average inventory per part is reduced from 120 units to 24 units. Beside that since each day's setup and production taken only 6 hours (120 + 240 = 360 minutes), 2 hours remain in an 8 hour workday for producing other part, problem solving equipment maintenance and so on. In addition the quality of the part is better because of the simplified, standardized setup technique the actual extra time available will usually close to 2 hours because of the low setup time variability.

Benefits of simplified setups

1. Quality
2. Cost
3. Flexibility
4. Worker utilization
5. Capital and lead time
6. Process and variability

Setup Reducing Methodology: Shingo & SMED

SMED → Single Minute Exchange of Dies- Shingo reduced setup time of a 1000 Ton press from 4 hrs to just 3 min!

Steps

1. Identify Internal & External steps or Online & Off line steps Internal setup > To do m/c is stopped
   External setup > Can be done while m/c is running

Setup worksheet:

Operation	Total Setup time	Elapsed
10T press	80 minutes	Setup time 65 mins

Set Number	Step	Internal/ External	Time (min)		Performed by	
1	Check in at operation, go to die storage	E		5	Setup	Person
2	Transfer new die	E		8	Setup	Person
3	Remove old die	1	10		Setup	Person
4	Return old die to storage	E		10	Setup	Person
5	Get new material	E		15	Operator	
6	Attach new die	1	12		Setup	Person
7	Adjust machine	1	20		Setup	Person
			42	38		

Without any issue, the 38 minutes lost time of the Press can be avoided by asking the setup person to do the tasks when the Press is idle for real minimum setting up activities. Just imagine the saving of 38 minutes on total lost time of 80 minutes! How much is saved by the change in setting activities methodology? Nearly 50% reduction of set up time loss is possible in this simple case. If one thinks of looking to have a ready usable die near the Press before itself, possibly another 10 minutes can be saved by these changes. It may be possible to reduce the essential setting operation timings by various changes. At the end, it may please to have a setting time loss of say 20 to 25 minutes as against the present 42 minutes.

3.2.1 1000 MM MILL CHANGE OVER PRESENT METHOD

S. No	Activity Code	Procedure	Time (Min)	Observations
4	d-e	Bottom Roll Fixing	45	This can be done simultaneously &need not be done sequentially
5	e-f	Universal Coupling Fixing	60	This can be done simultaneously when bottom rolls are fixed
6	f-g	Height level Correction	15	Should be eliminated through standardization of housing height bearing block etc.
7	g-h	Centre Line Correction	60	
8	h-i	Top Roll fixing	60	Rolls to be stacked in sequential manner. Waiting time for crane to eliminated by having dedicated handling facility
9	I-j	Top Clamp fixing	60	This can be done simultaneously by the workmen. Usage of Ring Spanner to reduce the time for clamping
		Sub Total	300	
		Grand Total	450	
Present Changeover Time 450 min ≻ 1Shift				

3.2.1A 1000 mm Mill Manpower Allocation During Changeover

❖ Manpower provided for Change Over (C/O) activities > 2 Permanent + 1 Trainee + 5 Temporary men = 8 Men
❖ Presently the C/O activities are done one after other
❖ Hence, at present man power utilization ><50%
❖ It is proposed to divided the total men with small teams and distribute them of doing activities simultaneously
❖ This will reduce the C/O time & improve manpower utilization considerably
❖ Above recommendation is also applicable to Section Adjustment

3.2.2 1000 mm Mill Change Over Present Method

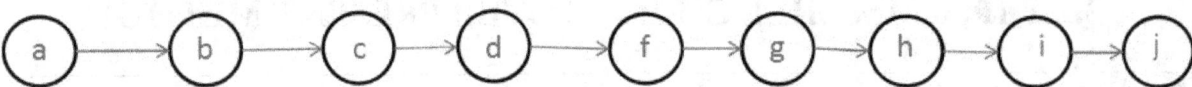

Total Change Over Time 450 Min

Remarks

➢ All activities are done one after another
➢ There are activities which can be done simultaneously
➢ Further, each activity can be improved to reduce the activity time which bring down overall C/O time considerably

3.2.1 1000 mm MILL CHANGEOVER – PRESENT METHOD

TIME (Mins)

S.No	Procedure	30	60	90	120	150	180	210	240	270	300	330	360	390	420	450
1	Top Clamps removal	■														
2	Universal Coupling removal		■													
3	Top & Bottom Roll removal &Mill cleaning			■	■	■										
4	Bottom Roll Fixing						■	■								
5	Universal Coupling fixing								■	■						
6	Height Level correction									■						
7	Center Line correction										■	■				
8	Top Roll fixing												■	■		
9	Top Clamp fixing														■	■

TOTAL TIME TAKEN 450 Mins

S. No	Activities Code	Procedure	Time (Min)	Remarks
1	a-b	Removal of Top Clamp	30	4+4 men to been gaged and both operations to be carried
2	a-c	Removal of all Universal couplings		out simultaneously to reduce to C/O time
3	b-d	Removal of Top and Bottom Rolls and Mill cleaning	90	Roll stacking platform and Crane should be available near the Mill while doing C/O; 4 men for Roll removing & 4 Men for Mill cleaning
4	d-e	Bottom Roll fixing	60	Both the operation to be carried
5	d-f	Universal Coupling fixing		out simultaneously to reduce the setting time
6	f-g	Height Level checking	15	Roll center distance locknut to be checked properly while assembling
7	g-h	Centre line checking	60	the Rolls by Rolls &Tool setters
8	h-i	Top Roll fixing	60	Both the operation to be carried
9	h-j	Top clamp fixing		out simultaneously to reduce the change over time
		TOTAL	315	

C/O > CHANGEOVER

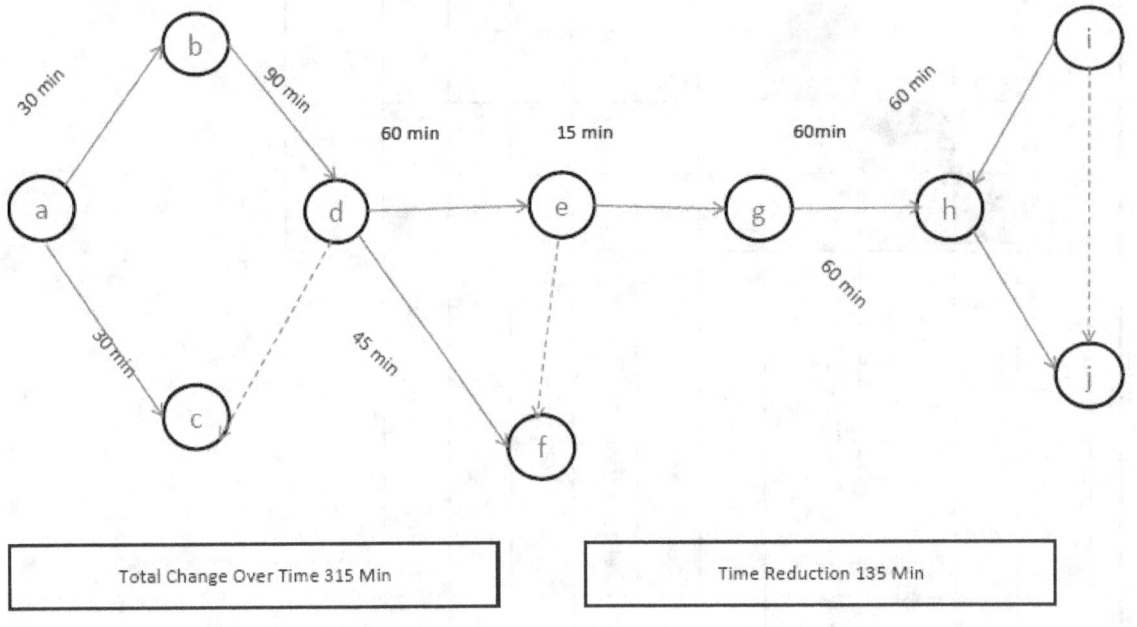

Total Change Over Time 315 Min

Time Reduction 135 Min

1000mm MILL C/O TIME REDUCTION BY SEQUENCING & PERFORMING CERTAIN OPERATIONS SIMULTANEOUSLY - STAGE -

3.2.2 C/O TIME REDUCTION SEQUENCING THE ACTIVITIES STAGE 1

TIME (min)

S.No	Procedure	30	60	90	120	150	180	210	240	270	300	330	360	390	420	450
1	Top Clamps removal	■														
2	Universal Coupling removal	■														
3	Top & Bottom Roll removal & Mill cleaning		■	■	■											
4	Bottom Roll Fixing					■	■									
5	Universal Coupling fixing						■	■								
6	Height Level correction							■								
7	Center Line correction								■	■						
8	Top Roll fixing									■	■	■				
9	Top Clamp fixing															

TOTAL C/O TIME 315 MIN C/O TIME REDUCTION >135min

3.2.3 1000 MM MILL CHANGEOVER TIME (PRSENT VS PROPOSED) STAGE-2

S. No	Activities Code	Procedure	Present Method (min)	Proposed Method (min)	Remarks
1	a-b	Top Clamps Removal	30		Operation 1 and 2 are to be carried out simultaneously to reduce the Change overtime
2	a-c	Universal Coupling Removal	30	30	Removal time per clamp can be shortened by using pneumatic nut runners ; Quick Lease coupling technique can be used
3	b-d	Top and Bottom Roll Removal and Mill cleaning	90	45	Stacking platform and Crane should be available near the Mill while doing C/O Dedicated handling facility is to be used
4	d-f	Bottom Roll Fixing	45	45	Operation 4 and 5 are to carried out simultaneously to reduce the change over time and Quick lease coupling technique can be used
5	d-e	Universal Coupling fixing	60		
		SUBTOTAL	**255**	**120**	

S. No	Activities Code	Procedure	Present Method (min)	Proposed Method (min)	Remarks
6	f-g	Height Level correction	15		Should be eliminated thro' Standardization of housing height Bearing block etc.
7	g-h	Centre line correction	30	30	Roll centre distance and lock nut to be checked properly while assembling the Rolls by Rolls & Tools fitters
8	h-i	Top Roll fixing	60		Operation 8 and 9 are be carried out simultaneously to reduce the change over time
9	h-j	Top clamp fixing	60	45	Rolls to be stacked in sequential manner, Waiting time for Crane to be eliminated by having dedicated handling facility
		SUBTOTAL	195	105	
		Grand Total	450	225	

*Investment required for Changeover improvements is given in the Mill Improvement Plans

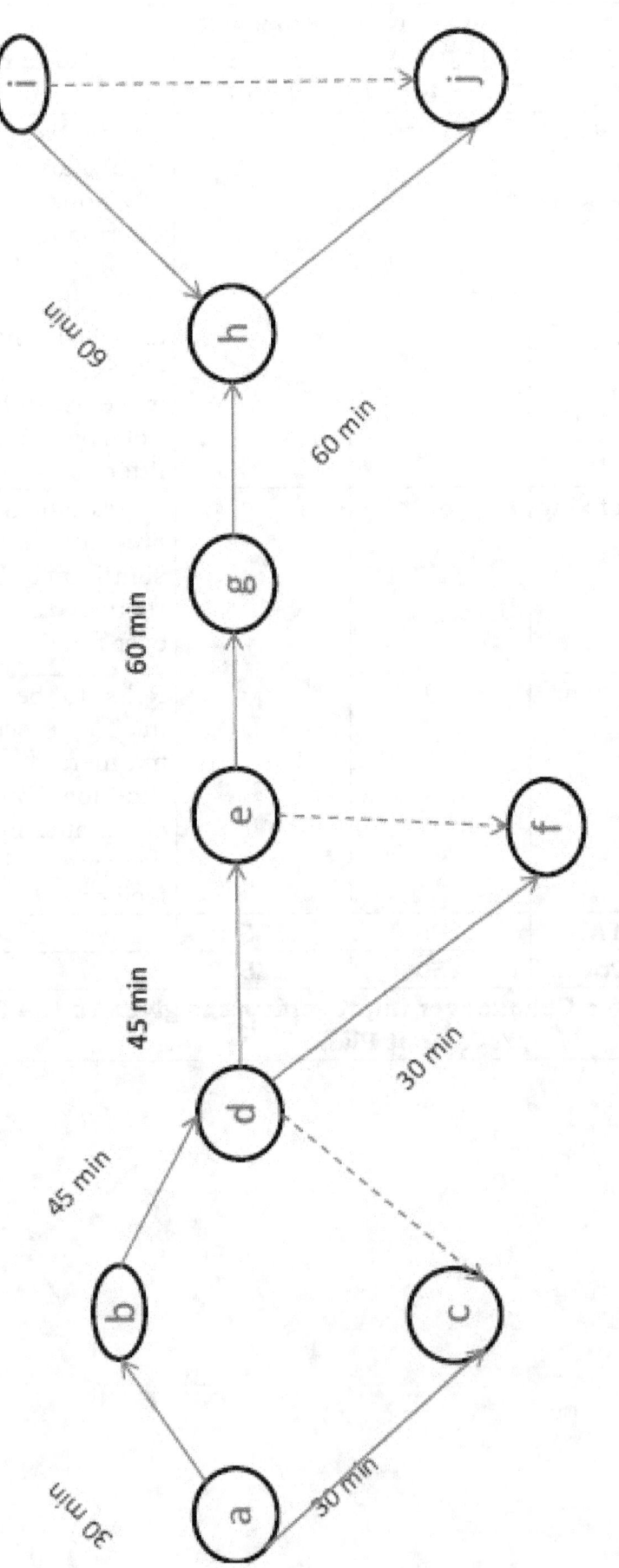

Total Change Over Time 255 Min

3.2.3 REVISED C/O TIME AFTER PROPER SEQUENCING & METHODS IMPROVEMENT - STAGE 2

3.2.3 1000 mm MILL CHANGEOVER TIME PROPOSED STAGE2

TIME(min)

S.No	Procedure	15	30	45	60	75	90	105	120	135	150	165	180	195	210	225
1	Top Clamps removal	■	■													
2	Universal Coupling removal															
3	Top & Bottom Roll removal & Mill cleaning			■	■											
4	Bottom Roll Fixing					■	■	■								
5	Universal Coupling fixing															
6	Height Level correction															
7	Center Line correction								■	■	■	■				
8	Top Roll fixing												■	■	■	■
9	Top Clamp fixing															

TOTAL C/O TIME >225MIN C/O TIME REDUCTION > 225min

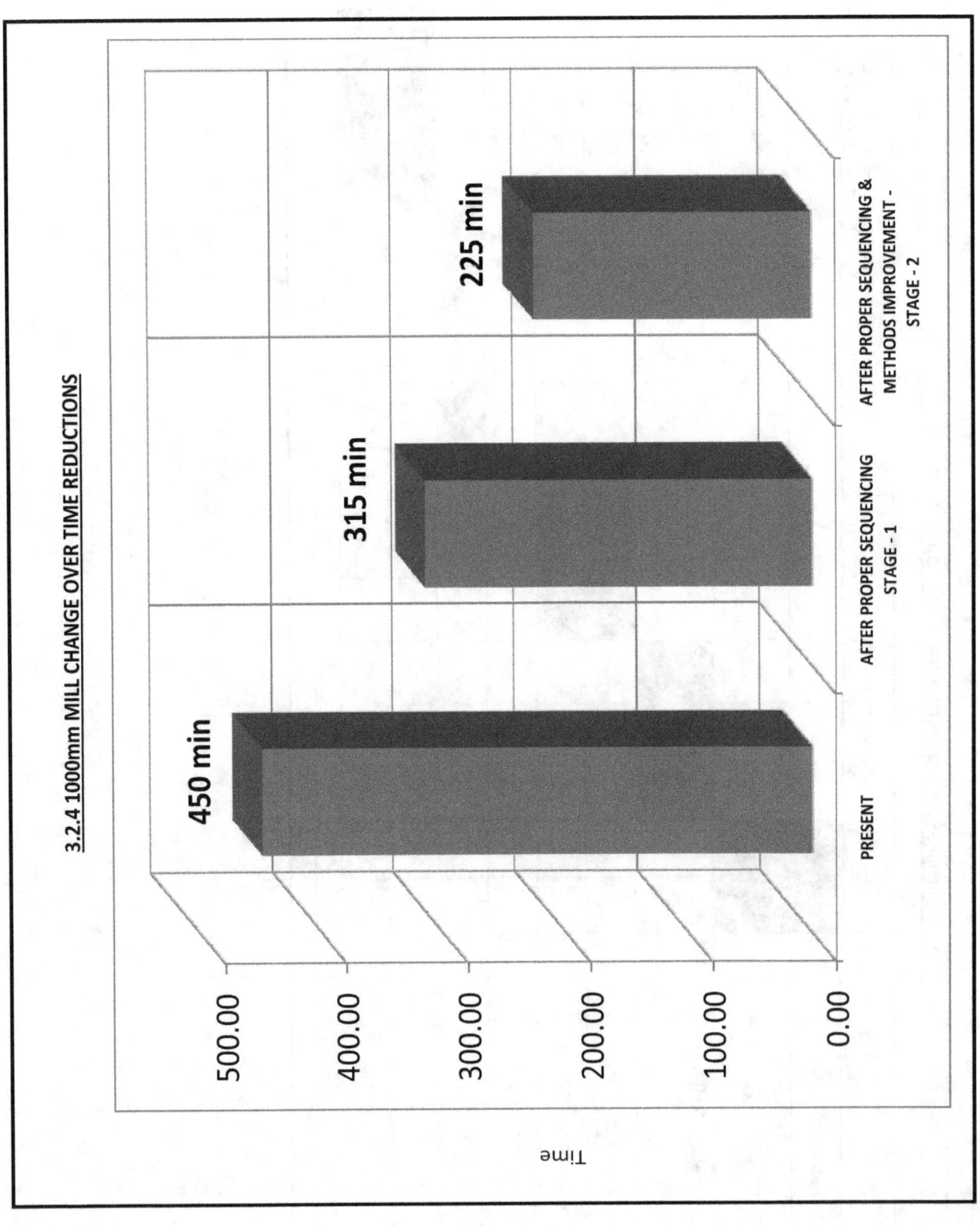

3.2.4 1000mm MILL CHANGE OVER TIME REDUCTIONS

3.2.5 Change Over Time Reduction Implementation Plan

❖ Presentation of Existing C/O method to Mill operatives.

❖ Video coverage of present method.

❖ Discussions with Mill operatives on C/O methods improvement.

❖ Considering suitable benefits such as.

  • Grade.

  • Onetime benefit etc. to operatives for establishing improved.

  • Changeover method.

❖ Arriving consensus on improved C/O method.

❖ Conducting Trails/Pilot implementation of revised method if required.

❖ Making suitable changes/modification on revised method if required.

❖ Establishing the revised method & Making continuous improvement.

12. Line Balancing Concepts Applied in Few Assembly Lines

In any Assembly operations, there could be say 3 to 10 men in a shift to complete all operation for the finished assembly product in a particular lay out with ongoing material handling.

By no means, the individual time taken for each operation can be the same because it is done in different machine or jigs and fixtures. The utilization of the 10 men may be different, say as follows:

Operation-1 -   60%

Operation-2 -   85%

Operation-3 -   55%

Operation-4 -   40%

Operation-5 -   80%

Operation-6 -   65%

Operation-7 -   70%

Operation-8 -   90%

Operation-9 -   60%

Operation-10 - 35%

All operators are supposed to work for 95% at least of the shift time.

Ask and see whether part of operation-2 can be transferred to operation-1. See the possibilities operations-3 & 4. Lastly see the possibility of combining operation 9 & 10. For this, may be the layout and material handling need to be changed. In critical machines, possibility of enhancing machine capacity can be thought of.

If so the man power can be reduced by 2 to 3 men per shift and even the production level can go up by say 20%. Endless possibilities are there for enhancing the productivity by reducing man power and increasing the production level.

Such an exercise is done in the following case study of 3 lines of a auto component manufacturing unit

LINE BALANCING CASE STUDY

Line	Present Output/ Day(Nos)	Present Manpower	After Line-Balancing	
			Proposed Output/ Day(Nos)	Proposed Manpower
Line1	2600	49	3400	32
Line2	2800	61	3600	46
Line3	3200	46	4000	29
Total	8600	156	11000	107
Production/ Day/Man	55 nos		103 nos	
Productivity Improvement			88%	

PRESENT LINE BALANCE/SHIFT LINE-1

S.No	Operation	Man Power	Cycle Time Sec	Set up Time Min	Dressing Time/Tip Change Time (Min)	Present Output (Nos)	Cycle Time/Present Output (Hrs)	Total Time Spent for Prod/7.5 Hrs	Idle Time Hrs/Shift	% of Working Time/Shift
1	C, less forge	1	8.00	45.00	39.00	1300	2.89	4.29	3.21	57.19
2	Turn head	1	8.00	45.00	26.00	1300	2.89	4.07	3.43	54.3
3	Copy turn	2	15.00	60.00	13.00	1300	2.71	3.93	3.58	52.33
4	Facing	1	13.00	45.00	26.00	1300	4.69	5.88	1.61	78.37
5	Wet end	1	6.00	30.00	6.50	1300	2.17	2.78	4.73	37
6	Chamfer	1	6.00	30.00	6.50	1300	2.17	2.78	4.73	37
7	F grooving	1	8.00	45.00	6.50	1300	2.89	3.75	3.75	49.96
8	IH	1	8.00	75.00	0.00	1300	2.89	4.14	3.36	55.19
9	Centerless II	1	8.00	45.00	39.00	1300	2.89	4.29	3.21	57.19
10	Finishlew C less	1	8.00	45.00	39.00	1300	2.89	4.29	3.21	57.19
11	Grs	1	8.00	30.00	24.00	800	1.78	2.68	4.82	35.7
12	Seat grind	2	16.00	60.00	19.50	1300	2.89	4.21	3.29	56.19
13	End touch	1	5.00	9.00	6.50	1300	0.9	1.16	6.34	15.48
14	Roll Mark	1	5.00	30.00	10.00	1300	0.9	1.57	5.93	20.93
15	Polish	1	12.00	24.00	0.00	900	1.5	1.9	5.6	25.33
16	Final Inspection	3	15.00	60.00	0.00	1300	2.71	3.71	3.79	49.44
17	Packing	2	10.00	30.00	0.00	1300	1.81	2.31	5.19	30.74

Plant 2

PRESENT LINE BALANCE

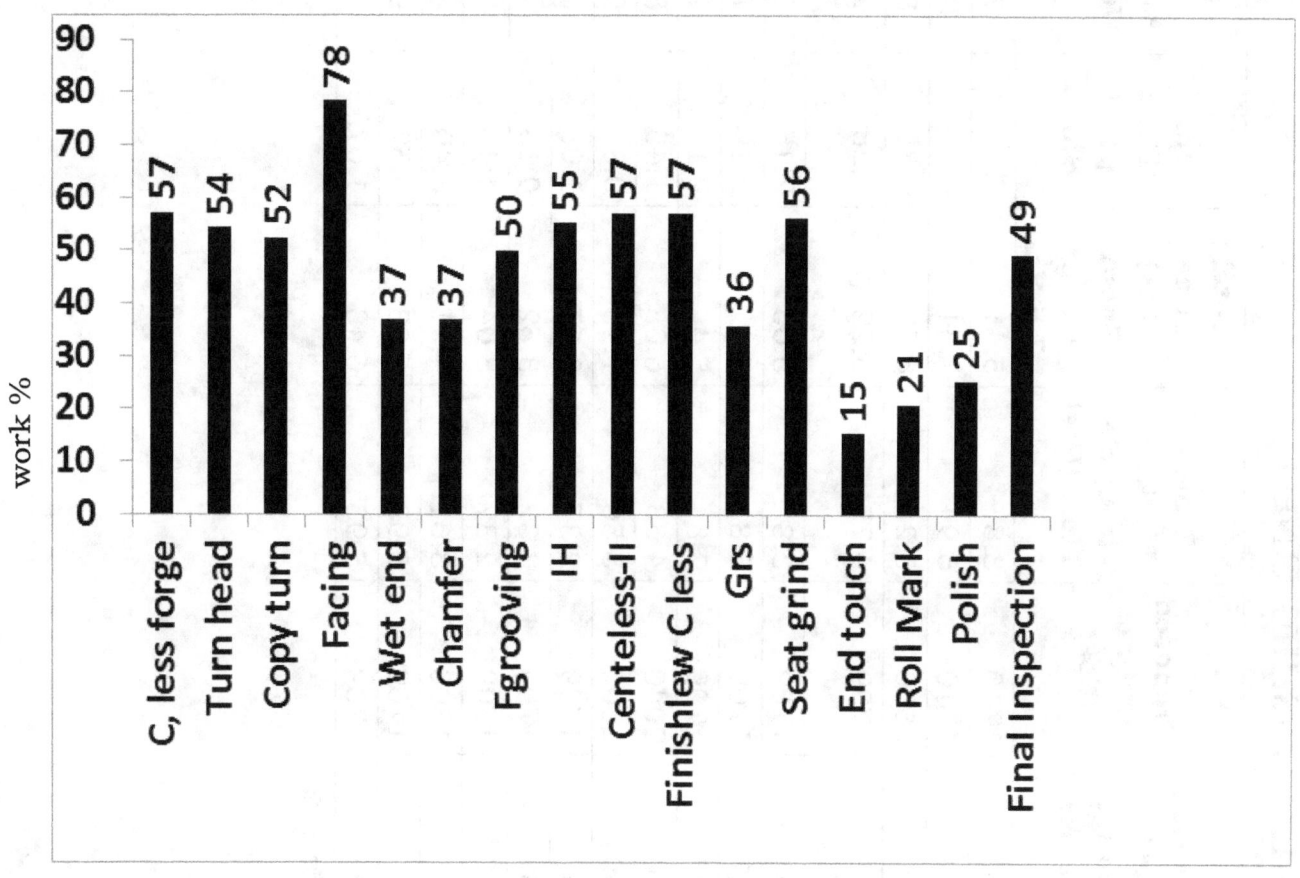

Operation – Plant 2

PROPOSED LINE BALANCE/SHIFT LINE-1

S. No	Operation	Man Power	Cycle Time Sec	Set Up Time (Min)	Dressing Time/Tip Change Time (Min)	Proposed Output (Nos)	Time of Work Acc to Cycle Time (Hrs)	Total Time (Hrs) Spent Out of 7.5 Hrs	Idle Time (Hrs/ Shift)	% of Work
1	C, less forge	1	8.00	45.00	51.30	1710	3.8	5.41	2.1	72
2	Gedee Weiler CNC	1	25.00	60.00	34.20	1710	5.94	7.51	0	100
3	Copy turn	2	15.00	60.00	25.00	2500	5.21	6.63	0.88	88
4	Wet end, chamfer, grooving	1	10.00	60.00	28.48	1709	4.75	6.22	1.28	83
5	IH	1	8.00	75.00	0.00	1709	3.8	5.05	2.45	67
6	Centerless II	1	8.00	45.00	51.27	1709	3.8	5.4	2.1	72
7	Finishlew C less	1	8.00	45.00	51.27	1709	3.8	5.4	2.1	72
8	Grs	1	8.00	30.00	61.20	2040	4.53	6.05	1.45	81
9	Seat grind	2	16.00	60.00	37.50	2500	5.56	7.18	0.32	96
10	End touch	1	5.00	9.00	8.55	1709	2.37	2.67	1.08	84
11	Burnishing		7.00	9.00	8.55	1709	3.32	3.62	0.13	
12	Roll Mark	1	5.00	30.00	10.00	1709	2.37	3.04	4.46	94
13	Polish		10.00	24.00	0.00	1300	3.61	4.01	3.49	
14	Final Inspection	2	25.00	60.00	0.00	1709	5.93	6.93	0.57	92
15	Packing	2	25.00	30.00	0.00	1709	5.93	6.43	1.07	86

Plant 2

PROPOSED LINE BALANCE/SHIFT

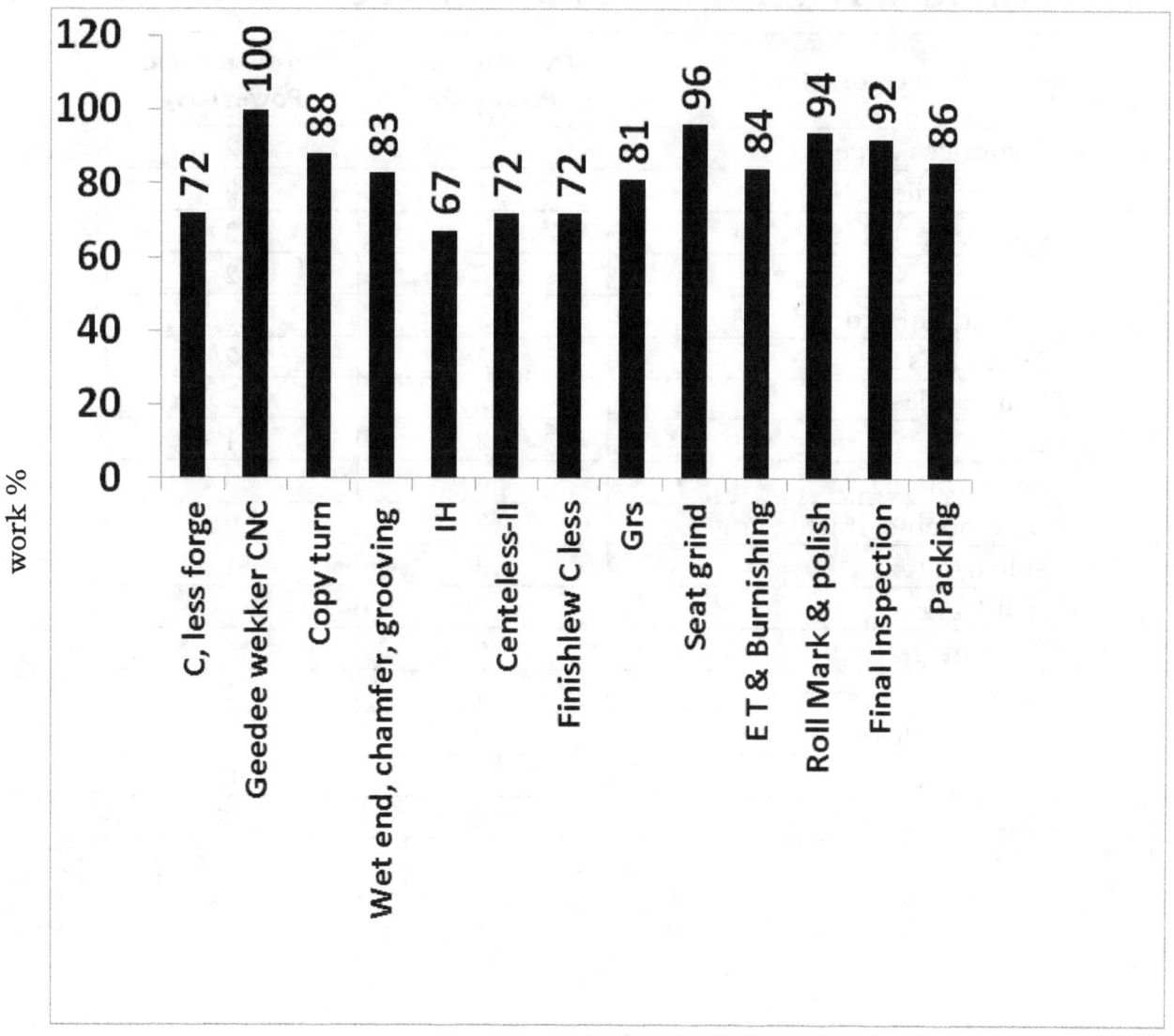

Operation – Plant 2

COMPARISION OF PRESENT AND PROPOSED MANPOWER BEFORE AND AFTER LINE BALANCING/IMPROVEMENTS

Operation	Present Man Power/Day	Proposed Man Power/day
Centerless forge	2	2
Gedee weiler CNC	4	2
Copy turn	4	3
OCG	6	2
Induction Harden	2	2
Centerless 2	2	2
Finish C less	2	2
GRS	2	1
Seat grinding	4	3
End touch & Burnishing	2	2
Polish/cutoff	2	1
Roll Mark	2	1
Final Inspection	6	4
Packing	4	4
Material Movement	2	1
Night shift	3	0
Total	**49**	**32**

Plant 2

PRESENT LINE BALANCE/SHIFT LINE-2

S. No	Operation	Man Power	Cycle Time Sec	Setup Time (Min)	Dressing Time/Tip Change Time (Min)	Prop Output (Nos)	Time of Work Acc To Cycle Time (Hrs)	Total Time (Hrs) Spent Out of 7.5 Hrs	Idle Time (Hrs/ Shift)	% of Work
1	C, less forge	2	9.00	45.00	42.00	1400	3.50	4.95	2.55	66
2	Turn head	2	9.00	45.00	20.00	1000	2.50	3.58	3.92	48
3	Copy turn	2	18.00	60.00	28.00	1400	3.50	4.97	2.53	66
4	Facing	1	15.00	45.00	20.00	1000	4.17	5.25	2.25	70
5	Wet end, Chamfer	1	11.00	45.00	23.33	1400	4.28	5.42	2.08	72
6	Grooving	1	8.00	45.00	9.33	1400	3.11	4.02	3.48	54
7	CNC	1	40.00	50.00	8.00	400	4.44	5.41	2.09	72
8	Turn Seat	1	8.00	45.00	28.00	1400	3.11	4.33	3.17	58
9	Centerless II	1	8.00	45.00	42.00	1400	3.11	4.56	2.94	61
10	IH/FH	1	8.00	75.00	0.00	1000	2.22	3.47	4.03	46
11	Profile Induction	1	8.00	75.00	0.00	2000	4.44	5.68	1.82	76
12	Finish C less	1	8.00	45.00	42.00	1400	3.11	4.56	2.94	61
13	Seat grind	2	16.00	60.00	42.00	1400	3.11	4.81	2.69	64
14	Face stamp	1	6.00	30.00	0.00	1400	2.33	2.83	4.67	38
15	End touch	1	5.00	9.00	7.00	1400	1.94	2.21	5.29	29
16	Roll Mark	1	5.00	30.00	0.00	1400	1.94	2.44	5.06	33
17	Cut off L/P	1	18.00	30.00	0.00	1000	5.00	5.50	2.00	73
18	Final Inspection	3	25.00	60.00	0.00	1400	4.86	2.86	1.64	78
19	Packing	2	25.00	30.00	0.00	1400	4.86	5.36	2.14	71

Plant 2

PRESENT LINE BALANCE/SHIFT

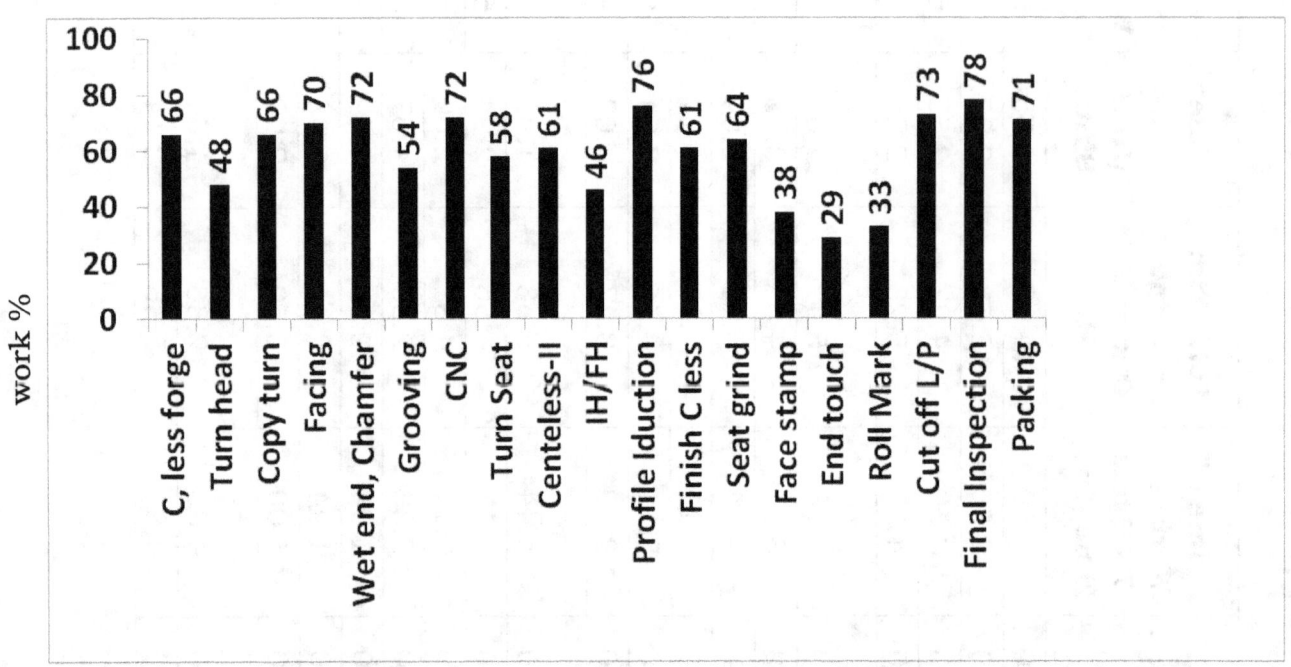

Operation – Plant 2

PRESENT LINE BALANCE/SHIFT - LINE-2

S. No	Operation	Man Power	Cycle Time (Sec)	Setup Time (Min)	Dressing Time/Tip Change Time (Min)	Prop Output (Nos)	Time of Work Acc Cycle Time (Hrs)	Total Time (Hrs)Spent Out of 7.5 Hrs (Prodn +Setup)	Idle Time (Hrs/Shift)	% of Work
1	C, lessforge	2	9.00	45.00	54.00	1800	4.5	6.15	1.35	82
2	Turn head(manual)	1	8.00	45.00	36.00	1800	4	5.35	2.15	71
3	Turn head and Face CNC	1	30.00	60.00	30.24	1512	12.6	7.05	0.45	94
4	CNCLT 16	1	26.00	40.00	17.54	877	6.33	7.29	0.21	97
5	CNCLT 20	1	40.00	60.00	11.40	570	6.33	7.52	0.02	100
6	Crack detection/ Run out check	1	13.00	30.00	0.00	1800	6.5	7	0.5	93
7	Seat turn	1	8.00	45.00	43.20	2160	4.8	6.27	1.23	84
8	Centerless II	1	8.00	45.00	54.00	1800	4	5.65	1.85	75
9	Grooving	1	8.00	45.00	9.00	1800	4	4.9	2.6	65
10	Wet End	1	6.00	30.00	9.00	1800	3	3.65	0	100
11	Chamfer		7.00	30.00	9.00	1800	3.5	4.15		75
12	Finish C, LES	1	8.00	45.00	54.00	1800	4	5.65	1.85	
13	Induction Hardening	1	10.00	75.00	0.00	1800	5	6.25	1.25	83
14	Face stamping	1	6.00	30.00	0.00	3600	6	6.5	1	87
15	Seat grind	1	18.00	60.00	54.00	1800	9	5.45	2.05	73
16	End touch	1	5.00	9.00	9.00	1800	2.5	2.8	4.7	80
17	Roll mark		5.00	30.00	10.00	1800	2.5	3.17	4.33	
18	Polish/LP	1	15.00	30.00	0.00	1260	5.25	5.75	1.75	77
19	Final Inspection	2	25.00	60.00	0.00	1800	12.5	6.75	0.75	90
20	Packing	2	25.00	30.00	0.00	1800	12.5	6.5	1	87

Plant 2

PRPOSED LINE BALANCE/SHIFT LINE-2

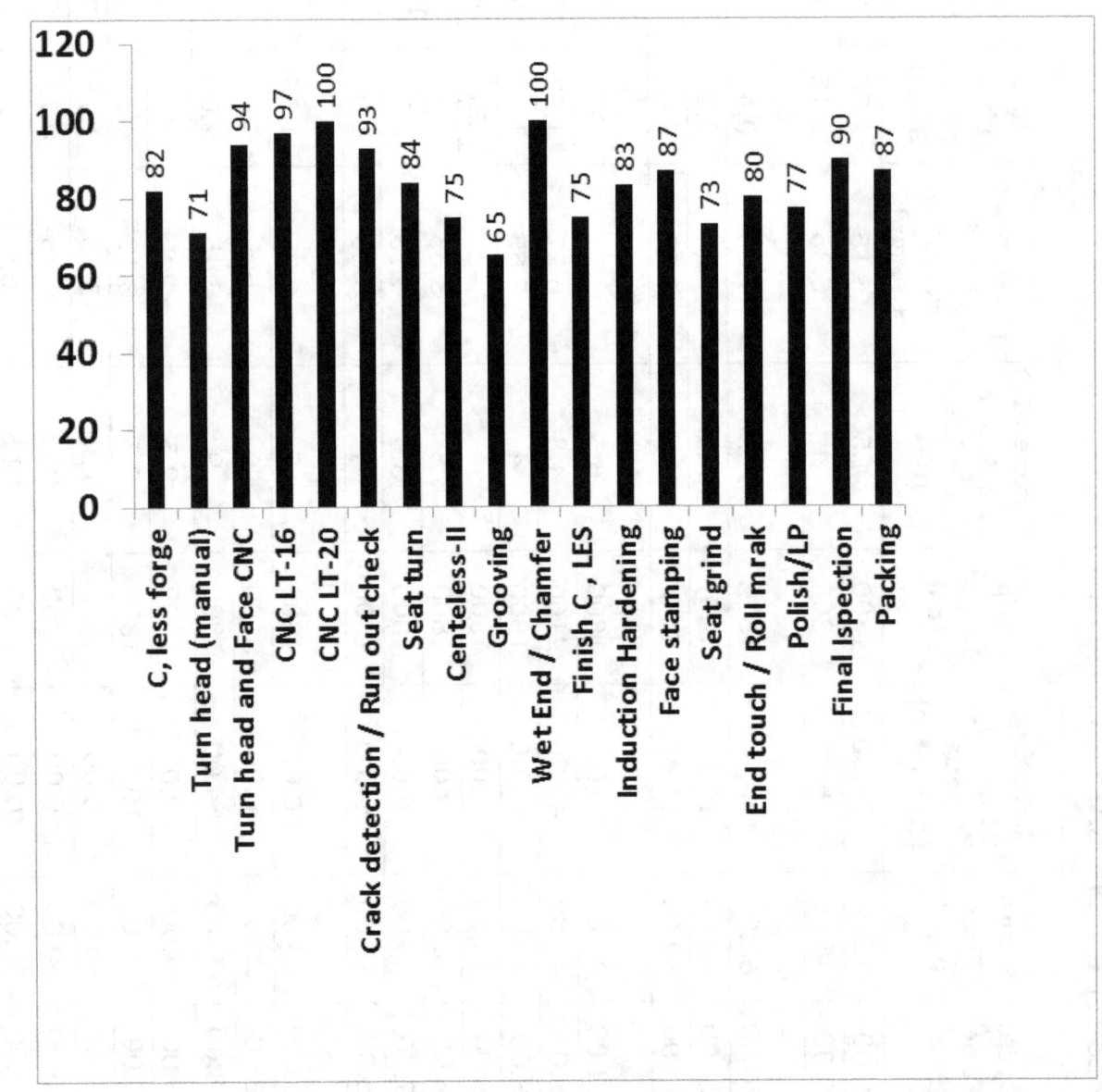

Operation – Plant 2

COMPARISION OF PRESENT AND PROPOSED MANPOWER BEFORE AND AFTER LINE BALANCING/IMPROVEMENTS

Operation	Present Manpower/Day	Proposed Manpower/Day
Centerless forge	4	4
Turn Head (manual)	4	2
TH & Facing CNC	2	3
ACELT 16CNC	2	2
ACELT 20CNC	3	2
Crack detection/Run out checking	2	1
Grooving	2	2
Wet end		
Chamfer	2	2
Turn seat	2	1
C, less II	2	2
Finish C, less	2	2
Seat grind	4	4
Induction hardening	2	2
Profile induction	3	3
Face stamping	2	1
Roll mark	2	1
Cutoff/LP	2	2
End touch	2	1
Final Inspection	6	4
Packing	4	4
Load movement	2	2
Nightshift	5	0
Total	**61**	**46**

Plant 2

PRESENT LINE BALANCE/SHIFT – LINE -3

S. No	Operation	Manpower	Cycle Time (Sec)	Setup Time (Min)	Dressing Time/Tip Change Time (Min)	Prop Output (Nos)	Time of Work Acc to Cycle Time (Hrs)	Total Time Spent (Hrs) Out of 7.5 Hrs (Prodn + Setup)	Idle Time (Hrs/ Shift)	% of Work
1	C, less forge	1	8.00	30.00	48.00	1600	3.56	4.86	2.64	65
2	Turn head	1	8.00	30.00	32.00	1600	3.56	4.59	2.91	61
3	Facing	1	12.00	30.00	32.00	1600	5.33	6.37	1.13	85
4	Copy Turn	2	15.00	40.00	32.00	1600	6.67	3.93	3.57	52
5	Wet end	1	6.00	20.00	8.00	1600	2.67	3.13	4.37	42
6	Chamfer	1	6.00	20.00	5.33	1600	2.67	3.09	4.41	41
7	Grooving	1	8.00	30.00	26.67	1600	3.56	4.50	3.00	60
8	IH	1	8.00	50.00	0.00	1600	3.56	4.39	3.11	59
9	Centerless II	1	8.00	20.00	48.00	1600	3.56	4.69	2.81	63
10	Finish C, LES	1	8.00	30.00	48.00	1600	3.56	4.86	2.64	65
11	GRS	1	8.00	30.00	36.00	1200	2.67	3.77	3.73	50
12	Seat grind	2	14.00	40.00	48.00	1600	6.22	3.84	3.66	51
13	End touch	1	5.00	9.00	8.00	1600	2.22	2.51	4.99	33
14	Roll mark	1	5.00	20.00	0.00	1600	2.22	2.56	4.94	34
15	Polish/LP	1	10.00	24.00	0.00	1600	4.44	4.84	2.66	65
16	Final Inspection	3	20.00	40.00	0.00	1600	8.89	4.78	2.72	64
17	Packing	2	25.00	20.00	0.00	1600	11.11	5.72	1.78	76

Plant 2

PRESENT LINE BALANCE/SHIFT – LINE-3

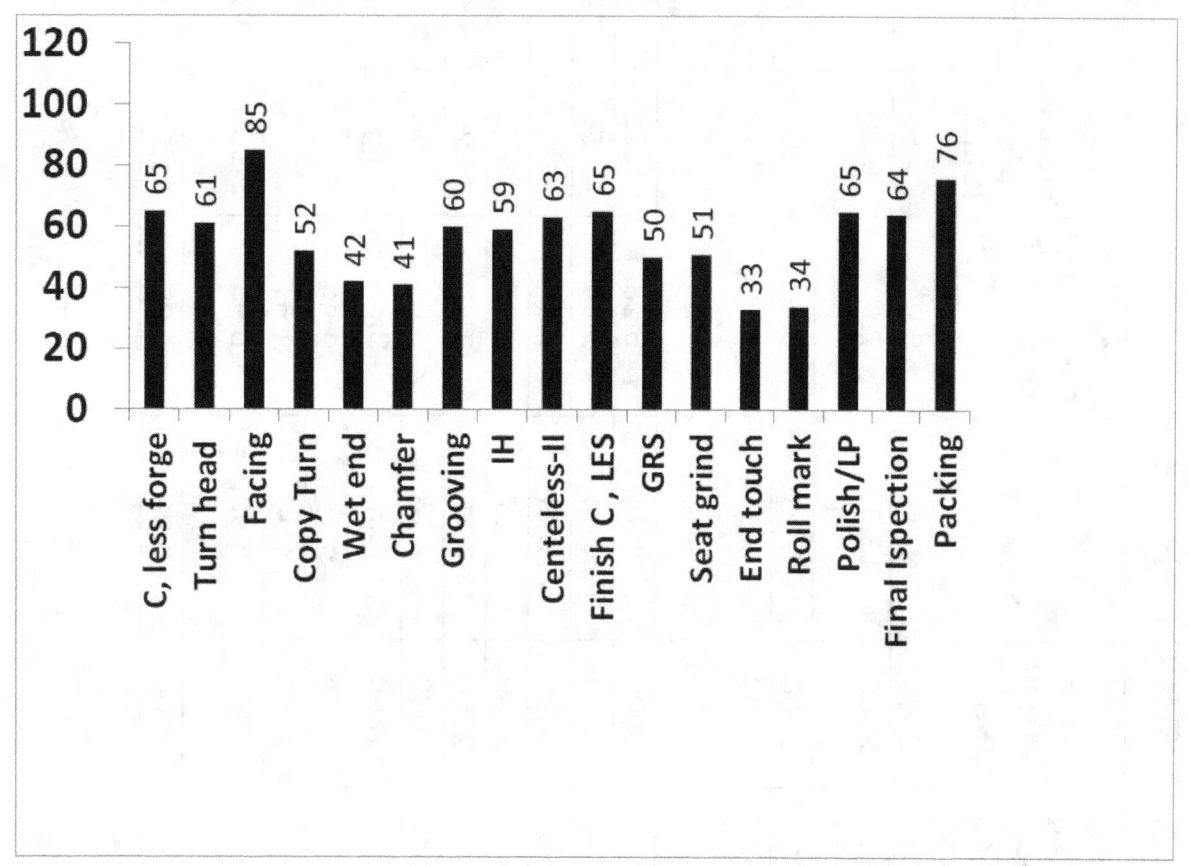

Operation – Plant 2

PREPOSED LINE BALANCE/SHIFT- LINE - 3

S. No	Operation	Man Power	Cycle Time Sec	Setup Time (Min)	Dressing Time/Tip Change Time (Min)	Prop Output (Nos)	Time of Work Acc to Cycle Time (Hrs)	Total Time Spent (Hrs) Out of 7.5 Hrs (Prodn + Setup)	Idle Time In (Hrs/ Shift)	% of Work
1	C, less forge	1	8.00	30.00	60.00	2000	4.44	5.94	1.56	79
2	CNC TJ & FACING	1	24.00	40.00	40.00	2000	13.33	7.33	0.20	98
3	Copy Turn	2	15.00	40.00	40.00	2000	8.33	6.44	1.06	86
4	Wet end, Chamfer, grooving	1	10.00	40.00	33.33	2000	5.56	6.78	0.72	90
5	IH	1	8.00	50.00	0.00	2000	4.44	5.28	2.22	70
6	Centerless II	1	8.00	30.00	60.00	2000	4.44	5.94	1.56	79
7	Finish C, LES	1	8.00	30.00	60.00	2000	4.44	5.94	1.56	79
8	GRS	1	8.00	30.00	36.00	1200	2.67	3.77	3.73	50
9	Seat grind	2	14.00	40.00	60.00	2000	7.76	6.3	1.20	84
10	End touch	1	5.00	6.00	10.00	2000	2.78	3.04	0.71	78
11	Roll mark		6.00	20.00	0.00	1500	2.5	2.83	0.92	
12	Cutoff	1	5.00	10.00	0.00	1600	2.22	2.39	0.50	93
13	Polish		10.00	10.00	0.00	1600	4.44	4.61		
14	Final Inspection	2	25.00	60.00	0.00	1709	5.93	6.93	0.57	92
15	Packing	2	25.00	20.00	0.00	1709	5.93	6.27	1.23	84

Plant 2

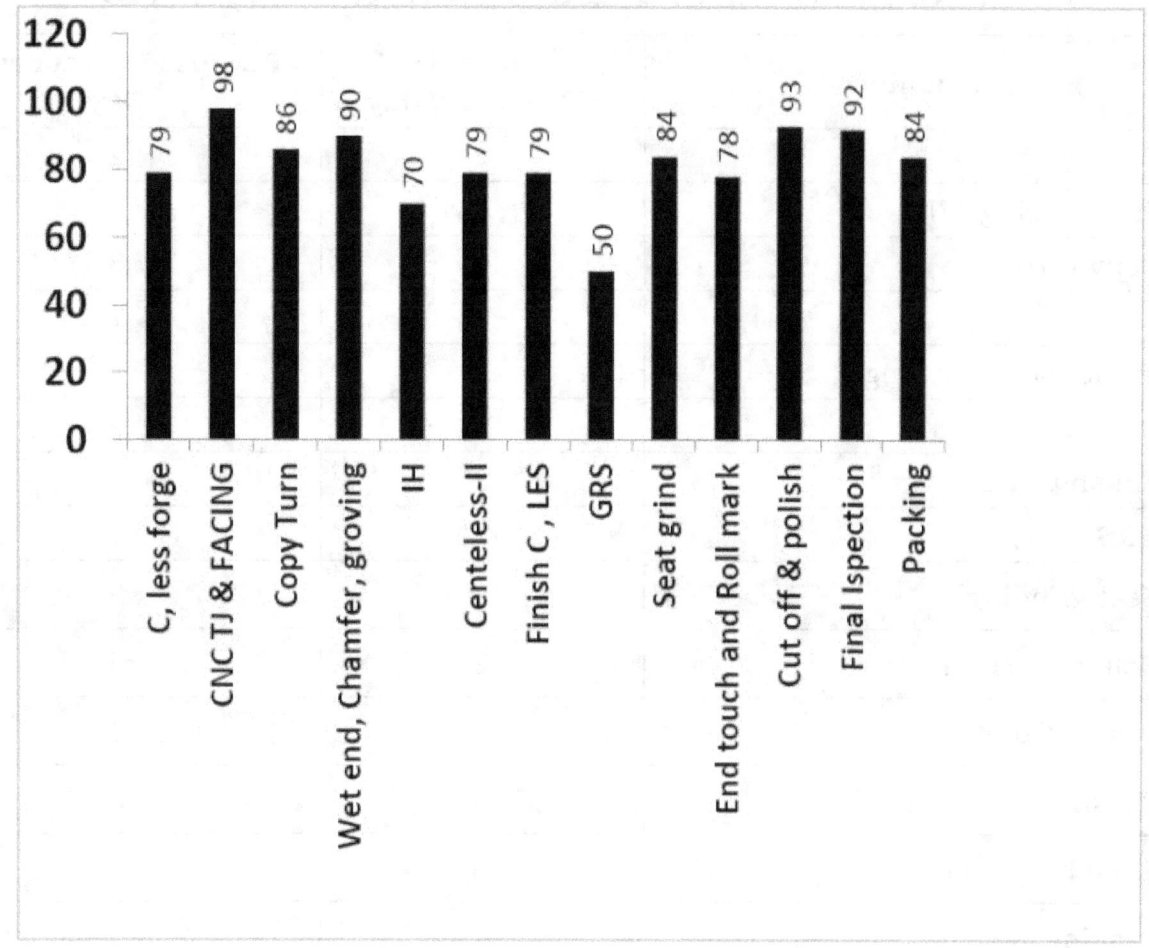

PROPOSED LINE BALANCE/SHIFT LINE - 3

Operation – Plant 2

COMPARISION OF PRESENT AND PROPOSED MANPOWER BEFORE AND AFTER LINE BALANCING/IMPROVEMENTS

Machines	Present Manpower/Day	Proposed Manpower/Day
C, forge	2	2
TH & Facing CNC	4	2
Copy turn	4	3
OCG	6	2
Induction hardening	2	2
C, less II	2	2
Finish C, less	2	2
GRS	2	1
Seat grinding	4	3
Roll mark/End touch	2	2
Polish/Cutoff	2	1
Polish	2	0
Final Inspection	6	4
Packing	4	2
Load movement	2	1
Total	**46**	**29**

Plant 2

13. At the End of Reading This Voluminous Book, What Do You Think on the Usefulness for Achieving Quantum Jump in Productivity?

Possibly the short answer could be, "average, good or excellent" for some of the readers.

At the far end of 53 years of solid experience from 1962 to 2015 let me confess that enhancing the productivity in some of the manufacturing units is as difficult as going to moon. At the same time, it is with lots of humility, I say that at the end I have come out successfully in about 20 units where I was a partner for such project work along with wonderful team members. A man with hearing aid impairment, and who had a major bypass surgery in 1994, had another minor surgery in 2007 and who had to undergo an encounter with thyroid primary tumor in the recent months, can accomplish so much in the field of enhancing productivity, it is most difficult for me to concede that your expectation and motivation and success quotient is just average.

The minimum Productivity enhancement was about 20% and the maximum in the vicinity of 75% to even 100%. The manpower reduction effected was in the range of 20 to 50% with all automation, lay out changes, capacity augment, lean manufacturing, set up time reduction, assembly line balancing, simplifications, methods improvements, process improvements and so on. Along with such high productivity enhancements, the machine productivity and yield improvement with low power consumption per unit of production were achieved to the delight of top management giving quality of products utmost importance and treating customers as gods with on time supplies along with lowest WIP at various stages.

Let me share with you a few of success mantra.

1. ***Be highly motivated, passionate, determined, committed with enormous perseverance. Be prepared for lots of road blocks and face it with dedicated, focused hard work for coming out with acceptable changes for productivity enhancement project in your manufacturing operations.***

Nothing can stop the man with right attitude and motivation from achieving his goals. The ladder of success works like any other ladder. Very people have climbed it with hands in their pockets. When in doubt, do the second reading of true motivational stories given in the initial Part 1 report.

Would you like to read the success mantra as told by great Swami Vivekananda?

"Take up one idea. Make that one idea your life. Think of it, dream of it, and live on that idea. Let the brains, muscles, nerves, every part of your body be full of that idea and leave every other thought. This is the way to success!"

"Each work has to pass these steps, ridicule, oppositions and then finally acceptance"
This was my case too when I initiated the killing of overtime culture and inflexibility, considered to be the terrorists of productivity enhancement. Over a period of time when the workmen tasted the blood of highest incentive amount in place of overtime wages, there is a tremendous mind set change in them and from their family members too. Likewise when flexibility practices are implemented properly, they are for it because everyone has to do other man's job which was never the case before and the atmosphere of cooperation from the workmen appears to be fantastic.

2. **Make sure to involve your team members for the total success of change management.**

Without their success you are doomed to fail. The difference between success and failure is on account of the cooperation from others. Be very pleasant and positive minded when you deal with others and give them full credit for what they do. When you choose to be pleasant and positive with others, you have also chosen how you are going to be treated. It does not matter who gets the credit, our focus is success of our project... The important thing about the success journey is that it starts with a thought which leads to action and you can be that important person or leader. As a leader never forget that in the middle of difficulty lies opportunity for productivity enhancement.

"You can accomplish anything in life, provided you do not mind who gets the credit."

- **Harry S. Truman.**

From my personal experience, I do recommend this success mantra by giving full appreciation to your team members without stealing an iota from them and for sure you will succeed on this project. The same holds good for our appreciation giving to our workmen also.

Take the cooperation of workmen and their view points.

"It is much easier to drive a horse in the direction it is going"

- **Abraham Lincoln.**

3. **Be prepared to move to Discomfort zone to look for success.**

"Unless you walk into the unknown Discomfort Zone, the odds of making a profound difference in your life are pretty low"

- **Tom Peters.**

"You have to leave the city of Comfort Zone and go to wilderness of your intuition. What you will discover will be wonderful. What you will discover will be yourself"

- **Allan Alda.**

Doing things differently, exploring untraded paths, taking that extra mile, all go a long way in making a mark as a Leader. One cannot embrace new horizon unless one lose sight of the shore. Please do not forget that you have already agreed for making use of GOD GIVEN TALENTS and as responsible supervisor, manager, or GM or this is the opportunity for you to reap lots of hidden benefits and name for you by scaling up on productivity. Think of coming months where you will not be criticized in front of others in the periodical Operational Review Meetings. Think of true professional happiness at factory and at home. Do not allow your family members to see your same old frowns on your face. At the end of this project success, they will see only SMILING FACE of yours. Let me assure you that all such blaming meetings can be converted to positive and constructive appreciation meetings which can be used for future expansion and various other improvements.

"Make the Best Quality Products at the Lowest Cost possible paying the highest affordable Wages possible which include you also"

- Henry Ford.

The biggest achievement can be this, you need not bend your head in front of superiors anymore and all your workmen would be equally happy when they see good incentive amounts in their pay slips!
Do remember, Start is the first step for this project. At the same time,

"There must be a beginning of any great matter, but continuing unto the end until it be thoroughly finished yields true glory"

- Francis Drake.

"If you want different Results, a change of Focus is required. Solutions, Innovations, Success come not from greater intelligence or Degrees, or Creativity, but a greater Focus on Outcome."

- Robert Louis Stevenson.

4. ***A personal communication to each of the readers aspiring for quantum jump in productivity***

Substantial Productivity increase is going to be your savior for you the management and the workmen, in other words for the entire company including the customers. If you do not achieve quantum jump in productivity with head count reduction, possibly someone else may be sitting in your chair.
Do initiate, do look for Quantum Jump in Productivity. If you think you can, you can... Display enthusiasm for high level of productivity.

"Nothing great is achieved without enthusiasm"

- Ralph Waldo Emerson.

You can overcome various difficulties as a team.

"The winds and waves are always on the side of ablest navigators"

- Edward Gibbon.

Do uncommon things. Do things differently. Do not be satisfied with unsatisfied satisfaction of low productivity. Go all out for productivity and manage higher productivity of all resources.

Do have a BIG DREAM ON PRODUCTIVITY.

"Nothing happens unless there is first BIG DREAM AND A PLAN."

- **Carl Sandburg.**

5. ***Do remember: "Talk doesn't cook rice," so says a Chinese proverb. Committed plans, Actions; Implementation can produce results on Productivity.***

   Our journey to Excellence will get more and more difficult, if we don't react to improve our productivity and efficiency levels from order to on time delivery, from problem to solutions, from choices to selection, from suggestions to decisions, from strategy to execution.

   Never give up, never, never give up, never, never, never give up the Productivity Oxygen supplies to the organization, without this oxygen supplies, the profitability will shrink and soon the company too may face death burial sooner than later.

   At the end of reading this book, can we together say, wholeheartedly, positively and decisively say,

   "We will do it. We will achieve it. We will succeed on this quantum jump in productivity with reduction of head counts in our company.

   We will restore sparkling and smiling faces through the changes and take the company to superior performance level"

   Be encouraged. Be challenged. Be motivated. Be courageous. Be reengineered. Be revitalized. Be committed. Be successful.. Be a team player and give credit o others. Go forward. Have faith for your productivity accomplishment. Make use of your GOD GIVEN TALENTS. Make your bosses and parents say very good of your achievements and take pride in it!! Be blessed on this marvelous job of your life.

   Most anxious to hear that this book reading has helped you to charge your performance battery to the level of Good if not Excellent by achieving quantum jump in productivity in your organization.

GOD BLESS YOU...

About the Author

K.C. Alexander

Holds a degree in Mech. Engg from Mysore University and post graduate degree in Industrial Engg & Management from University of Wisconsin, USA, Post graduate Diploma in SQC & OR from ISI, and a Diploma in Production Management from West Berlin, Germany. One of the founder members of Industrial Engineering Chapter in Kerala & Tamil Nadu in early 1961–62.

Put in a total of 53 years of experience with 35 years in senior positions at Murugappa Group companies and about 18 years as Consultant with a difference in many companies of repute at Chennai in the area of Productivity Enhancement in Manufacturing Operations and productivity linked wage settlements of about 40 numbers with union teams of different companies. All along the implementation of the productivity improvements with head count reduction and drastic changes in the shop floor were the priorities while working as employee or as consultant.

Now walking in the 80 the year of life on this planet and using the time for sharing the experience with manufacturing teams and for motivating them to excel on their task of productivity enhancement and possible head count reduction in their area of control.

About the Co-author

Dr. A.K. Raj, PhD

Holds a degree in Production Engg from P S G College of Technology and post graduate degree in Industrial Engg from P S G College of Technology, Coimbatore. Subsequently, I was associated with IIT, Madras for about 8 years and I was awarded PhD degree in Operations Management in the year 2013.

Put in a total of 30 years of experience in various positions at Murugappa Group companies in association with the author Mr. K.C. Alexander and 2 years experience as ERP Consultant in Oracle ERP Partner Company till the year 2013 subsequently, providing Management Consultancy to various organizations till date.

www.ingramcontent.com/pod-product-compliance
Lightning Source LLC
Chambersburg PA
CBHW081718220526
45468CB00008B/1896